MW00910107

Choose
the
NORTHWEST

Choose
the
NORTHWEST

Retirement Discoveries for Every Budget

**John Howells
and
Richard Harris**

GATEWAY
BOOKS

Copyright © 1996 by John Howells and Richard Harris

Edited and Designed by Donna S. Lee
Cover Design by Amy Neiman
Cover Illustration © by Susan Detrich / SIS

All rights reserved. No portion of this book may be reproduced, stored in a retrieval system or transmitted by any photographic, electronic, or mechanical process without written permission from the publisher, except that up to 300 words may be used in a published review of the book.

Printed in the United States of America

Gateway Books
Oakland, CA

Distributed by Publishers Group West

Library of Congress Cataloging-in-Publication Data

Howells, John
    Choose the Northwest : retirement discoveries for every budget \
by John Howells and Richard Harris.
      p. - cm.
    Includes index.
    ISBN 0-933469-28-4
    1. Retirement, Places of--Northwest, Pacific. 2.Retirees-
-Northwest, Pacific--Economic conditions. 3. Quality of life-
-Northwest, Pacific--4. Social indicators--Northwest, Pacific.
I. Harris, Richard, 1947- . II. Title.
HQ1064.U6N744 1996
646.7'9'09795--dc21   96-46203
                                                CIP

10 9 8 7 6 5 4 3 2 1

Contents

British Columbia

Washington

Oregon

The Northwest

INTRODUCTION

My book on retirement planning, *Where to Retire,* describes and recommends 150 communities around the nation as possible retirement choices. However, many readers find that when they narrow their choices to a certain section of the country, more detailed information helps in making final decisions. Others already know where they want to retire and want to zero in on that particular area from the beginning. Because of the wide variety and large number of potential retirement locations, the amount of information on each listing in *Where to Retire* had to be kept to a minimum, and some nice places were left out because of space limitations.

So, to better inform folks who want to sharpen their focus on a particular area, a series of regional retirement guides seemed to be in order. (This eases the job of a retirement writer, for it's far easier to present more information about a location than to make painful decisions as to what must be left unsaid.)

Thus started another odyssey of research and enjoyable travel as we visited new towns and revisited familiar places to create regional retirement guides. The first in this series was *Choose the Southwest,* which I completed with the invaluable help of my wife, Sherry. In this book, the second, I am joined by noted travel writer Richard Harris, who is well acquainted with this region.

Some of our visits were made by towing a fifth-wheel trailer and staying several days in each town. This gives us the flavor of what it's like to live in a community, something that can't be done by studying statistics and chamber of commerce handouts.

As a result, these new volumes contain descriptions of many new retirement locations, some places not covered in other publications, plus more in-depth information about previously discussed communities. This book evaluates over 80 different towns in the Northwest for your consideration and, by extension, many more places in surrounding localities.

What We Mean by "Northwest"

A lot of thought was given to the question of what should be covered in a retirement guide for the Northwest. Technically, one could consider the Northwest to start in Alaska. However, after much soul-searching, discussion and research, we decided not to include Alaska in our book on Northwest retirement. Why? Because Alaska is not a place the average reader would consider suitable for retirement. That is, Alaska attracts a particular type of retiree, one who is robust, adventuresome, and up to the challenge of 20-hour summer days and four-hour winter days. It's for someone who can adapt with the season, who is equipped with snowshoes, water skis, tennis racquets and plenty of books to read when it's too dark to use any of the above. Retiring to Alaska could be the subject of a book all by itself.

Idaho and Montana also are in the Northwest, but their mid-continental climate is markedly distinct from the region where the weather is controlled and moderated by the vast waters of the Pacific Ocean. Winters in Montana and Idaho are among the coldest in the nation, whereas winters in parts of the Pacific regions are exceptionally mild and permit year-round outdoor activities. Except for the mountainous and high-altitude inland areas, the Pacific Northwest enjoys mild winters as part of a true four-season climate.

We decided to include British Columbia because it's not only part of the Northwest, but because the mild climate of its coastal areas matches that of neighboring Washington and Oregon, and the lifestyle is similar. We anticipate that it will be the choice of fewer U.S. retirees than the other areas covered in this book, however, partly because of the difficulty of obtaining permanent residency and partly because its winters are cooler. But British Columbia enjoys some of the prettiest scenery imaginable, and it is certainly a pleasant place to live.

Technically, Northern California could be considered part of the Northwest, for its climate, topography and scenic values are indistinguishable from areas north of the California state line. But California's people, taxes and lifestyles tend to tie the entire state into one unit, with gradual changes from south to north as one travels the length of the state. California must also be the subject of another book.

Rain and Shine!

People who live in other parts of the country often have a warped vision of the Northwest. They tend to believe that it's a place of continual rain and humid weather. The reality is that the Northwest encompasses an astounding range of climates, from lush rain forests to bone-dry deserts. Places on or near the Pacific coast are indeed damp, with lots of rainfall, but as you move inland, precipitation levels are about the same as, or less than, the Midwest or Eastern portions of the continent. Moving farther east takes you into places with less rain than many areas of Arizona or New Mexico. People who choose to live on the coast don't seem to mind the extra rain, because it is gentle—without thunder and lightning, tornadoes or hurricanes—and there's plenty of sunshine and clear weather to compensate for the rain. The bonus is one of the mildest year-round temperatures in the country; it almost never freezes, and the thermometer rarely reaches the 80-degree mark.

Further inland, residents enjoy a four-season climate, but with remarkable moderation. Snow falls, but not very often, and it tends to disappear after a few hours. This climate encourages outdoor activities, something vital to good health and longevity. For those who want real winter, there are mountains within an hour or two's drive from anywhere in the Northwest where you can find all the snow anybody would ever want to see. You can live in it if you choose, or you can visit and return to your warm, dry home when you grow tired of the cold. In short, we believe that the Northwest offers one of the best climates in the country for those who like four-season living.

Quality of Life

Our travels have taken us through hundreds of communities, and we've checked out many, many local conditions before making the final selections for this book. However, because a town is not described here doesn't necessarily mean it wouldn't be a great place to retire. The bottom line is there is no "best" place to retire for everyone. Selecting your ideal retirement home is a highly individual decision and depends on personal lifestyle, future aspirations and, most importantly, what you consider to be an ideal quality of life.

The phrase "quality of life" means something different for every individual. When you ask New York City residents about their quality of life, you might hear them rave about the plethora of cultural events available to them. They enjoy everything from opera, jazz combos and stage plays, to world-class restaurants, museums and Fifth Avenue shopping. They'll tell you they can't imagine living without all the excitement that is characteristic of urban life. However, people in Florida brag about their beaches, seafood restaurants and great services for senior citizens.

When you ask the same question in a small town in Oregon, Washington or British Columbia, "quality of life" might be defined in terms of peace and quiet, outdoor activities and low-key cultural activities. People here prize the crystal-clear quality of the air they breathe, their sense of security, safety and knowing what to expect from neighbors and community. Quality of life here is enhanced every time they're treated to the sight of a doe and her fawn grazing in a forest glade. Miles of hiking and bicycle trails, winter skiing and summer gold-panning replace opera, gourmet restaurants and museums. Hooking a trout with a fly-cast in a sparkling mountain stream substitutes for sitting in a stadium and watching the Mets lose another game.

Yet Northwest retirement doesn't mean just outdoor activities. Many communities provide exciting cultural events and entertainment that rival those found back East—without the excitement of muggers lurking in the darkness after the performance. True, you won't see world-renowned personalities appearing in a musical, but the fact that your hair-dresser is performing in the play or your next-door neighbor works on set design makes up for the lack of professionalism. Who knows, you might decide to participate, something impossible for Manhattan theater buffs.

Because the vast majority of Pacific Northwest towns and cities are relatively small, many retirees discover an opportunity to become involved in politics. Folks living in large cities find their voices small and unheard, but in a smaller community their votes and opinions count. In some smaller cities of Oregon, retirees have become the dominant force in local politics.

However, if it's big-city convenience and formal cultural offerings you crave, Portland and Seattle or Vancouver and Victoria offer just about any kind of diversion or amenity you might desire. The good thing is, you can live away from the metropolitan areas, far out in the country, but still be less than an hour to the heart of a downtown mall, if that's what you desire.

Northwest Lifestyles

With such a wide range of climates and variety of cities and towns, a large number of lifestyles are possible in the Northwest. There's something to fit any personality or appetite and plenty of opportunity to acquire a taste for some new hobby, skill or whatever endeavor you'd care to try. Many of the activities listed below can, of course, be enjoyed in Eastern or Midwestern settings, but not as easily and not as a regular part of your routine.

Hunting and fishing are much easier to do in Northwest environs, because most lands, forests and streams are public property. Instead of being fenced and posted with keep-out signs, most unused land belongs to the U.S. Forest Service or the Bureau of Land Management. It belongs to all of us. Most towns listed in this book are located on the banks of a scenic river (or rivers) where you can hook a trout or salmon without ever leaving the city limits. Public boat ramps make it easy to slip your boat, canoe or raft into the water for fishing or leisurely cruising.

River rafting is another favorite sport for serious river fans. Some of the most famous whitewater rivers in the world cascade through the Northwest. Most Eastern whitewater rapids are a few miles long and can be covered in a matter of hours. Some Western rivers take as much as a week of rafting by day and camping at night. Since most of the land traversed belongs to the public, you can pretty much launch your boats and set up your tents wherever you darn well please. And even when rivers flow through private property on what are termed the "Wild and Scenic" stretches, the public is usually guaranteed access to the first 10 feet of river bank.

Rock hunting and prospecting are popular hobbies here that give you an excuse to get outdoors. No matter where you live in the Northwest you aren't far from a historic gold-mining location.

Again, because so much land is public, you can wander about at your pleasure. You can pan most streams for gold, you can break open rocks in search of ore or collect gemstones where you find them. Because vegetation is usually sparse in the dryer parts of the Northwest, rocks and minerals are exposed for easy examination. The exciting part is, should you by chance stumble across something valuable, you can stake a claim and start mining. Don't laugh; it's done all the time! (However, be aware that Congress is looking to change the laws concerning mining and prospecting.) It's not surprising that jewelry making is also a popular avocation out West; hobbyists often use semi-precious stones they've collected in the desert and polished themselves.

The beauty of the Northwest can't be overstated. Photographers love the Western ghost towns, mountain canyons and seascapes that cannot be found elsewhere. So do painters, writers, hikers, bicyclers, picnickers, and beachcombers!

Most all other social and recreational activities available to Easterners are enjoyed in the Pacific Northwest. Bridge clubs, literary groups, travel clubs, whatever you enjoyed before will entertain you here. If you can't find your niche, you can usually develop one at the local senior citizen center.

None of the Above

You may be one of those easy-to-please types whose interests are limited to television and gossiping with neighbors. We all know people who arrange their lives to fit the television schedule. Sunday is for football and *60 Minutes*; Monday morning is for soap operas; Monday night is for *Murphy Brown,* and so on. Shopping trips to the supermarket, browsing the downtown stores and visiting neighbors have to fit into the space between programs.

While some folks would view a lifestyle like this as boring, others see it as a perfectly natural way to live; after all, this is the way they've lived all their lives. When they had jobs, they didn't have the luxury of staying up late to watch David Letterman, and since they worked during the daytime, "soaps" were something they heard others talk about. Now, when they can do anything they care to, they choose to indulge themselves.

However, I suspect these folks won't be reading this book. For them it doesn't make sense to move away for retirement since they have everything they need right where they live. However, I would urge those who are thinking of moving to seriously consider the recreational and social facets of their new home base. Changing where you live is an opportunity to change your entire lifestyle. Your retirement can be a new beginning, not just a continuation of the same old groove (or maybe it's the same old rut).

Real Estate Prices

Throughout this book, we've tried to give the reader a flavor for current housing costs and real estate prices. We have grave doubts about doing much more than that. Why? Because it's virtually impossible to truly convey an accurate—and lasting—picture of a housing market in greater detail.

Part of the problem is defining the terms "average house" and "average sales price." Suppose we agree that an average house is a 1,500-square-foot, three-bedroom, two-bath home in a comfortable neighborhood. That's the easy part. What's difficult is determining the average cost of that average house. You see, statistics tell how many homes were sold in a given community and how much money changed hands. Presumably we can find the average sales price by dividing the total sales prices by the number of homes sold. But how many of those houses sold actually fit our definition of an "average house"? There's no way of knowing.

Let's suppose we're looking at a community with a sudden boom in upscale housing. (That happens frequently in today's affluent retiree market.) Perhaps a large, security-gated, country club development (the only one in the area) is selling homes at $500,000 each. At the same time, ordinary homes in average neighborhoods aren't selling so well. Say that 20 "average" homes sell for about $120,000 each, while ten $500,000 new homes are completed and sold. That brings the average sales price to $246,666, yet we know full well that an average home costs half that amount. At first glance, it would seem this community would be out of the question for many retirees who would otherwise love living here, but could not afford a house costing over $200,000. The fact could well be that a few of these average homes sold for far less than $120,000, maybe for as low as

$90,000, making this community affordable for those who need something economical.

A further problem arises when an author interviews real estate brokers about values of local property. Some real estate people will quote the average selling price as the cost of the average home which as we've seen, may be misleading. Others, realizing that the average selling price is unrealistic, will estimate the cost of an "average" home. And others, anxious to entice buyers to the community, may exaggerate and quote lowest-offered prices as the "average prices." In this book, we've tried to steer a center course between the tilts, but we'll be the first to admit that prices quoted here are subjective. Furthermore, changing market conditions could make them obsolete before this book is ready for its second edition.

Private Retirement Communities

Year by year, retirement becomes more of a big business, prompting impressive corporate investment. Planned retirement communities, often of astounding size, are popping up all over the country. Arkansas, Tennessee and North Carolina lead the trend, with other states following suit. Arizona's Sun City West, for example, has 7,100 acres, with more than 15,000 homes. The Northwest doesn't have as many planned communities as other parts of the country, but as more people enter the age of retirement, the supply of planned communities is growing to meet the demand. Almost every community mentioned in this book has at least one private planned development.

Often these places are "hermetically sealed" developments; that is, to enter the property you must be a member of that development or have good reason to be there. Wanting to price property is usually a good enough reason to visit, so you are welcome to look around and see if this is for you. Round-the-clock guards staff the gates, scrutinizing everyone who enters. Occasionally, after the project is sold out, the original developers are no longer interested in staffing the gates with expensive security guards. It then becomes the responsibility of the owners' association.

Many complexes restrict buyers to those of age 55 and older. Youngsters may visit, but not live there. This impacts the community in two ways. Obviously, your lives will be more tranquil without gangs of kids riding bikes, playing boomboxes and knocking baseballs through your living room window. But more importantly than that, you'll enjoy a lower crime rate. Burglaries, vandalism and theft usually occur in direct proportion to the number of teenagers in the neighborhood. The other side of the coin is that many retirees prefer living in mixed-age neighborhoods; they find young children and teenagers fun to be with.

Developers look for inexpensive land for their new complexes, so they buy square miles of desert or large tracts of forested land. They can then afford to put in roads and utilities, dam up streams to create lakes and ponds and lay out a golf course or two—all at a fraction of what land alone would have cost in other parts of the region. Since local wages in undeveloped areas are generally less than in large cities, quality housing becomes relatively inexpensive.

Two caveats. First: make sure you are going to be satisfied with the physical location of your new home. Most developments we've visited are located several miles from the nearest town. Why? Because that's where the corporation found the cheapest land. This could mean a 20- or 30-mile drive into town to the supermarket or to buy a bit of hardware for the shed you are building.

Second: beware of glib promises and super-salesmanship. When a retirement project is in its initial phase, there will be a beautiful to-scale plan of the development showing the future shopping mall, clubhouses, swimming pools and all the wonderful amenities to come. An enormous supermarket and hardware store are clearly part of the plan. Believe this when you see it. Sometimes, when and if the "mall" is completed, the supermarket turns out to be a convenience store. (This doesn't happen as often with the more established developers, however.)

After you visit a development, check with a real estate office and the newspaper's classified section to see what resales in the development are selling for. If homes are offered at prices drastically below those of the development's sales office, you may have trouble getting your price if you later need to sell out. Also, if you like the development, you could save money by buying a resale instead of a newly built unit.

An advantage to getting in on the beginning of a retirement complex is that it's easier to become involved socially and to make new friends with neighbors as they move in. You might, however, prefer a well-established neighborhood, where you can join existing clubs and activities instead of having to form them. Another point to keep in mind is that membership fees are involved in planned communities, either yearly or monthly. These fees can be reasonable or considerable, depending on the situation. By the way, the rule of thumb is that $100 in monthly fees is a financial commitment roughly equivalent to an additional $10,000 mortgage.

Retirees Welcome?

Legend has it that Oregonians and Washingtonians harbor resentment toward outsiders moving into their states, particularly toward Californians. Therefore, when my wife and I bought a home in a small community on Oregon's Rogue River, our California friends asked, "What do your neighbors think about having a Californian in the neighborhood?" Our reply was, "Oh, they don't mind. The family who owns the store is from Long Beach, the neighbors on our right are from Monterey, on the left from St. Louis and across the road, Los Angeles. Oh yes, there is one family in town from Oregon." We lived in Oregon for the next four years, and the truth is that the only people we heard complaining about Californians moving to Oregon came from California themselves!

It's true that at one time, natives were exasperated over the way affluent Californians—loaded with profits from sales of greatly appreciated Los Angeles homes—bid up the prices of local real estate and began trying to run local politics their way. However, so many Californians have moved into the Northwest that the natives have surrendered to the inevitable. The resentment was always mild, often in a joking sort of mood. And today, with the rebounding of the economy in the Northwest, the differences in prosperity levels between natives and newcomers aren't significant.

Today, most Northwest communities actively seek retirees, doing everything possible to lure them into the area. For good reason—according to studies done by government researchers, when 50 new retirees locate in a small community, the impact is equivalent to a $10-million industry moving in. Retirees spend money. About 90 percent of their income goes for local goods and services. They actually create jobs rather than take jobs. With half a million retirees relocating each year, we're seeing a massive redistribution of wealth, flowing from industrial metropolitan cities to rural and small-town America. A sign of the times: a McDonalds restaurant in Florida replaced the kids' playground with a shuffleboard court. The welcome mat is out for retirees!

Today's senior citizens, as a group, are more affluent than at any time in our country's history. Because of the fantastic real estate appreciation of the '70s and '80s, those who happened to buy homes when they were cheap now have tremendous equities with which to finance their retirement. (Unfortunately, we may be the last of the affluent retirees. Our children and grandchildren have to struggle to become homeowners; low downpayments and $100-a month mortgages are faded memories.) Today's average retired couple has $225,000 in total assets. Much of this is in home equity. These unused funds, when released and used for retirement, can permit retirees to upgrade their lifestyles dramatically. When spent in a new community, this money benefits local residents. That's why so many rural towns are begging retirees to join them.

Doing Your Own Research

Magazine articles and guidebooks commonly grade retirement communities, ranking the top places from one to ten, as if they were rating major league baseball teams. With a baseball team, we can check the scores; can't argue with that. But cities and towns don't receive scores except in somebody's mind. The fact that a freelance writer likes a city and ranks it number one in his magazine article doesn't prove a thing. For all we know, maybe the writer has never even seen the place!

Favorable ratings are too often awarded on the basis of conditions that don't affect retirees. For example: good schools, high employment and a booming business climate will boost a town's rating, while horrible weather and high taxes are often ignored. Quality grammar schools and juvenile recreational programs matter less to retirees than quality senior citizen centers and safe neighborhoods. Full employment and thriving business conditions can create high prices and expensive housing. Also, cultural amenities, such as museums and operas, receive high marks in retirement analysis. Yet how many times a month will you be going to the opera? The museum? Would you rather live in a town with two golf courses and no museums or two museums and no golf courses? To find your ideal location, you're going to have to do your own ranking.

It's best to start your retirement analysis early. A great way to do this is by combining research with your vacations from work. Instead of visiting the same old place each year, try different parts of the country. Even if you are already retired, you need to do some traveling if you plan on moving somewhere else. Your travels needn't be expensive, however. Pick up some camping equipment at the next garage sale in your neighborhood. Anywhere you want to visit in the Northwest will have a nearby state park with a campground; you can combine your retirement research with a camping vacation.

Check out real estate prices. Look into apartment and house rentals. Are there the kinds of cultural events in town you will enjoy? A cultural event could be anything from light opera to hoisting a glass of beer at the corner tavern; the question is, will you be happy you moved there? Just looking closely, as if you truly intended to move there, will tell you a lot.

While you are there, be sure to drop in on the local senior citizens' center. Talk to the director and the members of the center to see just what services will be available should you decide to move there. A dynamic and full-service senior center could make a world of difference in your everyday life.

When investigating a town, one of your first stops should be at the local chamber of commerce office. The level of enthusiasm and retirement advice offered by the chamber staff clearly tells you something about the town's elected officials and business-men's attitudes toward retirees. Most chamber offices love to see retirees move into their towns; they recognize the advantages of retirement money coming into the economy and the valuable contributions retirees can make to the community. These offices will do just about anything to help you get settled and to con-vince you that living in their town is next to paradise. However, don't be surprised if the person behind the counter isn't the least bit interested in your upcoming move. My experience has been that a few chamber of commerce offices are staffed with mini-mum-wage employees who seem to resent folks coming in to ask questions and interfere with the novels they are reading. When this is the case, you might guess that the level of services and senior citizen participation in local affairs could be somewhat inadequate.

Continuing Education

We just can't pass up the opportunity to climb on the soapbox and push an idea we're enthusiastic about, something that grows more popular as time goes by: continuing education for seniors. Throughout the country, community colleges, adult education centers and universities are adding classes and programs expressly tailored to older adults' needs. More than two-thirds of U.S. colleges and universities offer reduced rates or even free tuition to older citizens. You won't feel like the proverbial sore thumb in a setting where you have company your own age.

But continuing education for retirees is more than a pleasant learning experience; the classroom is a tool for retirement adjustment. Signing up for a class in Chinese cooking, fly-tying or rock polishing puts you in social contact with others from the community. An adult classroom is a great place to make friends with lively, stimulating people who share your interests, folks whose horizons are broader than *Monday Night Football* or tomorrow's *Family Feud* show. Taking classes is a quick, sure-fire way of becoming part of your new community.

Many schools will allow you to audit the more serious courses, that is, take the class but not have to worry about quizzes, tests, finals or term papers. You get the intellectual benefit and fun out of a course without the tension of having to do the homework or participate in class discussions.

If you have a trade or special skills of some sort, an even faster way of getting known in your new locale is to offer to teach a class. Community colleges and adult education programs are often strapped for cash to hire full-time teachers and therefore welcome the opportunity to add classes with part-time or volunteer teachers. If your skills are needed, schools often don't require a teaching degree, just experience and the ability to communicate it to others.

Once, when my wife and I moved to a small Oregon city, I taught a couple of community college classes in freelance writing. Not for the money—which was almost nothing—but for the opportunity of meeting townspeople with a common interest in writing. The class was a resounding success, for we made half a dozen friends and received an invitation to join a local writer's group. Our entrance into the town's social life was immediate and satisfying.

But even if you have no intention of taking classes, a community college or university can be important to your lifestyle. Most schools provide the community at large with a wide selection of social and cultural activities, benefits which wouldn't exist without the school's presence. You don't have to be a registered student to attend advertised lectures and speeches (often free) given by famous scientists, politicians, visiting artists and other well-known personalities. Concerts, ranging from Beethoven to boogie-woogie, are presented by guest artists as well as the university's music department. Stage plays, Broadway musicals and Shakespeare are produced by the drama department, with season tickets often less than a single performance at a New York theater. Some schools make special provisions to allow seniors to use their recreational facilities. And art exhibits, panel discussions and a well-stocked library are often available to the public.

What to Look For

To sum it all up, the following is a list of requirements we personally consider essential for a successful retirement relocation. Your needs may be different; feel free to add or subtract from the list, and then use the list to measure communities against your standards.

1. Safety. Can you walk through your neighborhood without fearful glances over your shoulder? Can you leave your home for a few weeks without dreading a break-in? Most retirees feel that safety is the most important condition of all in selecting a new home.

2. Climate. Will temperatures and weather patterns match your lifestyle? Will you be tempted to go outdoors and exercise year-round, or will harsh winters and suffocating summers confine you to an easy chair in front of the television set?

3. Housing. Is quality housing available at prices you're willing and able to pay? Is the area visually pleasing, free of pollution and traffic snarls? Will you feel proud to live in the neighborhood?

4. Nourishment for Your Interests. Does your retirement choice offer facilities for your favorite pastimes, cultural events and hobbies, be it hunting, fishing, adult education, art centers, or whatever?

5. Social Compatibility. Will you find common interests with your neighbors? Will you fit in and make friends easily? Will there be folks from your own cultural, social and political dimensions?

6. Affordability. Are goods and services reasonable? Can you afford to hire help from time to time when you need to? Will your income be high enough to be significantly affected by state income taxes? Will taxes on your pension make a big difference?

7. Medical Care. Are local physicians accepting new patients? Does the area have an adequate hospital? (You needn't live next door to the Mayo Clinic; you can always go there if your hospital can't handle your problem.) Do you have a medical problem that requires a specialist?

8. Distance from Family and Friends. Are you going to be too far away from those you care for, or in a location where nobody wants to visit? (If you would rather they wouldn't visit, you may do better even farther away.)

9. Transportation. Does your new location enjoy intercity bus transportation? Many small towns have none, which makes you totally dependent on an automobile or taxis. How far is the nearest airport with major airline connections? Can friends and family visit without driving?

10. Senior Services. Senior centers should be more than merely places for free meals and gossip; there should be dynamic programs for travel, volunteer work and education. What about continuing education programs at the local college?

OREGON

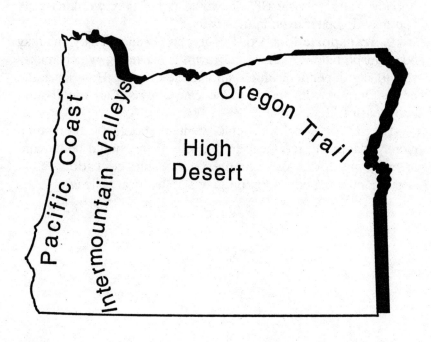

Pacific Coast

Intermountain Valleys

Oregon Trail

High
Desert

Oregon's dramatic collection of varied landscapes provides a broad range of choices for retirement living; there's something here for everyone. Rugged seascapes and coastal mountains contrast nicely with inland valleys and fertile plains. High mountain passes of the Oregon Cascades resolve into lava beds and the Ponderosa pines of the high desert, and then to the magnificent waterfalls and cliffs of the Columbia Gorge. You can test your luck with salmon, steelhead, sturgeon or bottom fishing—from the banks of a river, an ocean boat or in a sunny forest glade. The nice thing is, the overwhelming majority of acreage in Oregon is publicly owned, with national forests and deserts open to everybody—for hiking, camping and general outdoor enjoyment.

By now it should be clear that the general theme of Oregon retirement usually has something to do with outdoor recreation. Yet Oregon's fabulous natural beauty is only one reason the state is a strong contender for retirement consideration. Other reasons for retiring here are friendly neighbors, small towns occupying the banks of leisurely flowing rivers, and sophisticated cities with wonderful cultural environments. Oregon is also prized for its mild weather, a place where you feel obligated to spend time outdoors. Hiking and bike paths lead you through evergreen forests, along riverbanks, landscaped city parks, whichever you choose. Stroll along the beach in the early morning and watch for whales, accompanied by the sight and sound of ocean breakers crashing on the beach. You can hike forest trails, past whitewater rapids, or take your outdoor exercise in city parks, shopping malls and outlet stores.

But what about the weather? Doesn't it rain a lot in Oregon? Many people picture Oregon as a place of ceaseless rain, continual deluge, a place where ducks carry umbrellas. I admit that I once believed this myself. But after living in Oregon for four years, I learned the truth: Oregon weather has been receiving lousy press.

We enjoyed even more sunshine at our Rogue River home than we did when we lived in California, and the rainfall was almost identical, about 20 inches a year. Most Midwestern and Eastern locations get from two to three times that amount of rain, plus from four to ten times as much snow. We never owned a snow shovel when we lived in Oregon, and neither did our neighbors. The snow melted before we could shovel, anyway.

The exception—where this reputation for rain is somewhat deserved—is Oregon's Pacific Coast. Places like Astoria, Reedsport or Brookings usually receive more than 60 inches of rain per year. Yet that's only slightly more rain than some Florida cities catch, places like Miami or Pensacola. For those who live on the wet coast, the abundance of rain is more than offset by the absence of snow and ice. The rest of Oregon draws less rain than many places considered to have great climates. Finally, Oregon's rain, like California's, falls mostly in the winter months, between November and March; the summers are sunny and dry with nothing more than an occasional thundershower.

Take a look at the following chart. It shows Oregon towns for which the National Weather Bureau keeps official reports; I've randomly selected some cities from other parts of the United States for you to contrast. Note that Portland, Oregon, averages 37 inches of rain each year, about the same as Buffalo, New York (however, Buffalo also receives 92 inches of snow). Rainfall in places like Ashland or Grants Pass is around 20 inches a year—enough to keep things green, but not enough to raise the humidity or interfere with fishing.

Oregon Cities	Rain	Snow	Other U.S. Cities	Rain	Snow
Astoria	69	5	Murray, KY	47	13
Burns	10	46	Buffalo, NY	37	92
Eugene	46	6	Flagstaff, AZ	21	96
Grants Pass	22	4	Atlanta, GA	48	2
Medford	20	8	Cincinnati, OH	40	23
Pendleton	12	18	Charleston, SC	52	1
Portland	37	7	Little Rock, AR	49	6
Salem	40	6	W. Palm Beach, FL	60	—

Having defended Oregon's weather so strongly, I must admit that sometimes it feels like Oregon gets much more rain than statistics indicate. This is because rain tends to fall gently upon the landscape here, slowly, mostly in the winter, and over long periods of time while it builds up the accumulated totals. And, along the coast, low clouds can hang around for days upon end, even when it isn't raining, giving the impression of dampness.

Oregon Real Estate

At one time, Oregon offered some of the best housing bargains in the country, relative to the quality of life that goes with living here. Oregon escaped much of the inflationary real estate madness that swept some sections of the nation in the 1980s, partly because the state's economy was stagnated by the near-collapse of fishing and timber industries. As jobs disappeared, so did Oregon residents.

The worst years for the Oregon economy were from 1981 through 1987, which saw a dramatic drop in the number of Oregon's residents. Since the total population of the state is only about three million, so many people leaving the state had significant effects on the economy. You can imagine what this did to the housing market; buyers were in the driver's seat, and homes were bargains.

However, as you can see from the chart below, 1988 marked a turnaround in the economy. The flow of newcomers (a lot of them retirees) into Oregon became a font of new money and prosperity. We shouldn't be surprised that this demand on quality housing drove up real estate prices and turned places like Bend, Florence and Ashland into retirement communities. It also brought a wave of affluent, well educated and more sophisticated residents who are making a mark on the cultural as well as the economic aspects of Oregon.

California retirees are responsible for much of this immigration. In 1994, they accounted for 80 percent of the net migration into Oregon, and in 1995 they made up 55 percent of the migration, according to the Center for Population Research and Census at Portland State University.

Year	Increase	Year	Increase
1981-82	429	1988-89	34,050
1982-83	-25,250	1989-90	38,921
1983-84	8,100	1990-91	64,779
1984-85	50	1991-92	31,600
1985-86	-30,250	1992-93	43,700
1986-87	-13,600	1993-94	29,500
1987-88	36,550	1994-95	35,000

Oregon's overall cost of living is remarkably even throughout the state, hovering right around the national average. With a few exceptions, the main cost variables from one place to another are housing and heating/cooling expenses. Prices of groceries, automobiles and appliances don't vary to any great extent from one community to the next. So, especially for the smaller towns, you are pretty safe to assume that if we don't mention any particular living costs, housing aside, then they are about average.

Oregon Taxes

When it comes to taxes in Oregon, I must rely on the old adage of "good news and bad news." The good news is Oregon has no state sales tax. But the bad news is property taxes must be high to make up the deficit. The good news: a state referendum sent outraged property owners to the polls to vote a reduction in property taxes to a maximum of $15 per $1,000 valuation, with a prohibition against raising assessed values to make up for lost revenue. The bad news: voters didn't notice that the prohibition applied only to commercial property; private homes could be (and were) reappraised. It turns out that the tax reduction proposition was the brainstorm of business property owners. In some areas, as property tax rates dropped, the valuation of the homes climbed. Eventually, the good news should be that the reassessment loophole will be closed, because property owners are really outraged now! Other taxes Oregon doesn't have are: business inventory tax, real estate transfer tax, business tax, or a unitary tax on worldwide holdings.

If taxes are an important factor in your decision process, you'll need to ask about property taxes in the specific areas that you are interested in. Taxes can be twice as high on one house as on another home across the street—if the city limit happens to run down the middle of the road. And, when you find property taxes quoted for some towns in this book, don't accept them as gospel fact; sometimes a realtor or chamber of commerce states the basic tax rate and fails to mention the bonds and special assessments.

The scarcity of tax dollars and curtailed spending on education in some communities has had a curious side effect on medical care. Since funds for public education are in short supply in some school districts, and because some voters are reluctant to increase taxes to fund schools, the quality of education naturally deteriorates. What happens next is that young physicians looking for a place to open a practice tend to shun communities where their kids can't find quality schools. Therefore, many capable doctors (and dentists, too) choose larger or more education-minded communities to set up practice. As older doctors retire, new ones aren't there to take over. This problem isn't unique to Oregon; it's common in many areas of the country. Understand, this situation isn't the rule, but it happens often enough that in some instances, private doctors are reluctant to take on patients because of an overload. Should you have some kind of special medical problem and are used to having a wide selection of doctors to deal with it, better investigate your new community as to the medical care situation.

Where to Retire in Oregon

The marvelous thing about retirement in Oregon is the wide variety of places from which to choose. You can select a climate that precisely suits you and your retirement lifestyle. You can single out the town or city with the exact type of activities you enjoy or might want to learn to enjoy. Small town, big city, rural farmlands or tall-timber woods, they're all on the menu.

Let's take a closer look at Oregon's climates. Two major north-south mountain chains divide the state into distinct climatic and scenic zones. The first zone is the Pacific Coast, known for consistently cool weather—summer or winter—with mild temperatures and lots of rain in the winter but almost no snow or freezing weather. The entire length of this three-hundred-odd-mile coastline is heavily influenced by retirees, folks drawn there by the naturally air-conditioned weather plus the scenic and recreational treats granted by the ocean beaches and nearby mountains. The Oregon Coast has but two seasons: cool summer with mixed sun and clouds, and cool winter with mixed sun and rain.

The second area is in the center of the state, between the coastal hills—much in national forests or wilderness areas—to

> **Oregon**
> The Beaver State
> The 33rd state to enter the Union
> February 14, 1859
>
> **Sate Capital:** Salem
> **Population (1995):** 3,140,585; rank, 29th
> **Population Density:** 30.4 per sq. mile; urban: 70%, rural: 30%
> **Geography:** 10th state in size, with 96,003 square miles, including 1,091 square miles of water surface and 28 million square acres of forested land. Highest elevation: Mount Hood, 11,239 feet. Lowest elevation: sea level at the Pacific Coast. Average elevation: 3,300 feet.
> **State Flower:** Oregon Grape
> **Sate Bird:** Western Meadowlark
> **State Tree:** Douglas Fir
> **State Song:** Oregon, My Oregon

the west and the Cascade mountains to the east. A series of river valleys, mostly running north and south, form what I call the "intermountain valley" region. These valleys enjoy very mild, four-season weather. A small amount of snow can fall (some winters almost none), and it usually melts overnight. Freezing temperatures are rare, with daytime warming often into the 50s—

even in the coldest months. Spring, summer and fall weather is pretty much dry and sunny.

To the east you will encounter the Cascade mountain chain, with its high peaks, spectacular scenery, bountiful snowfall and very small towns or crossroads communities. Once past this rugged terrain, Oregon's high desert area spreads out to the Idaho border. As the term "high desert" implies, rainfall here is slight, as little as nine inches a year; spring, winter and fall are delightfully sunny and mild. However, the small amount of precipitation that does fall often turns into snow when winter clouds blow across the high desert. In higher elevations, snow can stick to the ground through the winter, much as it does in towns in the Midwestern and Eastern portions of the United States. Communities here vary from small, crossroads villages to nice-size towns with all amenities.

To my way of thinking, there is yet another region of Oregon that doesn't quite fit any of the above categories: the Oregon Trail and Columbia River Gorge. Towns along this northern band experience slightly different climatic and scenic features. The altitude here is much lower than the high desert country farther south, and fewer retirees have found their way into the area. Some places are more isolated, but perhaps that's what you're looking for.

Our discussion of Oregon is divided along the lines of the geographical and climatic sections outlined above. Since most retirees opt for the central, intermountain river valleys where the climate is the mildest, we'll begin our investigation here.

OREGON TAXES

Income Tax

Oregon's state income tax is based on modifications to the Federal adjusted gross income, and you may deduct a maximum of $3,000 federal taxes from your income. Seniors age 59 and over may include all eligible medical expenses if they itemize. Eligible pensioners are allowed a tax credit equal to the less of 9 percent of the individual taxpayer's "net pension income" or their Oregon income tax liability.

For persons filing as Single or Married filing separately:

If your taxable income is:	Your tax is:
Not over $2,100	5% of taxable income
$2,101 - $5,250	$105 plus 7% of excess over $2,100
Over 5,250	$325 plus 9% of excess over 5,250

Filing Jointly, Head of Household, or Widow(er) w/dependent child:

If your taxable income is:	Your tax is:
Not over $4,200	5% of taxable income
$4,200 - $10,250	$210 plus 7% of excess over $4,200
Over 10,500	$651 plus 9% of excess over 10,500

Sales Taxes

State: *none;* **County:** *none;* **City:** *none*

Property Taxes

Rates vary widely, from $8 to $15 per $1,000 of assessed value, not including bonds and special assessments which vary. Typically, total property taxes on a $100,000 home will run between $1,200 and $1,800.

Deferrals Under the Senior Deferral Program, the State pays your taxes to the county, maintains the account and charges 6 percent simple interest—which is also deferred until the taxpayer dies, transfers ownership, or ceases to live permanently on the property. Senior citizens need the following qualifications to participate in the program: they must be 62, live on the property and have a deed or recorded sales contract. Your total household income must be less than $24,500 for the year before you apply, and once on the program you need a federal adjusted gross income of $29,000 or less to continue. Any year your income exceeds $29,000, your taxes for the following year will not be deferred.

Estate/Inheritance Taxes

none

Licenses

Driver's License $26.25 for a four-year period.
Automobile License Plates cost just $30 for a two-year period, no matter how new or old the car.

Intermountain Valleys

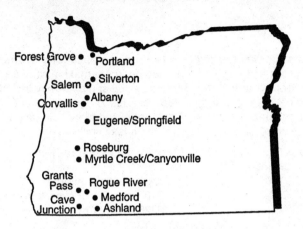

From the California state line north to the Columbia River, a series of valleys and gently rolling hills invite newcomers with an amiable climate and pleasant towns and cities. At low altitudes—just a few hundred feet—with mixed open fields and scattered forests, you are never far from mountains and foothills, and usually not much more than an hour's drive to the Pacific Ocean.

This part of Oregon contradicts the common belief that the state is continually being rained upon. Actually, Oregon's intermountain region gets far less rain than most places in the East or Midwest. Total rainfall varies from very light in the south around Ashland—about the same as Flagstaff, Arizona—and gradually increases as you travel north to Portland—which catches about the same amount of rain as Albany, New York. Winters are cool, with light to moderate snow, rarely sticking to the ground for more than a day. Below-freezing days are rare except at higher elevations. Warming trends begin in April, growing steadily warmer into the hot summer days of July and August. Sunny days are the norm, with little rainfall from May through October. Fall weather is pleasant and crisp, usually characterized by an Indian Summer in mid- to late October. Rain usually begins in November and alternates with bright, sunny spells until late spring, when the dry season begins, broken by occasional thundershowers.

Places suitable for retirement relocation along this 335-mile stretch of intermountain valleys range from small towns to medium-size cities, with Portland thrown in as a metropolitan area. Many folks who are looking for a likely retirement haven in Oregon begin their odyssey at the California-Oregon border and work their way north. We shall do the same in this book, starting with Ashland, one of our favorite Oregon retirement locations.

Ashland

Besides the activities connected with the Shakespeare theaters and the college, I like Ashland because it's small enough that I can walk anywhere in town I care to go. —Myrtle Franklin

About 19 miles north of the California-Oregon state line, a traveler's first sight of Ashland is a cluster of homes and buildings spreading up a mountain slope to the west of Interstate 5. At an elevation of 1,800 feet, the town overlooks a pleasant countryside of gently rolling hills, fields and sporadic remnants of forests that once covered the area. Off in the distance, about 30 miles to the east, the Cascade Range ascends, with Mt. McLaughlin rising majestically in white-frosted splendor. To the south, another 30 miles away, Mt. Ashland dominates the Siskiyou Mountain Range.

Among other things, the surrounding country is famous for pear orchards—the official fruit of the valley and once the major industry. According to one resident, "In April the trees look like they're in the popcorn business!" One local orchard has a special deal: for a fee you can climb the trees and pick cherries or whatever is ripe that week. For an excellent view of the area, drive up into the hills along Valley View, Mountain or Oak roads. Some claim that the scene from here is reminiscent of similar places in Austria.

This is an excellent retirement choice for couples with varied interests. It's for those who crave the intellectual stimulation of a college town as well as access to outdoor sports, all combined with a comfortable place for retirement living. Even though Ashland has only 19,000 residents, it's large enough to provide all necessary services and then some—without the crush of traffic congestion and hordes of strangers. "It's rare that I go downtown without seeing someone I know," said one retiree.

As a college town, Ashland is a textbook example of how the presence of a school can affect a community's ambience.

Whenever you combine a goodly number of students, professors and support staff with lots of retired couples, something happens. You create a demand for a higher level of services, nicer shopping facilities and quality restaurants. Because students are chronically short of money and because retirees like to watch their expenses, prices naturally remain at reasonable levels. Ashland's charming downtown is the result. Folks from Oregon towns near and far journey here to dine in restaurants serving French country cooking, wood-fired pizza or Thai cuisine, or perhaps to browse in used bookstores or look at fashions imported from Scotland.

Much of Ashland is beautifully landscaped and graced by lovingly restored turn-of-the-century homes, and the town is justifiably proud of these stately old houses. Stunning examples of large five-bedroom Victorian homes—which would look quite proper in San Francisco—sit next to smaller, one-bedroom Victorians whose style is also ornate, but on a much lesser scale. Residents take great pride in keeping these architectural jewels in their original form and in good repair. Some of the more spectacular Victorians command sites on the hillsides, sharing the spotlight with equally stunning but more modern homes.

Many Victorians do double duty as bed-and-breakfasts as well as residences for retirees; we've been told that as many as 80 bed-and-breakfasts provide accommodations for tourists, visiting scholars and theater devotees attending the Shakespeare festivals. During our last visit (Spring 1996) a close friend was in the process of remodeling a large garage behind her home into a "Victorian" cottage. She feels confident that as a tourist rental the house will supplement her retirement income nicely. "I don't plan on advertising," she said, "I should get enough overflow from the other bed-and-breakfasts to keep me as busy as I care to be." With a constant stream of visitors to the Shakespeare Festival and university functions, bed-and-breakfasts do quite well here.

Ashland's Lithia Park, located on a former Chautauqua ground, is a unique feature which dominates the upper reaches of the city. This gorgeous setting was developed by John McClaren, designer of San Francisco's Golden Gate Park, and it's become an important part of Ashland's ambience. Lithia Spring, which supplies water to the city, is said to have one of the highest concentrations of lithium in the world. Even prior to the coming of the early settlers, the Indians used the springs in care of their sick and aged. The development of Lithia water fountains began with an idea that Ashland could become a famous health resort similar to Carlsbad, Germany, where mineral water treatments were big business. Although resorts never materialized, the springs still supply mineral water for Ashland dinner tables.

Recreation and Culture One of the best climates in the country makes outdoor sports enjoyable year-round in Ashland. Fabulous hunting, fishing and hiking are all available in the Cascade Range or in even closer parks and preserves. Five lakes within 30 minutes of town provide favorite fishing holes, swimming, water skiing, or picnics. The ski season lasts from Thanksgiving through April, with up to 22 runs operating (snow permitting). Nearby rivers with crystal-clear waters offer catches of world-class salmon and steelhead trout. Whitewater rafting on the nearby wild-and-scenic Rogue River draws adventurers from all over the country. Ashland's low rainfall and infrequent snows make golf possible in all seasons. The local public golf course is Oak Knoll Golf Course—nine holes, par 35—with six more public courses in nearby Medford.

Ashland is internationally famous for its outstanding dramatic performances. Starting out as a seasonal Shakespeare presentation in an Elizabethan-era styled, open-air theatre, in 1935 Professor Angus Bowmer of Southern Oregon College conceived the idea of producing Shakespeare's plays in the abandoned Chautauqua shell. With the cooperation of local merchants and interested citizens, an Elizabethan stage was built.

In the years that followed, attendance at the Shakespeare plays continued to increase; the season constantly lengthened. The basic pattern of a four-play repertory evolved, eventually becoming a year-round production and drawing 300,000 visitors yearly to its three theaters. Performances aren't limited to Shakespeare; modern, classic and experimental drama also entertain the public. Everybody in town has an opportunity to get into the action, volunteering to help with costuming, ushering, or whatever is needed. Tourists are often surprised to encounter costumed actors on their lunch break, munching hamburgers in a downtown restaurant while discussing their roles in the current stage production.

Housing Costs At one time, Ashland was one of the best bargains in the country for college-town real estate. As in most of Oregon, those days are behind us. Home prices have risen dramatically over the past five years, which pushes the overall cost of living over Oregon's average. Still, depending upon where you are from, asking prices in Ashland may seem quite reasonable. A typical small, three-bedroom Victorian home will cost between $135,000 and $175,000. Larger homes, higher on the hill, sell for $200,000 and up. While this might seem high to Oregonians who used to purchase real estate for a fraction of today's prices, Californians and retirees from some other parts of the country find these outlays more than affordable.

It isn't all Victorians in Ashland; most homes date from the 1920s and later, with some new "Victorian" homes being constructed today as well as conventional housing on the city's outskirts. The advantages of these Victorian replicas are efficient plumbing and minimal upkeep. To provide more affordable housing, the city of Ashland is trying to annex nearby acreage to erect some low-cost housing.

Medical Care Ashland has its own hospital and a satisfactory ratio of doctor-to-patient relationships. There's an ambulance service plus a 24-hour emergency clinic. A full-service medical facility is at Rogue Valley Center in Medford, just about 17 miles up the interstate.

Crime and Safety Ashland is small enough to enjoy a very low crime rate, ranking in the country's top 25 percent in personal safety.

When Grandkids Visit About 16 miles south of Ashland, on the road up to 7,500-foot Mt. Ashland, is the Mt. Ashland Inn. The Pacific Crest Trail crosses the inn's parking lot, inviting you to climb through groves of ponderosa and red-barked manzanita. In mid- to late summer, the alpine meadows blossom with colorful wildflowers such as larkspur, lupine and white bear grass.

Important Addresses and Connections
Chamber of Commerce: 110 E. Main St., Ashland, OR 97520.
Senior Services: 1699 Homes St., Ashland, OR 97520.
Newspaper: *Daily Tidings*, 1661 Siskiyou Blvd., Ashland, OR 97520.
Airport: Medford.
Bus/Train: Greyhound makes a stop in town.

ASHLAND	Jan.	Apr.	July	Oct.	Rain	Snow
Daily Highs	45	64	91	69	20	10
Daily Lows	30	37	54	40	in.	in.

Medford

We wanted to find a place away from Southern California's rush and crush, but we couldn't bear the thought of moving back East where we'd have to fight snow and ice in the winter. We feel Medford is a good compromise. —Roberta Johnson

On the spine of the Cascades, about 80 miles from Medford, one of the scenic wonders of North America awaits your admiration. A deep blue gem known as Crater Lake, the deepest in the United States, is the centerpiece of a national park of the same name. Boundary Springs, just inside the park, gushes forth to become the Rogue River as it begins its 215-mile journey to the Pacific Ocean. The scenic beauty of the river is legendary as it falls through gorges and canyons, rushing and swirling through rapids of whitewater thrills. It widens as it passes through the Rogue River Valley, then narrows sharply on the other side of Grants Pass as it cuts through the hard igneous rocks of the mountains of the Siskiyou National Forest on the way to the Pacific. Old-growth pines and twisted madrone trees grace the banks of the river as deer graze in fields and pastures along the way. Osprey fish for steelhead and rainbow trout, while blue heron skim majestically along the sparkling waters. Several excellent retirement possibilities sit on the banks of the Rogue, from Medford to the beginning of the Wild and Scenic portion of the river past Merlin. The southernmost river location we'll look at is Medford, about 17 miles north of Ashland.

Because the city of Medford is only 20 minutes north of Ashland, along the interstate, one might argue that it should be described as part of an Ashland-Medford complex. But they are quite different. Although Medford's spacious shopping mall serves as Ashland's major shopping center, Medford is a modern city as opposed to a sleepy college town. Medford's population is 55,000, with a shopping area of 154,400. Instead of sitting on the edge of a mountain slope as does Ashland, Medford occupies the middle of the Rogue River Valley and is more or less flat, surrounded by rich farmland and dairies that spread out beginning at the edges of town.

Medford's pleasant downtown city center is old-fashioned, with turn-of-the-century buildings and varied business enterprises. Although the city center supports some interesting restaurants and shops, the truth is that most major shopping happens at the large Rogue River Mall on the outskirts of the city. There you'll find just about every kind of store you can imagine. This shopping center brings folks from as far away as Grants Pass.

Recreation and Culture Medford's benign climate encourages a wide variety of year-round sports activities. For bicyclers and hikers, Bear Creek Greenway offers two nature and bike trails, as well as trails in Holmes Park. One private and one public 18-hole golf course supplement the five nine-hole public golf courses in the Medford area. Two private tennis clubs and 23 public courts are available for play. Skiing at Mt. Ashland is only 34 miles south of Medford.

Eight months of the year, Medford theatergoers take advantage of Ashland's Shakespeare Festival, which includes classic plays by other playwrights as well. During the summer, the Peter Britt Festivals in Jacksonville supplement Medford's four theatre groups, and musical entertainment is provided by the Oregon Cabaret Theatre, Rogue Music Theater and the Rogue Opera association.

Housing and Other Costs Medford offers a wide range of real estate, with the average cost of three-bedroom homes between $95,000 and $120,000. Several condominiums have units selling around $80,000 for a large two-bedroom. Apartment were renting for $500 to $600 for two bedrooms. Taxes are about $14 per $1,000 valuation. You'll find some especially nice upscale neighborhoods around the Country Club section—one of Medford's few hilly areas—along Barnett Road, Black Oak Drive and Hillcrest. In that general area is also a large retirement complex, sitting high on a hill with a view of the entire valley below. The cost of living here is right about average for the state.

Medical Care Medford has the largest, most comprehensive medical facility in the area. Rogue Valley Medical Center is a 305-bed, non-profit facility, a referral hospital for the entire south-central part of the state. Providence Medford Medical Center is another state-of-the-art hospital offering heart care, rehab and senior health programs. Medford Clinic is an outpatient complex with 63 physicians and surgeons on staff.

Crime and Safety Even though Medford has the advantages of a metropolitan area, it avoids many ills found in large cities. According to FBI crime reports, the personal safety rating is above the national average for desirable retirement locations.

Nearby Retirement Possibilities A few miles west of Medford is the historic town of Jacksonville, site of another famous festival. The ongoing Britt Festivals are the oldest outdoor music and performing arts festivals in the Northwest. Five events are presented each summer, featuring world-class artists, and the entire community becomes involved in one way or another. Concertgoers combine theater with picnics, sipping wine and sampling cheeses while they relax and listen to classical music, jazz and bluegrass or watch ballet and light opera.

Once the site of a major gold strike, Jacksonville lost its chance to become the largest town in southern Oregon back in 1883 when the Oregon & California Railroad pushed its tracks northward. When the railroad requested a $25,000 "bonus" to place a station in Jacksonville, the city fathers unwisely refused to pay. Instead, the station was built at a crossroads called Middle Ford. Middle Ford shortened its name to Medford and grew while Jacksonville languished. In some ways this was fortunate, because "progress" passed the town by, saving its historic old buildings from the wrecking ball.

Jacksonville's shady, tree-lined streets, 130-year-old brick hotels, commercial buildings and restored Victorian homes assured its designation as a National Historic Landmark Town in 1966. Antique stores, boutiques and interesting restaurants line the main street while quiet residential neighborhoods are set back from the commerce. The town was once used as a movie set; they just covered the pavement with a thin layer of dirt to make things look authentic and used the downtown streets for a Western film. Except for the evening traffic for the outdoor Britt Festival, Jacksonville is basically quiet, a place many folks have selected for retirement because of its small-town, old-fashioned atmosphere. The surrounding countryside and north toward the community of Gold Hill are favored by horse breeders, with pastures and white-fenced ranches spaced at frequent intervals.

When Grandkids Visit Try a campout at beautiful Diamond Lake. About 80 miles northeast of Medford, the lake has boat rentals so you can make inroads on the rainbow trout population. Don't try it in the winter; the resort is open, but it's so cold that even the trout wear earmuffs.

Important Addresses and Connections

Chamber of Commerce: Medford/Jackson County: 101 E. 8th St., Medford, OR 97501; Jacksonville: 185 N. Oregon St., Jacksonville, OR 97530.

Senior Services: 510 E. Main St., Medford, OR 97504.

Daily Newspaper: *Mail Tribune,* First at 6th, Medford, OR 97501.

Airport: Medford's airport is the air hub of the region.

Bus/Train: Local bus system, with special rate for seniors and Greyhound serve the area.

MEDFORD	Jan.	Apr.	July	Oct.	Rain	Snow
Daily Highs	45	64	91	69	20	8
Daily Lows	30	37	54	40	in.	in.

Rogue River

> *We first thought about settling on the coast, and we almost bought there. But our car just seemed to keep wanting to head this direction, for Gold Hill and Rogue River. Finally, we decided this was the place for us, and we've never been sorry.*
>
> —Kay Campbell

North of Medford and just off Interstate 5, the town of Rogue River sprawls along the banks of its namesake. The city of Rogue River counts about 2,000 inhabitants, but when folks hereabouts refer to "Rogue River," they include the surrounding countryside, an area containing a total of 14,000 people. Grants Pass is the nearest "heavy-duty" shopping area, with Medford 18 miles to the east.

With an elevation of 1,000 feet above sea level, the town of Rogue River sits in the heart of a region where three mountain ranges meet: the Cascades, the Siskiyous and the Coast Range. This creates the weather so typical of the Rogue Valley· warm, dry summers, cool evenings, and moderate winters.

This is small-town living at its best. There are quiet streets shaded by mature trees, and affordable homes for those who prefer to be within walking distance of stores and the library. An adults-only mobile home park is conveniently located close to shopping, as is a "clubhouse" community which is primarily for senior citizens. Excellent medical facilities are in Grants Pass, only eight miles away. For emergencies, the town has an ambulance service.

To the east of Interstate 5, a sprawling countryside of homes sitting on generous acreage, small farms and forested homesites captivate the get-away-from-it-all crowd. We have California friends who recently purchased 38 acres of woods, pastures and abandoned mining claims, complete with a two-story home for half what they got for their Southern California tract home on an ordinary-size lot. The mining operations left two ponds which are perfect for swimming on warm summer days.

Recreation and Culture   The city is within two hours' drive of both mountain skiing and ocean beaches. Lakes and streams with fine fishing are nearby, but many residents and visitors prefer to fish right in the Rogue itself, as it winds through the valley and the heart of town. The river's native trout, salmon and steelhead are justifiably famous among anglers.

The city boasts several parks—Coyote Evans, Fleming, and Anna Classick—which feature facilities for horseshoes, tennis, and boat ramps. Valley of the Rogue State Park, three miles away on Interstate 5, offers complete camping and RV facilities on the river. A public golf course is located in Gold Hill (Laurel Hill, 9 holes, par 31).

A popular yearly event is the "Great Bath Tub Race." Contestants float down the river from nearby Gold Hill to Rogue River. It's a wild and woolly race with winner-take-all in prize money! Another hilarious event is the "Rooster Crow." Contestants try to coax their roosters to crow for the audience. The rooster to crow the most in 30 minutes wins a cash prize for his master. (Don't feel left out if you don't happen to have your own rooster with you; you can rent a bird at this event.) It's great entertainment to observe the outrageous tricks they try. Some stand in front of the cage flapping their arms to encourage the cock to crow, while others shout or threaten to cut off access to hens for a week. Last year's winner crowed 96 times to take first place. The event is held the last Saturday in June, along with an old-fashioned, small-town parade.

Perhaps inspired by Ashland's theater spirit, the Rogue River Community Theatre Group brings people of all ages together for Wednesday night workshops. "Thespians and wanna-be thespians can soliloquy to their hearts' content, study acting, improve, create and recreate scenes," according to the group's spokesman.

Housing Costs When people speak of Rogue River, they aren't just talking about the relatively small commercial and residential area where the interstate and Rogue River intersect. They include a large area extending east of town for 20 minutes driving time, including the community of Wymers. The countryside varies from flat farming lands to rolling, forest-covered hills. In town, of course, building lots are small, with new homes fitting between older homes and an occasional mobile home or manufactured home park. Away from the town proper, homesites are measured in acres rather than yards. In town, you can easily find homes priced under $100,000, and a three-bedroom place on five acres or more outside of town might sell for $150,000. Rentals are limited, since most homes are owner-occupied, and apartments and condos are scarce.

Crime and Safety As with all small Oregon towns, the crime rate in Rogue River is exceptionally low.

Nearby Retirement Possibilities Also off Interstate 5, the little town of Gold Hill presents a pioneer image, with historic buildings and a Western atmosphere. It's just a few minutes' drive to Rogue River, so it shares much of the same interests. The population is about 1,000, so everybody has a chance to know all the neighbors. Because it's so small, anybody can run for a city office, and it appears that everybody does, with very active political jousting at every election.

This is an area of inexpensive housing, with many homes on acreage rather than lots, and you have the right to place a mobile home on your property if you wish. Some nice river-frontage places were for sale during our visit, with prices over $200,000, and other river-front lots held more modest mobile homes.

When Grandkids Visit Think about a kayaking or rafting trip on the Rogue. You can rent for the day, and professional companies offer guided trips from one to five days. The most ambitious starts downriver, at Grave Creek, and rides the rapids for 32 miles along the "Wild and Scenic" section of the Rogue.

Important Addresses and Connections

Chamber of Commerce: 510 E Main St., Rogue River, OR 97537.
Senior Services: 132 Broadway, Rogue River, OR 97537.
Weekly Newspaper: *Rogue River Press,* 105 Gardner, Rogue River, OR 97537.
Airport: Medford.
Bus/Train: Senior Club has a van for local rides. Nearest Greyhound bus stop is in Grants Pass, eight miles away.

Grants Pass

The people are friendly, the weather is great, the fishing is good, and we are out of the rat race.   —Francis Stroup

Grants Pass is only about eight miles north on the interstate from the town of Rogue River, but it presents yet another retirement style: somewhere between a small town and a small city. If Grants Pass appears to be larger than its credited 19,000 people who live within the city limits, that's because it's the everyday shopping center for a large area surrounding the city.

A picturesque aspect of Grants Pass living is the way the scenic Rogue River winds through the town, lazy and swirling, with park-like lawns reaching down to the waterline in people's backyards. Three sides of Grants Pass are flanked by mountains, low and pine-covered. The roaring, whitewater sections of the river don't start until farther downriver, around Hellgate Canyon. Mobile home parks and cozy homes sit in close proximity to the riverbanks, allowing sportsmen to reel in steelhead and salmon just a few yards from their back doors. The city built boat ramps at strategic locations so you can put in your craft and drift along slothfully while you fish.

Houses within walking distance of the town's center are predominantly older, frame buildings, mostly single family, neat, well cared for and, best of all, affordable. Newer housing tends to be away from downtown, often built on an acre of land or so, with trees and natural shrubbery planted as low-maintenance landscaping devices. Although there are a few modest-looking neighborhoods, we found none to be run-down or shabby. Just a few blocks from the main north-south street is a lovely neighborhood of expensive homes. To the north, where hills are in transition to mountains, you'll find a mix of expensive homes on landscaped lots and inexpensive places with large, wooded yards.

Downtown Grants Pass recently earned the distinction of a National Historic District because of its tastefully restored historic buildings and older homes. Like many downtown cities nowadays, the city center's business is shifting to the shopping malls on the outskirts. But Grants Pass merchants are fighting back. The city center is sprinkled with antique and collectibles shops, ice cream parlors, and sidewalk espresso stands, and there's a large Safeway and some hardware stores still serving local shoppers. Next to downtown, Riverside Park is located on the Rogue River and is a wonderful place for picnicking, hiking or fishing along the river's edge.

Another feature of the area is that Oregon becomes mountainous at this point, with forests and rugged hills covering much of the landscape. A 15-minute drive from downtown takes you to wonderfully secluded and wild-looking properties where you will be plagued by deer eating your flowers and black bears raiding your garbage cans. (We used to live there, so we know!)

The Grants Pass retirement community is exceptionally active, engaging a large number of volunteers in worthwhile programs. This is important, because without sales-tax revenue, Oregon has little money to spare for senior services. If some things are to happen, they must be done with volunteer labor. Because of chronic under-employment locally, the competition for part-time jobs is brisk, so those who need meaningful work in order to feel fulfilled find satisfaction in volunteer jobs. Isn't it a good feeling to know that at least somewhere people still consider you vital and dynamic? By the way, some official sources claim that 50 percent of Grants Pass residents are retirees. I'm not convinced this is accurate, but if you retire here, you will have lots of people your own age to mix with.

Recreation and Culture Grants Pass has four public golf courses, and skiing isn't far away at Mt. Ashland. But outdoor recreation here naturally centers around the legendary Rogue River. It draws sportsmen from far and wide to ride kayaks or rafts down its thrilling rapids, or to fish for steelhead, rainbows and salmon. Whitewater enthusiasts who have braved rapids all over the world will testify that rafting Oregon's Rogue River is the ultimate whitewater experience because of the river's incredible beauty. However, the raft ride isn't really dangerous, provided you go with an experienced boatman. None of the rapids are over class three, and cowards like me are always given the option of walking around the more exciting stretches.

Some wonderful hiking trails follow the river, the best of which is the Rogue River Wild and Scenic Trail. This fairly gentle trail begins at Grave Creek (downriver from Merlin) and follows the river downstream 40 miles to Foster Bar. You can make arrangements for a van to take you back home from several stopping points along the way.

Public golf courses include Colonial Valley, 9 holes, par 29; Grants Pass Golf Club, 18 holes, par 72; Paradise Ranch, 9 holes, par 28; Red Mountain, 9 holes, par 28.

Grants Pass is filled with fun during the "Boatnik Festival" at Riverside Park, which lasts four days over Memorial Day weekend. The main event is a thrilling hydroboat race. This caps "Amazing May," a month-long eclectic mix of activities to kick off the summer season. Horse races at Grants Pass Downs spice up August's entertainment calendar.

Grants Pass is also the site of the region's largest outdoor agricultural Growers Market, where you can buy farm-fresh fruits, vegetables and flowers every Saturday morning from Easter to Thanksgiving, and also on Wednesdays in the summer.

For educational diversion, Rogue River Community College's wooded setting makes for a beautiful campus in keeping with the area's forest and hill environment. The school offers a wide variety of classes for seniors as well as regular students. Should you have special expertise in some field that you'd like to share, talk to the administration; they're often receptive, and will pay a token hourly wage for you to teach. This is a great way to become acquainted with those with like interests.

Housing and Other Costs The overall cost of living here is slightly below Oregon averages, but the cost of home ownership varies widely in Grants Pass and the surrounding communities. There appears to be plenty of affordable housing in the $65,000 to $100,000 range, as well as luxury places over $300,000. Being located on the river can boost the price of a home by $50,000. The median price of homes sold in Grants Pass in 1995 was $110,000 and outside the city, $125,000. Recent building of nice apartments means that rentals are plentiful, with apartments starting at $350 and home rentals at $600.

Medical Care Three Rivers Community Hospital and Health Center is the result of a merger by Southern Oregon Medical Center and the Josephine Memorial Hospital. The result is a 148-bed hospital with 119 physicians affiliated with the facility. This change gives the Grants Pass region a boost in medical care.

Crime and Safety For some reason the crime rate in Grants Pass is higher than expected—not horrible, just above national averages. However, I can testify from experience that during the four years we lived in the Grants Pass area, we never felt threatened at any time. As a matter of fact, out in the country where our home was located, we seldom bothered locking our doors unless we were going to be gone for a weekend or longer.

Nearby Retirement Possibilities Downriver from Grants Pass, the small town of Merlin bills itself as the "Gateway to the Wild & Scenic Rogue River." A dozen or more river outfitters, boat rental companies and fishing guides stand ready to prepare you for the river. Most homes around Merlin are modestly priced, set on large, tree-shaded lots. Just a short distance from the commercial area, generous acreages harbor sprawling ranch homes and farm houses. For an interesting journey back in time visit nearby Pottsville. Although it sounds like a town, it's really a large farm with a collection of historic gas engines, antique farm implements and steam engines from the turn of the century. It's located on Pleasant Valley Road, off of the Merlin-Galice Highway.

Downriver from Merlin is the famous Hellgate Canyon, where dramatic rock walls rise 250 feet above the rapids, a favorite with kayakers and photo buffs. Here's where they filmed the famous "jump" segment of the movie "Butch Cassidy and the Sundance Kid." We watched scenes from "River Wild" (with Meryl Streep and Kevin Bacon) being filmed in Hellgate Canyon and other places along the Rogue River.

About 15 miles farther downriver, the little community of Galice marks the point where most river-rafters inflate their rubber boats and drop them in the water for whitewater adventure. This is the beginning of an 84-mile segment of the Rogue River set aside by Congress under the National Wild and Scenic Rivers Act of 1968. Galice is a lovely location, with riverside homes priced accordingly. Across the road from the river, prices are much more affordable. This stretch of the river is popular with gold miners, with several of them making a living by panning or digging in mountain canyons.

The town of Murphy is located just off Williams Highway about five miles to the south of Grants Pass, where Murphy Creek meets the Applegate River. Murphy has a rural feeling, with inexpensive housing, yet is close to Grants Pass. It features a market, a popular steak-house restaurant and several retail establishments. Homes and small farms are clustered nearby.

The community of Williams is also in the Applegate Valley, located about twelve miles south of Grants Pass. Like Murphy, it's a mix of ranches, rural residences and a town center with several businesses. Williams is known for its artists and musicians, and for peace and quiet, accentuated by some of the most gorgeous scenery in the Rogue Valley.

When Grandkids Visit Take them on a jet boat ride down the Rogue River. This is a neat way of seeing the river, its wildlife and scenic wonders, and having a good time in the bargain. The boats roar through Hellgate Canyon, stop for lunch in Galice, and continue south to Grave Creek before turning around.

Important Addresses and Connections

Chamber of Commerce: 1501 N.E. 6th St., Grants Pass, OR 97526.
Senior Services: 306 N.W. D Street, Grants Pass, OR 97562.
Newspaper: *Daily Courier*, P.O. Box 1468, Grants Pass, OR 97526.
Airport: Medford, shuttle service available.
Bus/Train: A private bus service in town at $1 a ride. Also Greyhound/Trailways Bus inter-city service.

GRANTS PASS	Jan.	Apr.	July	Oct.	Rain	Snow
Daily Highs	49	69	94	69	28	4
Daily Lows	34	40	56	42	in.	in.

Cave Junction

My parents moved here years ago, and when we came to visit, we fell in love with the place. We went right home to Riverside, California, and began packing. Later, our daughters decided to move here, so all our family, including grandchildren, live here.
—Dodie Wandermark

Some folks love small towns and rural life and can't stand the thought of living in a city, even one the size of Grants Pass. They might turn their attention to a series of small settlements dotting the winding roads that cross the coastal mountains to the ocean.

An example of this are the small communities scattered along the scenic road leading to the ocean at Crescent City. This area is known as the Illinois Valley, named after the Illinois River that runs through here. "Wide-spot-in-the-road" type communities such as O'Brien, Kirby, and Selma straddle this two-lane pavement. Most residents live on generous plots of land, in homes of modest construction, often built by the owners themselves.

The heart of Illinois Valley is Cave Junction, a crossroads town of 1,235 inhabitants. It's also known as the gateway to the Oregon Caves: a fascinating complex of nearby limestone caverns (a place you must take your grandkids!). Cave Junction is strategically located halfway between ocean fishing or beach-combing and shopping Grants Pass at Safeway, WalMart or Fred Meyers. The just-opened senior citizen center is located here.

This is also the heart of Oregon's wine producing region. Three small wineries operate in the Cave Junction area, and tasting rooms proudly offer samples of their vintages. Since these are family-owned and operated enterprises, you may have to call ahead to visit the tasting room.

People living here forfeit the benefits of city life, accepting instead the solitude and charm of country living. However, let's agree on something: in order to fit into this rustic world, you have to bring a considerable amount of "country mentality" with you. You'll not find Greyhound buses zipping through here, and the nearest airport is 58 miles away (Medford). You'll have to adapt to local norms and cannot expect your neighbors to change to your way of thinking. But that's part of country living.

The altitude in Illinois Valley is about 1,400 feet, so expect more snow than you would in the Rogue Valley, where the elevation is less than 500 feet. Local residents claim that while it might snow six inches overnight, the white fluffy stuff almost always vanishes within a day or so after it stops falling. This four-season climate is one thing retirees here swear by.

Recreation and Culture Hunting and fishing are big here. Bird hunters go after pheasant, quail, pigeon, geese and ducks. The Illinois, Rogue and Applegate Rivers provide salmon, steel-head and trout, while Selma's 160-acre, man-made Lake Selmac is the state's premier trophy bass lake. A 55-mile drive to the coast affords surfcasting, rock fishing and deep-sea adventures.

In addition to the natural outdoor recreation here, Cave Junction also has a golf course. The Illinois Valley Golf Club is an 18-hole, par 72 layout. For continuing education, Rogue River College in Grants Pass is 22 miles away. Many classes there are tailored for senior participation.

Housing Costs You won't find much upscale housing here; this is the low-end, economy mode of country living. As a matter of fact, the federal government recently designated this as an area in need of economic assistance. The lifestyle here is not only rustic, but strictly down-scale. You probably won't be surprised to learn that the Illinois Valley is a great place to look for low-cost housing. A high-quality, elegant, three-bedroom house might sell for about $80,000, according to local homeowners. In general, real estate sells for less here than in almost any other retirement area in the state.

Medical Care For medical emergencies, it isn't necessary to travel to Grants Pass; Cave Junction has its own medical clinic and an excellent ambulance service. But it's comforting to know that top quality medical care isn't far away.

When Grandkids Visit Take 'em to the Oregon Caves, just a short drive away. The formations and twisting tunnels will keep their attention, and the climbing up and down isn't too difficult.

Important Addresses and Connections

Chamber of Commerce: 201 Caves Hwy, Cave Junction, OR 97523.
Senior Services: 520 W River St., Cave Junction, OR 97523.
Weekly Newspaper: *Illinois Valley News,* 319 S Redwood Hwy., Cave Junction, OR 97523.
Airport: Medford.
Bus/Train: None.

Myrtle Creek/Canyonville

We came here from San Diego, traveling about in our motorhome, looking for a place to retire. What impressed us about Myrtle Creek was the way local people went out of their way to welcome us.
— Gail Black

Continuing north, Interstate 5 crosses the mountains at Stage Road Pass and then plunges down into the Umpqua River Valley.

(By the way, before you reach Myrtle Creek, try to stop for lunch at the Wolf Creek Inn. This is a restored hotel and stagecoach station, owned and operated by the state of Oregon. The Inn is not only a historical museum portraying life in the latter 1800s, but it also serves delicious food at moderate prices.)

The Umpqua Valley is characterized by small farms, rolling hills and stretches of wooded, and sometimes scantily populated, country. Lumber is the area's mainstay. With only 19 people per square mile, this valley presents many quiet areas to explore as retirement possibilities if you like small-town or country living. The snow-capped Cascade Mountains guard the valley to the east, and the lower Coast Range hills loom in the west.

The first retirement choices you'll encounter after traversing the mountain passes will be the twin towns of Myrtle Creek and Canyonville. Neither place is quite on the valley floor; they're sheltered by the hills and ravines at the foot of Canyon Mountain. Canyonville is a little more than 10 minutes by inter-state from Myrtle Creek. Both towns present a distinct Western motif, with small businesses in the downtown areas and comfort-able, single-family homes shaded by large trees. Myrtle Creek is just a short distance from the highway, which makes access to shopping and city conveniences easy from both Canyonville and Myrtle Creek.

Called the "Gateway to the 100 Valleys of the Umpqua," some compare the region geographically and climatically with Italy and the south of France—not in small part because of the way vineyards thrive here. Because the altitude is only 600 feet, the weather is unusually mild, even though four distinct seasons are evident. As one resident put it, "We don't get much cold weather here, yet it snows enough to prove that it's winter. But most of it falls on the hills and mountain slopes. Not much sticks to the streets." Between the two towns and the intervening area, the population can be guesstimated at 8,000.

Canyonville is the third-oldest settlement in Oregon, and it works hard to maintain its appearance as a pioneer town. The business center displays several interesting antique shops and stores which carry out this Old West theme. The first wagon trains passed through here in 1843, and Canyonville soon evolved as an important supply station for fur traders, miners and early immigrants. The town was a welcome resting place for pio-neers after wagons passed through the "Dreaded Canyon" on the famous Applegate Emigrant Trail. This history is commemorated each August by a "Pioneer Days" celebration, complete with music, arts and crafts, logging demonstrations and great food.

One of the features of Canyonville is the gambling casino operated by the Umpqua Indian Tribe. It was being enlarged during our last visit; soon to have 250 slot machines and a 500-seat bingo hall, plus an RV park. All of this is within walking distance from downtown Canyonville and presumably will draw tourists, create business for merchants and possibly provide part-time jobs for seniors.

Eight miles north of Canyonville, just off Interstate 5, at the confluence of Myrtle Creek and the South Umpqua River, the delightful little town of Myrtle Creek is one of the area's best kept secrets. You'll know when you've traveled exactly 108 miles north of the California border, because the Interstate 5 offramp here is labeled "Exit 108." For the record, that's also 80 miles (90 minutes' drive) from the Pacific beaches should you choose to retire here. Myrtle Creek's population is about 3,600, large enough to support public facilities such as a library, adequate shopping, clubs and organizations and churches for most faiths.

The Senior Center in Myrtle Creek also serves Canyonville, and its members are quite active in community affairs and volunteer projects. When we visited, a number of retirees were busy putting up Christmas decorations on Main Street, precariously perched on ladders, draping decorations and illumination from light standards and power poles. With a high percentage of residents retired, active socialization is important here. "We work hard at relaxing," said one volunteer.

A Greyhound/Trailways bus will stop in both towns on its daily run, but you have to place an advance reservation, so the driver will know to stop for you. The towns aren't so small that they don't have a cable TV company. There's also a UHF TV station, which is a CBS affiliate.

The nearby town of Riddle, on the opposite side of the interstate, is usually considered part of Myrtle Creek-Canyonville area. Folks in all three communities join in local activities.

Recreation and Culture The setting here naturally encourages outdoor activities. Since 80 percent of Douglas County is timberland—part of one million square miles of the Umpqua National Forest—you're never far from a park or a woodland camp for family enjoyment. Local hunters are said to go after deer, elk, black bear, cougar, fox, wild turkey, quail and pheasant, as well as Canadian geese and ducks. (Sounds like they're busy as well as ambitious.) Others find outdoor recreation in panning for gold in the South Umpqua River. The oldtimers didn't get it all, just most of it. For golfers, the good news is that an 18-hole course is in the first stages of development in Myrtle Creek, scheduled to be ready for play by the spring of 1997.

From the Myrtle Creek intersection on Interstate 5, it's only a 13-mile drive to Roseburg and access to the wonderful programs and cultural offerings of the Umpqua Community College. See the section on Roseburg (below) for more details about continuing education and other programs given by the excellent community college there.

Housing Costs According to property specialists in this area, the price of a moderate three-bedroom home starts at $69,000, which is said to be about $20,000 lower than similar properties in nearby Roseburg. A broker pointed out a sale she had made the previous week: a three-bedroom, two-bath home with a two-car garage; 1,504 sq. ft. on a 150x150 lot: $82,000. She claimed that a comparable home in the Roseburg area would sell for $120,000. It's possible. Rentals are never too plentiful in a small area like this; single family homes are the norm, with few condominiums or apartment buildings.

Medical Care Myrtle Creek has a small hospital staffed by 13 doctors. The nearest large hospitals are in Roseburg, some 15 miles from Myrtle Creek and 28 miles from Canyonville. An excellent ambulance and paramedic service stands by to whisk you to the hospital in case of an emergency. Most local residents support the ambulance with a $15 yearly donation, for which they receive free emergency assistance; others pay a nominal fee if the service is needed.

Crime and Safety Crime levels are exceptionally low, as you would expect of an area of this nature.

When Grandkids Visit Nearby South Umpqua Falls is a great place for picnics, swimming and loafing. The falls tumble over an unusual scenic bedrock formation. There's a viewing platform, a fish ladder and a great picnic area. All are wheelchair accessible. Another possibility is a visit to the Tiller Ranger

District, where you can tour a restored fire detection lookout and historic Civilian Conservation Corps-era buildings.

Important Addresses and Connections

Chamber of Commerce: Myrtle Creek: 59 Main Street, Myrtle Creek, OR 97457; Canyon City: 250 Main St., Canyonville, OR 97417.

Senior Services: 425 N.W. Second, Myrtle Creek, OR 97457.

Weekly Newspaper: *Umpqua Free Press*, 119 S Main St., Myrtle Creek, OR 97457.

Airport: Portland or Medford.

Bus/Train: A Greyhound bus will make a stop in Myrtle Creek or Canyonville, but you must phone Roseburg to notify the driver in advance.

MYRTLE CREEK	Jan.	Apr.	July	Oct.	Rain	Snow
Daily Highs	48	63	84	67	33	7
Daily Lows	34	39	53	43	in.	in.

Roseburg

A lot of things have been happening with the college in the last five years. There's been a large increase in cultural activities, and that makes living here much more interesting.

—Bonnie Girardet

Roseburg is slightly larger than Grants Pass, with 19,000 inhabitants, and like Grants Pass is an important commercial center. As the largest city in the Umpqua Valley, Roseburg naturally assumes the role of major shopping center for the surrounding localities. As the largest town between Grants Pass and Eugene, it has also become the cultural and social focus for this region because of the way Umpqua Community College reaches out and invites everyone to join in the school's programs. No less than a dozen small towns circling Roseburg look upon that city for their "downtown" activities. For large-city conveniences, Eugene is 67 miles to the north.

The altitude here is less than 500 feet, which accounts for the mild weather the Umpqua River Valley enjoys. Snow that sticks to the ground is rare, and rainfall registers a mere 33 inches— about the same as in Chicago—except that Chicago also receives 39 inches of snow! According to local boosters, the area enjoys one of the lowest wind velocities anywhere in the United States.

The region's rich soil, combined with a gentle climate, encourages cultivation of such crops as melons, berries, nuts, plums and apples. Grapes do well under these conditions, so it's no surprise that the Umpqua Valley is one of Oregon's premier wine-producing areas. Within a short drive from Roseburg you can tour the region's eight wineries, which grow chardonnay, pinot noir, gewürztraminer, reisling, zinfandel and cabernet varietals.

This area is also renowned for covered bridges, mid-1800 restored homes and the nationally acclaimed Douglas County Museum of History and Natural History.

Recreation and Culture Ocean fishing, crabbing and beachcombing are but an hour's drive to the west. An hour's drive in the opposite direction takes you into superb trout fishing and camping country, along the beautiful North Umpqua river. Faithfully, the North Umpqua delivers catches of trout, salmon, bass. It's one of the world's only rivers with a native run of summer steelhead.

You needn't travel far to enjoy famous recreational sites like nearby Crater Lake National Park, Diamond Lake, and the Wild and Scenic North Umpqua River, or to more quiet and lesser known sites like Yasko Falls and Skookum Lake. Highway 138 provides access through the forest and is part of the National Scenic Byway System. Over 390 miles of maintained hiking trails are complemented by cross-country skiing and snowmobiling trails to a total of more than 600 miles. A very popular hiking path is the 79-mile North Umpqua Trail.

Two public golf courses are open for play: Roseburg Municipal Golf Course (9 hole) and Sutherlin Knolls (18 holes) in nearby Sutherlin.

The Hoffman Center Tennis Complex offers 12 outdoor, lighted courts and the Paul Jackson Tennis complex has 3 indoor courts, both located at Stewart Park. Indoor courts are also available during the winter at the Douglas County Fairgrounds by advance reservation.

Roseburg is justifiably proud of its Umpqua Community College, a school that believes in total local involvement and that actively encourages senior citizen participation. The 100-acre campus is situated on a bend of the North Umpqua River, offering a spectacular educational setting. Concerts, plays and musical productions by the school's theater department are supplemented by presentations by the Umpqua Actors Community Theater.

Internationally recognized musical fare is provided by the Umpqua Symphony Association and the Roseburg Community Concert Association. Regular showings of works by local artists are presented by the Umpqua Valley Arts Center. The college's "Gold Card" program is extended to seniors to encourage their participation in the school. Gold Card holders may take credit, non-credit and community education courses for a tuition of $15 per class; some classes are free.

Housing and Other Costs Apartments and houses are available for rent in most areas of Roseburg. Homes for sale can accommodate a wide range of tastes, locations and economic resources, from mobile homes to luxury homes with acreage. Several retirement complexes also offer many amenities. Prices in town and the surrounding communities vary widely. The cost of living here is about average for the state.

Medical Care Roseburg is also the center for medical care for the many smaller communities in the surrounding country-side. Besides a large Veterans Hospital (with 417 beds), two private hospitals serve the medical needs of the Umpqua Valley region: the Mercy Medical Center and Douglas Community Hospital. There's also a specialized cancer treatment center, a kidney dialysis center, an outpatient surgical center and two fully staffed emergency clinics.

Crime and Safety Like most Oregon towns, Roseburg ranks above average in personal safety.

Nearby Retirement Possibilities Actually, the city of Roseburg isn't really the retirement attraction here as much as are the surrounding areas. Many retire in the half dozen or so small communities that depend upon Roseburg for shopping, cultural events and city conveniences. They consider the city as their "downtown," but at the same time they take full advantage of rural life. We've visited pleasant communities such as Winston and Dillard and Lookingglass, to the south and west of town— and also Sutherlin, to the north—and we consider them to have excellent potential as lower-cost retirement locations. Homes here tend to be unpretentious, set on generous pieces of land, with small farms dotting the hilly countryside.

Sutherlin is the site of an RV park that's owned by RV travelers who've opted for full-time retirement living in their motorhome, travel trailer or camper. Residents own their lots and rent them out when they're on the road. The organization has several similar parks in various parts of the country, where visiting members can "boondock" (stay for free) or rent a landscaped space for longer stays. (For more details about the RV retirement lifestyle, see my book *Retirement on a Shoestring*.)

Each year, a countywide Timber Days Celebration is held in Sutherlin, usually the second week in July. The event is a tribute to the timber industry, and events include axe throwing, pole climbing, saw bucking and log rolling. Contestants come from all over the world to participate, and the local residents add a historic touch by growing beards and wearing old-fashioned clothes for the annual parade. Other activities held during the celebration are a black powder shoot, horseshoe pitching and, of course, a dance and crowning of a queen.

When Grandkids Visit Don't miss the famous Wildlife Safari, a 600-acre, drive-through zoological park in nearby Winston. It's a reverse zoo: hundreds of exotic animals roam freely through the park's 600 acres. Giraffes, lions and rhinoceroses look you over while you drive about, securely locked in your automobile, through the animals' world. Should a rhinoceros become interested in your vehicle, consult Gary Larson's *Far Side* cartoons for an appropriate reaction.

Important Addresses and Connections

Chamber of Commerce: P.O. Box 1026, Roseburg, OR 97470.
Senior Services: 621 W. Madrone, Roseburg, OR 97470.
Newspaper: *News Review*, 345 N.E. Winchester St., Roseburg, OR 97470.
Airport: Eugene or Medford with shuttle bus service.
Bus/Train: There are a local bus system, Greyhound/Trailways intercity service and an Amtrak connection in Eugene.

ROSEBURG	Jan.	Apr.	July	Oct.	Rain	Snow
Daily Highs	48	63	84	67	33	4
Daily Lows	34	39	53	43	in.	in.

Eugene/Springfield

We're centrally located, a pretty place with four distinct seasons and lots of outdoor activities, and the crime rate is not bad.
—Dina Fortier

The biggest "industry" here is the University of Oregon, with an enrollment of nearly 18,000 students. Eugene is proud of its status as one of Oregon's intellectual communities; one-third of its population has completed four or more years of college. As if the university didn't provide enough academic life for the community, Eugene also supports Lane Community College, which enrolls even more students through its many branch faculties than does the university!

Like Ashland and Corvallis—the two other university towns featured in this book—academic life and the excitement of learning spills over into the community, making this one of the nation's premier college-town retirement destinations. Ongoing schedules of lectures, concerts, plays and sports offerings, many of which are free, provide a constant source of entertainment and academic interest for the retirement community.

Eugene's business center is highlighted by a large pedestrian mall for a pleasant shopping experience. Because of the large student population, the center is well-patronized, and it is graced with excellent restaurants and upscale shops. A large old building known as the Fifth Street Market houses a family of unique craft and specialty retailers, bookstores and restaurants, all of which make shopping downtown Eugene a treat. Toward the outskirts, two large shopping malls—one enclosed, the other open-air—offer shoppers a vast array of goods, food and services. Eugene's open-air Saturday Market is a popular, ongoing event from April to Christmas.

The Willamette River runs through the heart of the metropolitan area, with the McKenzie River joining the Willamette to the north of town at an elevation of just 426 feet above sea level. The Willamette River also divides Eugene from its sister city, Springfield, which has 47,000 inhabitants, compared with Eugene's 113,000.

Springfield's town center is definitely small-town style, since by common consent, Eugene has become the shopping and commercial center. Buildings here are small, with light traffic on the quiet streets. Downtown Springfield makes up for size by its contented charm. The housing around the town center is also low-key, with comfortable and quiet neighborhoods. By the way, Springfield enjoys one of the best senior centers we've encountered in Oregon, or anywhere for that matter. Facilities are excellent, the staff dedicated and retirees seem unanimously pleased with their center. The center regularly features such activities as health seminars, outdoor hiking and birdwatching, charter bus trips to places of interest and arts and crafts programs, as well as a wide variety of classes.

Eugene/Springfield's weather is mild enough that retirees can enjoy the outdoors all year. On the average, only 15 summer days a year reach or exceed 90 degrees, and most days are gloriously sunny. Rainfall is heavier here in the mid-state than in the more southerly parts—43 inches or so of rain each year, with very little snow—still far less than in most Eastern or Midwestern cities. Precipitation falls mostly in the winter, from November through April. This keeps the countryside green the year round and rewards the rest of the year with typically gorgeous and sunny Oregon springs, summers and falls. This gentle weather makes possible year-round enjoyment of Eugene's exceptional park system. Nearby Spencer Butte Park is famous for its coniferous forest that surrounds Spencer Butte, the highest point in the Eugene area, at 2,000 feet.

Recreation and Culture Much outdoor activity centers around the Willamette and the McKenzie rivers, which are fed pure water from distant glaciers and springs. A series of dams on the Willamette form long lakes which offer exceptional trout fishing and boating, with facilities for picnicking, miles of bicycle trails and river walks. For ocean fishing, clamming and beachcombing for driftwood or Japanese glass fishing floats, Pacific beaches are a 90-minute drive west through gentle, low mountain country and the Siuslaw National Forest. A short drive in the opposite direction is the Deschutes National Forest, crowned by the Mt. Washington and Three Sisters wilderness areas.

College basketball, baseball and other sports events are open to the public, and the university stadium accommodates over 40,000 fans for PAC Ten football games, city sports events and large outdoor concerts. The 10,000-seat McArthur Court regularly hosts indoor events such as basketball, volleyball and cultural programs. The local minor league baseball team is a farm club for the Atlanta Braves. Public golf courses include Fiddler's Green (18 holes, par 54; seniors play 9 holes for $3 or 18 for $5), Laurelwood (9 holes, par 35), Oakway (18 holes, par 61) and Riveridge (18 holes, par 71). There are also 23 tennis courts and sports programs for seniors that are sponsored by the city.

Because of the university, cultural and social activities are endless in the Eugene/Springfield area. Eugene has its own symphony, ballet and opera companies. Eugene also enjoys seven museums, a science and technology center plus a planetarium. The Hult Center for the Performing Arts houses two theaters—a concert hall and a playhouse—which regularly feature plays, concerts and performances by local, regional and national talent. If you've always wondered why Bach is considered such a great composer, you must make it a point to attend the critically acclaimed Oregon Bach Festival.

Housing and Other Costs Near the university, residential streets are restrained, with plenty of older homes providing housing for students and retirees alike at reasonable prices. Away from the center of town, Eugene's housing is varied and neighborhoods attractive. Prices for an average 3-bedroom, 2-bath, 1,600-square-foot home can range from $100,000 to $125,000. In Springfield, across the river, housing costs are about 10 percent lower for comparable homes in similar areas. The overall cost of living seems to be a bit above Oregon average, due to the vigorous economic development underway in the Eugene area.

Medical Care The Eugene/Springfield area has two main medical facilities, both offering state-of-the-art treatment in 25 specialities, plus 24-hour emergency care. The largest is Sacred Heart General Hospital, with 432 beds and a large intensive care unit, and the other hospital is McKenzie-Willamette Hospital with 114 beds. In all there are nearly 500 physicians and surgeons in the metropolitan area.

Crime and Safety According to the FBI national statistics, Eugene is just about average, as far as crime is concerned. Springfield fares a bit better, ranking in the top 40 percent for personal safety.

Nearby Retirement Possibilities Northeast of Eugene is a delightful area of farms, woods and small, crossroads communities where most homes enjoy spacious acreage settings. Mohawk, Marcola and Mabel are some landmarks to head for if you care to investigate this area. Numerous small farms checkerboard the countryside, interspersed with forested tracts, meadows and homes set back from country roads. Buildings here tend to be casual, a mixture of older homes and new, some places obviously do-it-yourself architecture and others top quality.

When Grandkids Visit Take them to the Lane County Historical Museum and look at the displays about the Oregon Trail pioneers. Exhibits include covered wagons, photos, maps and photos of the historic trek to settle the West.

Important Addresses and Connections

Chambers of Commerce: 1401 Willamette St., Eugene, OR 97401; 101 S A St., Springfield, OR 97477.

Senior Services: 996 Jefferson St., Eugene, OR 97401; 215 West C St., Springfield, OR 97477.

Newspapers: *The Register-Guard* (daily), 975 High St., Eugene, OR 97401; *The News* (bi-weekly), 1887 Laura St., Springfield, OR 97477.

Airport: Eugene.

Bus/Train: Local bus service, Greyhound and Amtrak.

EUGENE/SPRING.	Jan.	Apr.	July	Oct.	Rain	Snow
Daily Highs	46	60	82	65	40	6
Daily Lows	33	34	50	41	in.	in.

Albany

Albany's an all-around nice town. It's very green, and within an hour's drive you can be in the mountains, the beach, or in a big city. We have an active senior community [and] don't have crime problems.
                                                              —Lee Carter

Pioneers who followed the offers of free land in Oregon knew they'd found a good thing when they saw a fertile prairie on the banks of a beautiful river. For them, this was the end of the Oregon Trail. This fortuitous location on the Willamette River started Albany on its way to becoming a prosperous river town. The downtown waterfront area developed as a steamboat landing, with passengers traveling to and from Portland for a $1 fare. A railroad reached Albany in 1871, and heavy industry sprang up on the edge of town, around the railroad tracks. Albany became known as the "hub city" because of its location and commercial importance. It was a time of prosperity; beautiful Victorian mansions blossomed and intricately decorated smaller homes graced the city's exceptionally broad streets.

Then, when Highway 99 pushed through the town's outskirts—and later Interstate 5—Albany began to change, attracting
even more industry and businesses of all kinds. Fortunately this
boom occurred away from the center of town, along the railroad
and highways. Thus the older part of the city was spared the
modernization that destroyed the old homes and historic downtowns of so many similar places. Today Albany is credited by his-
torians and architects with having the most varied collection of
historic buildings in Oregon. Represented are home styles from
the 1840s through the 1920s, including examples of every major
style popular in the U.S. since 1850. These are concentrated within an area of approximately one hundred square blocks, and
some are always up for sale at any given time. The vintage
Albany Trolley takes you through the historic districts in appropriate style. Finding treasures and collectibles while shopping or
enjoying dinner at one of many fine restaurants is a perfect way
to end a memorable day in historic Albany. Albany is worth a
slight detour off the interstate if only to step back into the past
for a moment.

The downtown, too, escaped modernization and offers shoppers and strollers an intriguing glimpse of yesterday's splendor.
This preservation keeps the area from falling into decay as many
other downtowns tend to do when residents begin to shop at
highway strip malls instead of in the town center. Nice restaurants and shops invite browsing and relaxing.

Eight venerable covered bridges in the area are all located
within a short distance of town, and they date from the 1930s. A
self-guided tour of these bridges takes you on a beautiful drive
through green fields on well-paved country roads. There is a
public park and swimming area beside Larwood Bridge, a perfect
spot for a picnic.

Albany (population 29,000) and nearby Corvallis enjoy the
highest air quality in the Willamette Valley. This is due to a gap
in the Oregon Coastal Range which draws continuous ocean
breezes to refresh the atmosphere. These breezes, along with the
valley's low elevation at this point (only 210 feet), are responsible for the mild climate that residents here enjoy.

Recreation and Culture   Four of Albany's 23 city parks
have tennis courts, and nine have hiking and bike paths. The
local public golf course is Golf Club of Oregon (18 holes, par

70). There are also two golf courses in nearby Corvallis: Golf City (9 holes, par 28) and Marysville (9 holes, par 36).

Oregon State University is located just 11 miles to the west, in Corvallis, and Albany residents take full advantage of the cultural and academic events there. But they also have the programs at Linn-Beton Community College in Albany, on the way to Corvallis, to choose from.

The world's largest logging event, the Albany Timber Carnival, is held every July 4th weekend. Albany also hosts one of the nation's largest Veteran's Day celebrations. Medal of Honor recipients, dozens of bands and a banquet highlight the day.

Another well-known event is Albany's Great Balloon Escape and Wine Fest. The sky fills with all the colors of the rainbow as the balloons lift off each morning during this three-day event, also held in July. On the ground, you find live musical entertainment, foods and crafts to enjoy, while tasting some of Oregon's finest wines.

Housing and Other Costs Albany has a wide range of housing alternatives varying in style, age, cost and surroundings. According to the local chamber of commerce, a two-bedroom apartment rents for between $425 and $550 a month and a three-bedroom home from $650 to $900 a month. A new, 1,500-square-foot home, three bedrooms with an enclosed two-car garage, runs between $140,000 and $165,000.

Medical Care Albany has a hospital and several nursing homes. Between Albany and the medical facilities in Corvallis, folks here enjoy more than adequate medical care.

When Grandkids Visit Take a guided tour of Albany's historic homes; start at the Visitor's Center on S.W. Second Street. Or, you can pick up a map at the center and do a self-guided tour. If that isn't enough, you could tour the area's covered bridges—the largest collection this side of New England.

Important Addresses and Connections

Chamber of Commerce: 435 1st Avenue N.W., Albany, OR 97321.
Senior Services: 489 Water Street, Albany, OR 97321.
Daily Newspaper: *Albany Democrat-Herald,* 600 Lyon S.W., Albany, OR 97321.
Airport: Portland or Eugene.
Bus/Train: Local bus service, Greyhound and a connection to Amtrak.

ALBANY	Jan.	Apr.	July	Oct.	Rain	Snow
Daily Highs	46	61	82	65	40	6
Daily Lows	33	38	51	42	in.	in.

Corvallis

We prize our quality of life, freedom from traffic problems and our safe environment. The college draws a lot of interesting things to do: the symphony, speakers, sports, events, a state-of-the-art library, along with good hospital facilities.

—Georgia Ostenson

Because Corvallis is just 11 miles from Albany, it might seem logical to lump the two towns together when describing them as retirement possibilities. But Corvallis clearly falls into a separate category: it's a college town. Oregon State University's park-like campus helps Corvallis enjoy that special atmosphere created whenever students, teachers and senior citizens mix. The city is ranked 14th nationwide for most educated residents per capita. The town is positioned about 80 miles from the Cascade Mountains and 50 miles from the Pacific Ocean beaches at Newport. The population is 46,000, and the elevation is 224 feet.

Residential areas are neat and cheerful, homes are well maintained and streets are often spiced with young adults cruising about on bikes or roller blades. The Corvallis downtown area, as you might expect in a college town, is upscale and user friendly, with quality shopping and excellent places to eat. Strolling through downtown is a pleasant experience as well as healthful exercise.

A few years ago, the Corvallis and Albany chambers of commerce started an innovative approach to attract retirees to the area. Called the "Sun Bird" program, it attempts to place out-of-state visitors in vacant rental units for the summer. The plan started for two reasons. First of all, a great deal of student housing fell vacant during the summer, when students went home for the long vacation term. The second item was that the chambers of commerce of both cities traditionally receive a pile of inquiries from retirees who live in the Southwestern states, inquiring about someplace to spend the summer and escape the 100-plus-degree weather of places like Phoenix or Dallas.

The Sun Bird program was a success, in fact, too much of a success. Today, school housing isn't going vacant. "Nowadays the school pretty much operates at full capacity the year round," said a chamber of commerce worker, "but we still get the requests, and we still try to locate housing for them." This has been a source of new residents, as some decide that going back to an oven isn't worth it. By the way, the head of the Corvallis chamber said that the majority of inquiries about retirement in Oregon come from folks who retired in hot climates and are now thinking about making a change.

Weather in the Corvallis area is typical of the intermountain valleys, with dry, sunny summers and wet winters. In fact, there's less than a 10 percent chance of rain during the summer months. Residents try to plant native shrubbery that thrives with little or no supplemental water. Like the rest of the area the surface soil does dry out in summer, so lawns and gardens need watering July through September. Rainfall is about 40 inches, most of it falling between November and March. As one Corvallis resident pointed out, "Some folks think Oregon is nothing but rain, but the fact is, 32 states out of 50 get more rain than we do!" Snowfall more than an inch deep occurs less than one time per year on average.

Recreation and Culture   More than 60 miles of hiking and bike paths wind through city parks and along the Willamette River. Just north of town, the McDonald Forest maintains 10 miles of interpretive trails, as well as many miles of roads and trails for hiking, horseback riding and biking.

Fishermen love the convenience of the Willamette River flowing through town; it makes fishing for steelhead trout most convenient. Rainbow trout and steelhead are also found in the tumbling streams of the nearby Coast Range mountains. For ocean fishing, clamming or crabbing, you need only drive 50 miles to the beaches at Newport.

Local public golf courses are Golf City (9 holes, par 28) and Marysville (9 holes, par 36). There's also a golf course in nearby Albany, the Golf Club of Oregon (18 holes, par 70).

A rich variety of cultural activities are available through the Corvallis Arts Center: community festivals, summer open-air concerts, a community orchestra, and year-round performing arts at the Majestic Theatre. Oregon State University offers the public a host of plays, concerts, lectures, films, dance productions, art exhibits and more.

Housing Costs   As is the rule in college towns, apartments and condominiums are common, so there are a large number of rentals, even though you may have to compete with students to acquire one. Since Corvallis has the second-highest income per capita in Oregon, it isn't surprising that housing is more costly. The average home sales price was $126,000, although it isn't difficult to find properties priced much lower. Again, rentals can be in short supply because of heavy student demand. According to one real estate person, the average rent of a two-bedroom apartment starts at $450, when available.

Medical Care   The Good Samaritan Hospital is the largest medical facility in Corvallis. An alternative is the Corvallis Clinic, the largest multi-specialty physician clinic in Oregon. It has branches in nearby Albany and Philomath.

Crime and Safety   Personal safety is very high in Corvallis. The city comes in seventh for safety out of 32 Oregon towns ranked by the FBI in their crime statistic tables.

When Grandkids Visit   They'll be interested in canoeing on the Millrace, a canal constructed in 1851 to generate water power for flour mills and a sawmill. They can paddle along a lazy, two-mile stretch of water, past blackberry bushes, geese and people's backyards. Several outfits rent canoes for the day.

Important Addresses and Connections

Chamber of Commerce: 420 N.W. Second, Corvallis, OR 97339.
Senior Services: 2601 N.W. Tyler Ave., Corvallis, OR 97330.
Daily Newspaper: *Gazette Times,* 600 S.W. Jefferson Ave., Corvallis, OR 97333.
Airport: Portland or Eugene.
Bus/Train: There is an excellent local bus system, and Greyhound provides intercity service with a stop in town. An Amtrak connection is in Albany, 10 miles away.

CORVALLIS	Jan.	Apr.	July	Oct.	Rain	Snow
Daily Highs	46	61	82	65	40	6
Daily Lows	33	38	51	42	in.	in.

Salem

We thought we'd have a difficult time making friends and keeping busy here. First thing we did was join a church group and register for senior classes at the university. Before long, we had TOO much to do and more friends than we had before we retired.
—Sharon Dearman

Sometimes called the "Cherry City," Salem is known for flowering orchards in the surrounding countryside. Fertile soil brings bountiful crops of strawberries, raspberries, pears, filberts and walnuts. The region is becoming known for wine, especially pinot noir, reisling and chardonnay.

Salem is the third-largest city in Oregon, with a population of 118,000, and its appearance gets a double boost from being both the site of Oregon's state capital and the home of Willamette University. These institutions help keep the downtown alive and thriving. A great deal of commerce and business is generated by both entities. The city has one of the best libraries we've ever seen, not only for the book collection, but also for public conference rooms available for residents to use as meeting places, classes, lectures and social affairs. The library is one of the focal points of the community for many retirees, a place to meet people and make friends.

As you might expect of a state capital, the downtown center is vibrant, with nice restaurants, shopping and excitement in the air, yet with an informality not expected in a political city. During our last research trip to Salem, a retired couple invited us to one of the local micro-breweries for a snack. The place is famous for good hamburgers in addition to its homemade beer. While we were ordering our hamburgers, a couple walked in and sat at the table next to us. They turned out to be Oregon's Governor, John Kitzhaber, and his wife, Sharon. Both were dressed casually; he wore his "trademark" blue jeans, sport coat and tie. Our friends exchanged pleasantries with the Governor, and we returned to our conversation. By the way, Governor Kitzhaber is a good friend to retirees. He is a medical doctor and the architect of Oregon's unique health care program—which is often looked at as a possible health-care model for the nation.

Salem is more than a one-university town. Besides Willamette University (a quality private school with 2,500 students), there's

Chemeketa Community College, with a wide variety of adult educational programs to serve the surrounding area, and Western Baptist College, a private co-educational school that's been in Salem for more than 40 years. Nearby is Western Oregon State, located 17 miles west of Salem at Monmouth.

Although most of the countryside around Salem is flat, conforming to the Willamette River's meandering course at this point, some beautiful residential areas are on hilly to almost mountainous tracts. These hills are wooded and have a rustic, country feeling, even though they are only 15 minutes from the center of town. In these neighborhoods, homes are designed to blend with the forest setting.

Recreation and Culture As you can tell from the golf courses listed here, you'll have plenty of opportunity to whack the balls around. Public play can be found at Auburn Center (9 holes, par 27), Battle Hill (18 holes, par 72), McNary (18 holes, par 71), Meadow Lawn (9 holes, par 32), Salem Golf Club (18 holes, par 72) and Evergreen Golf Club (9 holes, par 35). Hunting, fishing and skiing can be enjoyed in the nearby mountains, and of course, the ocean beaches are just a ninety-minute drive from Salem.

Willamette University's contribution to senior learning is an excellent example of why college town retirement is such a good idea. Called the Institute for Continued Learning, this program costs $80 per person for the entire year, including summer sessions, and is designed for seniors, although spouses can participate regardless of age. This fee includes participation in all seminars, held each Tuesday and Thursday four hours each day; use of gym, swimming pool and exercise equipment; free tickets to Willamette athletic events; and the use of Copy Center Learning Resource Center (VCR tapes, etc.). Seminars and lectures are given by noted scholars on a wide variety of subjects, ranging through literature, music, art, history, philosophy and current events. Taking classes in a university environment such as this one is a superb way for newcomers to make friends in their new community—friends with common interests and ideas.

Housing and Other Costs The cost of a typical new, 1,500-square-foot, three-bedroom home begins at $100,000. The rental market was very tight at the time of our last visit, but occasional apartments were available from $450 to $700, and homes were renting from $850. The cost of living index for Salem is two percent above national average, ranking it 95th lowest in a field of 252 U.S. cities.

Salem has several nice retirement complexes, some of which we investigated. These are particularly appropriate for singles or couples who wish to down-size their living accommodations. None of the residences we checked out required "buy-ins," that is, requiring a large sum of money to "buy" your apartment. We found studio apartments going for as little as $915 a month ($750 in nearby Woodburn), one bedrooms for $1,260 and two bedrooms for $1,500. These include some or all meals in the facility's elegant restaurant-style dining room, once-a-week maid service and TV cable. Many of Oregon's larger towns have similar accommodations, and it's worth an investigation to see if you fit into this lifestyle. For many people, Social Security checks would just about cover all their basic living expenses, and the quality of life is excellent. These kinds of places aren't restricted to Salem, they can be found all over the state.

Medical Care Health care in Salem is excellent with one large hospital, numerous medical clinics, and a large regional rehabilitation center.

When Grandkids Visit Visit the Gilbert House Children's Museum on Salem's Downtown Riverfront. They can explore innovative and exciting hands-on exhibits in the sciences, arts and humanities.

Important Addresses and Connections

Chamber of Commerce: 220 Cottage St. N.E., Salem, OR 97301.
Senior Services: 1055 Erixon Street N.E., Salem, OR 97301; 930 Plymouth Drive N.E., Salem, OR 97303.
Daily Newspaper: *Statesman-Journal,* 280 Church St. N.E., Salem, OR 97301.
Airport: Eugene or Portland.
Bus/Train: Local mass transportation system, plus Greyhound and train service to Portland.

SALEM	Jan.	Apr.	July	Oct.	Rain	Snow
Daily Highs	46	61	83	65	40	6
Daily Lows	34	38	51	42	in.	in.

Silverton

My family moved here years ago, and we knew we'd found our home. Silverton is relatively quiet, but close to any amenities you desire. I like it here for the beauty, the people, and the economic stability. I've retired here and intend to stay!
—a chamber of commerce volunteer

Silverton probably could be lumped together with Salem as a place to retire—they are so close together—but it does have a distinct flavor and character all its own. Whereas Salem is a dynamic city with sophistication and excitement at every corner, Silverton is much lower keyed and more old fashioned—with Victorian architecture instead of modern governmental construction. Neighborhoods are quiet, well landscaped and almost rural in appearance. Silverton is one of those Oregon communities that is too big to be called a town and too small to be a city; the population is 6,400, but it looks much larger.

Only 15 minutes from Salem, Silverton is just a short distance from the mainstream, yet years apart from the pressures and problems of urban life. The community remains an agricultural center, much as it was when the town was established back in 1854. Driving through the Silverton countryside, you can easily see the diversity that nature has given the community. Silver Creek, whose waters race and roar to form the ten magnificent waterfalls at Silver Falls State Park, after which the town is named, slows to a more civilized pace as it meanders through the center of town.

Newcomers use many words to describe Silverton: quaint, charming, quiet, beautiful, architecturally intriguing, and more, but mostly they say that Silverton feels like home. An amazing number of perfectly preserved Victorians set the mood here, with elegant homes on large lawns shaded by 100-year-old trees. Some of the better homes occupy view sites on the hillsides east and west of town. There isn't much new construction here, due to problems with building permits; it seems that all homes are on septic tanks, and the county won't permit new systems.

Recreation and Culture All recreational activities available to Salem residents are accessible to residents of Silverton, too. In addition, Salem's Chetmekta Community College holds classes here. With the interstate nearby, a drive to Portland takes only 50 minutes, so the top-quality events in that city are freely available to Silverton folks. Although Silverton doesn't have its own golf course, nearby Woodburn Golf Course (a nine-hole, par 33 layout) is the cheapest place to play golf in the entire state: for two bucks, you can play all day!

Housing Costs   Silverton's real estate market is described as vigorous, with growing sales and increasing prices. Housing costs are generally 10 percent higher than in Salem. There are no condos and very few apartment units. Besides the Victorians, many pleasant neighborhoods of conventional homes are priced starting at $110,000, going to $140,000 and up. Property taxes are about the same as Salem: $16.34 per $1,000 valuation.

Medical Care   Silverton residents are proud of their 38-bed hospital, which is staffed with health professionals and volunteers. Many specialties are represented by the 21-member medical staff, including family practice, general surgery, obstetrics and gynecology, emergency medicine and internal medicine.

Nearby Retirement Possibilities   Originally founded in 1844, the tiny town of Aurora received a boost in population in 1856 when a wagon train of religious immigrants braved the Oregon Trail to found Oregon's first religious colony. A museum in the town's center displays some of the original furniture, tools and household goods that the settlers brought with them. A success from its inception, Aurora was distinguished by substantial homes and business buildings. Since the town today is practically the same size as it was a hundred years ago, there are few new buildings; the homes here are mostly original. The architecture is unique, neither strictly Victorian nor antebellum. Today many of these stately old homes are used as antique shops. In fact, 24 antique outlets are located here.

About halfway between Salem and Portland, Aurora depends upon other towns for all but basic services. This may not be a logical choice for many retirees because of the small-town character (only 624 inhabitants) and because real estate for sale can be scarce. New construction is out of the question here, so you must depend on resales of old homes. But in any event, Aurora is worth a side trip off the interstate if only to soak up some Oregon history.

When Grandkids Visit   Be sure to visit Silver Creek Falls Park, about 15 miles above Silverton in the hills; this is Oregon's largest state park, with 8,000 acres. There are 10 spectacular waterfalls, with six of them over 100 feet high.

Important Addresses and Connections

Chamber of Commerce: 424 S Water St., Silverton, OR 97381.
Senior Services: None.
Weekly Newspaper: *Silverton Appeal Tribune-Mt Angel News*, 399 S Water St., Silverton, OR 97381.
Airport: Portland or Salem.
Bus/Train: None.

Portland

I feel as if I'm living in the middle of a forest, with huge trees and wildlife, but I'm only a little more than ten minutes by free-way to downtown Portland.
—Karen Kovalik (near Lake Oswego)

Originally called "Stumptown" back in 1844, this settlement of tents, shanties and cabins grew from a wild and exciting river port to a genteel, sophisticated city with great retirement potential. Stumptown's name change was decided by a toss of a coin: "Heads it's Portland; tails, it's Boston." Obviously, the coin came up "heads."

Portland likes to bill itself as "The Biggest Small Town in the West." But in fact, Portland is a large metropolitan center—the largest between San Francisco and Seattle. High-rise buildings tower above the city, while parkways lined with museums and galleries grace the ground levels. Portland's city limits embrace half a million inhabitants, but surrounding suburbs and small towns merge into one unit of a million and a half people. Little more than invisible city limit lines separate one community from its neighbors.

Despite this large population, Portland does manage to maintain a measure of small-town atmosphere, similar in style to San Francisco, with a natural division of neighborhoods. Each of the city's districts feels like a small town unto itself, somehow distinct from adjoining areas. The overall impression, then, is not of one large city, but a group of friendly neighborhoods.

Portland's benign climate, hilly setting and attractive landscaping are also reminiscent of San Francisco. Ex-San Franciscans coming here—from one of the most expensive places in the

United States—are pleasantly surprised at the affordability of lovely San Francisco-style Victorian homes, which would cost a fortune where they came from. Here, it's possible to purchase one at a California tract-home price. We know of least one San Francisco publisher and several authors who made the switch to Portland from "Baghdad by the Bay." They feel right at home because of subtle similarities: sophisticated, yet relaxed restaurants and meeting places and a rich variety of cultural offerings, from opera and concerts to street musicians and entertainers.

By way of indicating the intellectual atmosphere, one of the central city's most prominent highlights is Powell's Bookstore, America's largest multi-storied department store of new and used books—its coffee shop is a place to meet friends. By the way, Portland happens to be one of the few oases of wonderful restaurants in a wasteland of boring, ordinary Oregon eateries. Whereas most smaller towns offer occasional excellent restaurants amidst a horde of pizza parlors and hamburger emporiums, Portland is a gourmet's heaven. Mundane restaurants here are in the minority. Cooks here even know how to make digestible pizza, rare in the hinterlands of the United States.

Unlike many American cities, where shopping malls have destroyed the downtown business community by luring consumers away from the center, Portland manages to keep its downtown area alive and well, a pleasant place to visit or shop, very user friendly. To keep the center healthy, the city built an award-winning public transit system during the 1970s, featuring a 15-mile light rail line. Senior rates are half-fare. To encourage use of the downtown area, the transit system offers free public transportation in a 340-square-block downtown area known as "Fareless Square." A combination of pedestrian-only streets and free buses makes shopping downtown Portland a pleasure. Well-preserved buildings, upscale shops and restaurants, plus good law enforcement complete the picture of a "small-town big city."

With unusual foresightedness, the city's founders provided for a large number of parks, some rather large, which contribute to a feeling of uncrowded spaciousness. Council Crest Park is the city's highest point, at 1,073 feet, towering almost a thousand feet above the downtown riverfront area. Portland's 5,000-acre Forest Park is the largest forested municipal park within a city limits in the United States. While meandering along the trails here, it's easy to forget that you are actually inside the boundaries of

Oregon's largest city and not in a protected wilderness area. A corridor of foothills connects the park with the Coast Range, and over 100 bird and 60 mammal species make this their home, so it's not unusual to spot deer. Rolling hills and lots of shade trees extend this natural feeling into Portland's neighborhoods. Portland's second motto is "City of Roses," and residents try to live up to that reputation, with marvelous displays of flowers of all descriptions thriving in the Portland area's mild climate.

The city limits of Portland straddle the Willamette River and are bordered by the mighty Columbia on its northern edge. The streets are laid out in quadrants, with Burnside Street marking the north-south line and the Willamette River the east-west division. From the central city, residential districts spread in three directions (on the north is Vancouver, Washington) with many possible choices for retirement living.

Portland's weather is temperate—warm, pleasant summer weather and cool (seldom cold) winters with long periods of intermittent rain. The total rainfall here, despite popular belief, is surprisingly normal. It just seems like more rain because it falls slowly, over long time frames during the winter, but dry summers make amends for wet winters. Snows aren't terribly common and seldom stay for more than a few hours.

The Northwest District North of Burnside and west of the river, touched on one side by Forest Park, Portland's Northwest District is an area densely populated by 1920s-era apartments, renovated Victorian homes and older bungalows. The Northwest District's commercial area is endowed with upscale retail shops, restaurants, coffee houses, theaters, microbreweries and book shops. Housing may be a bit on the expensive side, but rentals are plentiful and not outrageous. This is a neighborhood for those who like to be in the middle of lots of activity.

Southwest Hills This scenic neighborhood embraces some of the most expensive property in the area. Thirty percent of the residents earn over $100,000 per year, and housing costs reflect this affluence. Although Portland's city center is just a short drive from Southwest Hills, the district's quiet streets and almost crime-free atmosphere makes downtown seem leagues distant. Prices of homes drop as you move south from the more hilly parts. Directly south of the Southwest Hills area, still on the west side of the river, you'll find a large collection of nice residential neighborhoods, almost any of them suitable for retirement.

East of the Willamette Probably two-thirds of Portland lies to the east of the Willamette River and south of the Columbia. Property tends to be more affordable here, with some lovely islands of inexpensive Victorians set in San Francisco-style neighborhoods. The boutique-and-gourmet flavor of Portland's Northwest District is replicated in these places, although on a smaller scale. One of these Victorian neighborhoods captivated the hearts of two of our friends a few years ago (native San Franciscans, by the way) who decided to transfer their interests to Portland and have never regretted it. We enjoy visiting them in their lovely old (and affordable) mansion. However, you need to investigate this side of the river carefully, because one of Portland's worst areas—a small section known as the Eliot Neighborhood—also sits on the east side of the Willamette River.

Connecting Suburbs To the east are Gresham and Fairview. Gresham is a city of about 73,000 people, the fourth-largest city in Oregon and home of Mt. Hood Community College. The school offers a wide variety of programs geared toward continuing education. The 40-acre campus even has a small trout pond where kids and adults can fish. Gresham sits at the line's end of Portland's rapid transit system; from Gresham City Hall you can ride to downtown Portland in short order.

On Portland's southern fringe, Milwaukee, Tigard and prestigious Lake Oswego, with its Lakewood Center for the Arts, make nice choices for retirement living. A vintage electric trolley provides a leisurely connection to downtown Portland. Lake Oswego and the surrounding forested areas rank among our personal favorites for suburban retirement possibilities. While property here can be expensive (and gorgeous), some neighborhoods offer affordable homes set on heavily wooded lots, with rural style, winding roads (sometimes unpaved), that seem totally out of place so close to an urban center. Lake Oswego's crime rate is in keeping with the rural setting: the lowest in Oregon, according to FBI statistics.

On the western edge of the Portland area are Beaverton and Hillsboro, with a wide variety of housing and lifestyles available for retirees. Hillsboro bears the monicker "Silicon Forest" (as opposed to California's "Silicon Valley") because of the computer and high-tech industries that bring talented people from all over the world to work for Hillsboro's technology companies. The city has its historic neighborhoods as well as new subdivisions, and it tries to maintain a small-town atmosphere with items like a Saturday Farmer's Market and a downtown drug store soda fountain. Hillsboro's medical needs are served by a modern, fully equipped hospital and hundreds of professional health care providers. Just out of town, valleys and rolling hills provide an ideal environment for grapes, wineries, and rural retirement locations, not too far removed from city conveniences.

Recreation and Culture Portland sports fans glory in two major league home teams: the Portland Trailblazers (NBA Basketball) and the Portland Winterhawks (WHL Hockey). Other spectator sports include horse racing, greyhound racing and Indy car meets. Fishermen on the Willamette and Columbia rivers bring in Chinook salmon and steelhead trout, and the forests surrounding Portland furnish hunting opportunities, with plentiful deer in season.

There are too many golf courses around the Portland area to begin to list individually. I've counted over 15 public courses as well as several private golf clubs. Tennis players will be pleased to find both indoor and outdoor courts for their games.

The Portland Center for the Performing Arts is the focal point for the city's major cultural events. Unlike many such centers, this is a decentralized complex with buildings in separate locations, several blocks from each other. The Civic Auditorium showcases performances of the Portland Opera and the Oregon Ballet Theater. The Portland Repertory Company, whose plays are staged in the Willamette Center Theater, is one of the city's most renowned companies. Another notable ensemble is the Chamber Music Northwest orchestra, which performs concerts during June and July at Reed College and Catlin Gabel School.

Every Saturday and Sunday, from March until Christmas Eve, the city turns the waterfront area under Burnside Bridge into a celebration of arts-and-crafts displays, entertainment and a food extravaganza. This is our favorite event here, and we have to visit every time we pass through town: the Portland Saturday Market. Northwest artists gather together here to display their beautifully handcrafted creations—priced from one dollar to one thousand—while a bewildering assortment of booths serve gourmet snacks and serious food treats.

Housing and Other Costs It's interesting to note the rising real estate values in Portland since the late 1980s. In one of my previous books, I described this area as one of the best real estate bargains in the entire country. At the time Oregon was undergoing a severe recession and economic adjustment, and Portland didn't escape the malaise. But the downward spiral slowed, bottomed out, and finally reversed itself.

Still, prices have a long way to climb before they enter the realm of the expensive or overpriced. Real estate can sound like a bargain to folks coming from other parts of the country. Property is simply not a steal anymore. You'll have no problem finding three-bedroom homes in livable neighborhoods for $80,000 to $100,000. We've looked at spacious two-bedroom places in upscale, exclusive areas for $125,000. In fact, real estate price ranges seem to have an exceptionally wide variation in the Portland area. And of course, since Portland is a metropolitan area, apartments and condos are plentiful.

As for the general cost of living, Portland is nine percent above the national average, making it the highest cost place to live in the state (except for Bend, whose cost of living is skewed by costly winter heating bills). Of 252 U.S. cities ranked in the ACCRA survey, Portland comes in 111th place, making it still a very affordable place to live.

Medical Care As you might expect from a metropolitan area, Portland's medical facilities are excellent. There is no shortage of doctors, dentists, chiropractors or other medical specialists, and the selection of hospitals and medical clinics are too extensive to mention here. Suffice to say that Portland has it all when it comes to health care.

Crime and Safety According to FBI reports on Oregon cities, Portland ranks just below Grants Pass for personal safety. Nationally, it ranks about average for cities of similar size. That's not to suggest that Portland is crime free by any means; like all large cities, its suburbs are the most tranquil, with more crime found on the fringes of downtown.

When Grandkids Visit Be sure and visit the Washington Park Zoo, where the kids can see local animals like beaver and river otter, as well as exotic African and Alaskan critters. A train winds along a four-mile trail through wooded hills and groves.

Important Addresses and Connections

Chamber of Commerce: 12420 S.W. Main St., Portland, OR 97223.
Senior Services: There are centers city-wide; check a phone book.
Daily Newspaper: *The Oregonian,* 1320 S.W. Broadway, Portland, OR 97201.
Airport: The Portland Airport, on the northeast edge of the city.
Bus/Train: Excellent urban and inter-city transportation, plus Greyhound and Amtrak service.

PORTLAND	Jan.	Apr.	July	Oct.	Rain	Snow
Daily Highs	44	60	80	64	37	6
Daily Lows	34	41	56	45	in.	in.

Forest Grove

I love it here because Forest Grove is a fun, quaint little city in a beautiful country setting.
                                                    —Diane Bogard

Forest Grove is an example of small-town living (pop. 15,000) at the edge of the Portland area, isolated from the metropolitan tangle by the rich farmlands, vineyards and woods of the Tualatin Valley. The town offers urban amenities in a striking rural setting, just an easy, 24-mile drive to the heart of Portland, along Highway 26 and the Sunset High-Tech corridor. The Forest Grove area is also home to five award-winning wineries.

Forest Grove was named for a large grove of Oregon white oak situated on a knoll rising over the Tualatin Plains. The largest giant Sequoia in Oregon is located at the corner of Pacific Avenue and B Street: 32 feet in circumference and 152 feet high. While the downtown area is 210 feet above sea level, an uplifting of hills in the northwestern portion of Forest Grove slopes to over a thousand feet.

The town has aged gracefully, preserving the charm of its historic homes and tree-lined streets, while making room for high-tech industry and the stability a diverse economy entails. The 55-acre, tree-shaded campus of Pacific University is located near the center of Forest Grove, and its graceful old buildings bestow a college-town charm to the area. The school was founded in 1849, one of the oldest educational institutions in the West, and is the source of a constant supply of music, art, theater and special lectures open to the public.

Recreation and Culture Forest Grove has easy access to all of the amenities of the Portland area, yet it is closer to Pacific beaches and to the Tillamook Forest, a vast area of the Oregon Coast Range which offers hiking, fishing, hunting and other recreational opportunities. Hikers seeking a challenge may want to try the King Mountain or Elk Mountain trails off Highway 6 in the heart of the Tillamook Forest. Closer to Forest Grove is Henry Hagg Lake and Park, nine miles southwest of Forest Grove, with boating, fishing, swimming, hiking, picnicking and bicycling.

Forest Grove Educational Arboretum is located on the grounds of the Oregon Department of Forestry in Forest Grove, displaying a wide selection of native trees and other plants in a natural setting with a stream and small wetland area. Another wetlands, located outside Forest Grove just north of the Tualatin River, Fernhill Wetlands provides critical habitat for waterfowl and other wildlife. In addition to the many golf courses around Portland, Forest Grove has its own public golf course: Sunset Grove, 9 holes, par 36.

Besides the theatrical productions at the University's Tim Miles Theater, community thespians offer a variety of performances in a restored historic theater.

Housing Costs The real estate market is characterized as "vigorous" by local real estate brokers—presumably that means more expensive than elsewhere—with three-bedroom homes typically selling in the $110,000 to $125,000 range. There were a few condos offered starting at $40,000 and apartment rental units seem plentiful, although these are often occupied by students. Taxes are about $14 per $1,000 valuation.

Forest Grove has five retirement complexes featuring apartments geared toward senior activities, at least one advertising "parties and music, bingo every day." One apartment group is specifically reserved for low-income people over 62 years old, and offers state-subsidized rentals for those who qualify.

Medical Care Since it's only a half-hour from Portland, people have access to medical facilities there, but Forest Grove also has a small hospital, an ambulance service and at least two medical clinics.

Crime and Safety Despite its proximity to Portland, Forest Grove's crime rate is the second lowest in Oregon.

When Grandkids Visit Check out the Oregon Electric Railway Museum and their collection of streetcars and interurban coaches which have been lovingly restored to running condition. Jump on a trolley for a ride to a creekside picnic area.

Important Addresses and Connections

Chamber of Commerce: 2417 Pacific Ave., Forest Grove, OR 97116.
Senior Services: 2030 Elm St., Forest Grove, OR 97116.
Weekly Newspaper: *The News-Times,* 2038 Pacific Ave., Forest Grove, OR 97116.
Airport: Portland.
Bus/Train: Van for disabled seniors, bus to Portland, local bus system.

FOREST GROVE	Jan.	Apr.	July	Oct.	Rain	Snow
Daily Highs	45	61	82	66	45	5
Daily Lows	34	42	53	47	in.	in.

The High Desert

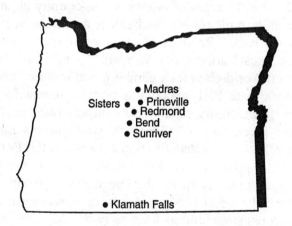

On the sunny side of Oregon's spectacular Cascade Mountains, Oregon's high desert country basks in a moderate climate that boasts an average of 263 days of sunshine a year. Rainfall is low enough to qualify this region as a desert, but the sun doesn't get hot enough to discourage vegetation growth, as happens in many desert terrains. Rainfall here is light, from 6 to 11 inches, mostly falling in brief thunderstorms.

The high desert country is not only a place of four seasons, it's a place where winter insists on its due share of time. Most moisture falls in the winter, and much of that is converted to snow. Since it only takes an average of one inch of rain to make a foot of snow, the white stuff can really pile up here in season! Snowfall averages 38 inches, with occasional heavy overnight buildups. Unlike most of Oregon, snow tends to stick around in the high desert. While an average of 15 days a year have temperatures above 90 degrees, rarely is 100 degrees reached.

A passion for recreation entices many people to the high desert. Kayakers and rafters shoot through the exciting triple waterfalls of the Deschutes River. The Deschutes, Metolius and Crooked Rivers offer fantastic fly fishing, with more than 500 miles of streams and rivers stocked with trout and steelhead. Deer hunting brings bountiful trophies.

Mountain bike cyclists can choose off-road riding in lush forests, on mountain peaks, through lava fields or across desert flats. Mt. Bachelor's ten lifts, six of them high speed, give alpine skiers 3,228 skiable acres of slopes. Cross-country skiing on the 56 kilometers of trails on Mt. Bachelor is a popular winter sport. Snowmobilers have 560 miles of groomed trails to choose from in the Deschutes National Forest, with 175 miles of that in the Bend District. World-class rock climbing and miles of hiking trails at Smith Rock State Park makes it a popular retreat for climbers and hikers. Backcountry hikers and campers head into the solitude of the Three Sisters Wilderness, while others hike in the more than 2.5 million acres of national forests in the Bend area.

One of the great winter sports destinations in the West, Mt. Bachelor is 25 miles from Bend. The majestic, 9,065-foot peak catches more than 300 pristine inches of powder snow a year. The 60 ski runs, stretching as long as two miles, are serviced by high-speed express chairs to fulfill the resort's motto, "They come to ski, not to wait." Even if you don't ski, it's worth a winter trip to have dinner at a ski lodge or in the summer for a glorious eagle's view of the surrounding country.

Bend

We moved here from Southern California, and at first were worried about whether we could take the snow. But we put on snow tires and had no problem whatsoever. —Janie Johnson

The city of Bend (pop. 29,000) is central Oregon's boom town and also the retail hub of the region. Bend manages to blend high growth and urban sophistication with a relaxed quality of life. Its only major growing pains are traffic-clogged highways and streets.

Although tourism and retirement revenues nourish Bend's expanding economy, commerce and industry have also advanced remarkably in the past few years. Because of all this fast growth, Bend's historic city center failed to escape the curse of strip malls that's destroying downtowns all over the country. Shoppers, seduced by low prices and easy parking deserted downtown Bend's traditional stores in favor of the massive chain stores and factory outlet complexes out on the highway.

However, Bend's downtown boosters are investing in an effort to alleviate this curse of center decay. They've tried to make walking, shopping or dining in downtown Bend a quality recreational experience. Galleries, restaurants, outdoor eateries, boutiques and specialty shops are spaced within easy walking distance of one another. Remodeling and upgrading of stores and offices is helping stave off decline. Drake Park's Mirror Pond, the jewel of downtown Bend, is a small lake with ducks, Canadian geese, and a pair of swans from Queen Elizabeth's royal swannery in England. Wide stretches of green grass bestow a restful counterpoint to the old brick and masonry buildings that compose Bend's business area. An old-fashioned horse-drawn coach offers to show you the turn-of-the-century buildings and other highlights of downtown Bend.

Recreation and Culture   With over 160 lakes and 120 designated recreation sites accessible to Bend residents, you'll find ample opportunities for hiking, fishing, camping, bird watching, hunting, skiing or snow mobiling. In the summer, the lava landscapes of Paulina Peak and Newberry Crater beckon campers and hikers alike. A minor league team, the Bend Bandits, play at Vince Genna Stadium from May through September.

In addition to the convenience of outdoor recreation opportunities near the city, golfers can choose between 20 top-rated courses within driving distance, offering every kind of challenge. The local public golf courses are Aubury Glen (18 holes, par 72), Orion Greens (9 holes, par 31), Pine Meadows (18 holes, par 72) and River's Edge (18 holes, par 72).

The place for continuing education, Central Oregon Community College, has 3,200 credit students, but also 3,500 non-credit students, many taking classes for personal growth instead of occupational goals. The college library is open free of charge to district residents.

August is the month of central Oregon's premier outdoor music festivals. The Cascade Festival of Music presents live music from symphony to jazz in Bend, and the nearby Sunriver Music Festival brings internationally renowned artists to that community. Two theatrical groups perform regular dramatic and musical presentations.

Housing and Other Costs Although lower-cost housing is available, the average price for a home in Bend in 1995 was $118,000. This marks a significant increase over past years, reflecting the pressure of a growing population, and making Bend one of Oregon's more costly places. The average price for a place on rural acreage was about $180,000. Property values outside the city of Bend are determined to a large extent by the availability and quality of water.

Condominium and apartment building flourished in the last few years, especially on the southeastern edge of the city. Condo prices there start at $65,000. Apartment rentals in Bend average $500 for two bedrooms, and $650 to $800 for three bedrooms, with houses starting at $700. Property taxes in Bend are about $15 per $1,000, but less outside city limits, as low as $9.55 per $1000 in some places.

In the cost-of-living derby, the Bend area finishes in the highest category of all of Oregon, with living expenses about 16 percent above national averages. However, this is mostly due to costly winter heating bills.

Medical Care There are a total of four hospitals in the central Oregon area, and all are accommodated by an emergency air ambulance service. The hospital serving Bend is St. Charles Medical Center—a comprehensive facility with 181 beds and 188 physicians on call. The facility maintains a trauma center and an upgraded intensive care unit.

Crime and Safety For some reason—it's certainly not obvious from our visits—Bend doesn't have a particularly high safety rating compared to other towns of its size. According to FBI statistics, Bend only ranks just a little above Portland in safety.

When Grandkids Visit Take a short six-mile drive south on US 97 to the High Desert Museum. Indoor and outdoor displays comprise a living history museum of plants and animals of the high mountain desert region in their natural settings. This state-of-the-art museum has exhibits on geology, geography, flora, fauna and human history. Stroll along the shady paths and watch the fascinating animals, or enjoy the historical exhibits, including a settler's cabin, a historic sawmill and a logging display. Wildlife programs give you a close-up look at birds of prey, and watching the river otters play is a favorite of all.

Important Addresses and Connections
Chamber of Commerce: 63805 N. Hwy. 97, Bend, OR 97701.
Senior Services: 1036 N.E. 5th St., Bend, OR 97701.
Newspaper: *The Bulletin,* 1526 N.W. Hill St., Bend, OR 97701.
Airport: Redmond, 16 miles north.
Bus/Train: No city bus, but Dial-A-Ride and Call-A-Cab service substitutes. Greyhound and an Amtrak connection are available in Chemult, 60 miles to the south.

BEND	Jan.	Apr.	July	Oct.	Rain	Snow
Daily Highs	37	56	84	62	11	38
Daily Lows	18	30	54	34	in.	in.

Sunriver

We can't retire for another four years, but we're ready for it. Our major regret about buying in Sunriver is that we can't spend enough time here. But in four years, we will!
—Ralph W. Summers

About a 20-minute drive from Bend is a place for those who fancy living as if on a year-round vacation. Sunriver is central Oregon's largest resort and residential community and has earned its reputation as a quality retirement locale. Surrounded by the Deschutes National Forest and crisscrossed by the confused Deschutes River, Sunriver's 3,340 pine-covered acres offer quality living with endless visual and recreational pleasures.

This is a mature development (started in 1968) combining down-home charm and upscale amenities in its private residences and condominiums—a unique blend of city and country life. Approximately 1,500 people make Sunriver their full-time residences and hundreds of other families spend up to several months a year here—all enjoying Sunriver's activities, amenities, special events and restaurants. Hiking trails and 80 miles of paved bike paths pass by each living unit. More than 650 condominiums are scattered throughout the property, with undeveloped forest serving as green belts in between. A shopping mall and full complement of services makes Sunriver fairly self-sufficient. All utilities including gas, electric, telephone and cable TV are underground. Additionally, Sunriver has its own 5,500-foot, paved and lighted airstrip, open all year 'round, with aviation fuel and services.

Better than half of the full-time residents here are retired, most moving here from other states. Many are pre-retired couples who live here as time permits. They stay here part of the year—whichever is their favorite season—and rent out their property during the other seasons. One of our close family friends owns a house here, but spends most of her time in California. "One advantage of having a place here," she says, "is that if my kids don't want to use the place in the winter ski season or for summer golf, I just call the management company, and they generally find tourists who are happy to rent my place by the day or week." Income from winter ski tourists and summer fishing and golf enthusiasts just about covers our friend's house payments. This is all done through one of several management companies that advertise the rentals, collect the rent and clean after each tenant leaves.

Sunriver has no hospital, so residents depend on Bend for major problems. But Sunriver's Department of Public Safety has emergency medical technicians on staff as well as an ambulance.

Recreation and Culture Sunriver places year-round recreation at residents' convenience: two 18-hole golf courses, 26 tennis courts, 30 miles of paved bicycle paths, two large swimming pools, stables, marina, whitewater rafting, canoes, an ice rink and a private racquet club. The thousands of acres of surrounding National Forests are available for hiking, biking, riding, climbing, fishing, sailing, skiing and all the other mountain, lake and river recreational activities. Mt. Bachelor, only 18 miles away from Sunriver, offers world-class downhill and cross-country skiing with a season that usually extends from late November through June. Cross-country skiing is also popular on the fairways of Sunriver and in the adjacent forest lands.

Housing and Other Costs Property prices in Sunriver have a wide range, and as you might expect, they are not inexpensive. Houses are priced from $125,000 to nearly $1 million, condominiums from $70,000 to $275,000 and lot prices from $40,000 to $265,000. The nice thing about the layout of the resort is that most buildings have ample wooded space separating one from the next, so even condos don't seem crowded.

Although official statistics aren't available, our guess is that the cost of living is relatively high here, partly due to the upscale surroundings and lifestyle, but also because of the added transportation expense of driving to Bend for major shopping and entertainment.

Crime and Safety The community has its own security force instead of a police department, and my understanding is that crime rates are low.

When Grandkids Visit Ask about the nearby nature center for tours. The facility features a 12-foot reflecting telescope, perhaps the only one in the region. The clear air in this vicinity makes for great observations of the stars.

Important Addresses and Connections

Chamber of Commerce: 57100 Mall Dr., Bldg. 15, Sunriver, OR 97707.
Airport: Redmond.
Bus: There's a shuttle service to Bend to use other public transportation.

SUNRIVER	Jan.	Apr.	July	Oct.	Rain	Snow
Daily Highs	37	56	84	62	10	46
Daily Lows	18	30	54	34	in.	in.

Sisters

We moved here from a big city and were delighted to find ourselves living and working with easy-going neighbors. This is a real break from a high-stress job in a hectic city environment. And we're close enough to cities without having to live there.
—Adrienne Van Bemmel

Because the rugged Cascade Mountains blocked the way, most of central Oregon was bypassed by pioneers following the Oregon Trail to the north during the 1840s. However, in 1859, Willamette Valley residents discovered a route east through the

Santiam Pass, the first of several routes that later became wagon roads through the Sisters country to the gold mines of eastern Oregon and Idaho. Today three main highways converge from the west near the Santiam Pass and run through the town of Sisters: one going to Eugene, one to Albany and one to Salem. Sisters is 160 miles southeast of Portland and 110 miles east of Eugene, Albany, or Salem, and only 20 miles west of either Bend or Redmond. These scenic highways are modern and well maintained, although snow and ice may be encountered from late November through March.

The town was named for the snow-capped Three Sisters mountains (called Faith, Hope and Charity by early-day pioneers), each peak topping 10,000 feet in elevation. During the early years, Sisters gained importance as a supply stop for travelers, ranchers and others, as well as a shopping center for local farmers and ranchers. Eventually, automobiles and trucks replaced wagons, and traffic began zooming through town without stopping. Sisters fell into decline, losing population while business languished. By the 1960s the town seemed to be gasping its last breath.

Then, in 1969, a recreational development company decided to promote Black Butte Ranch as both a resort and residential area. The ranch needed a shopping community for its visitors, so Black Butte developers offered Sisters business owners up to $1,500 each if they would remodel their buildings with Western-style storefronts and motifs. An 1880s Western building theme was formally adopted as part of the city's building code, one of the strongest such codes in Oregon. This introduced a charming Old West look to Sisters' downtown section, changing it from a generic, wide-spot-on-the-highway settlement to a delightfully inviting place to shop, dine and meet friends. The town once again attracted shoppers from surrounding areas, giving its spiffy looking commercial district the impression of a much larger place than its 820 inhabitants would deserve. For heavy-duty shopping or city conveniences, folks drive about 25 minutes to either Redmond or Bend.

Even though this is a small town, we've decided to include Sisters because of its attractive setting and unusually active community. Sisters' calendar of events is loaded with interesting happenings such as winter carnivals, summer market fairs, musical festivals and even a rodeo. There's a comfortable look to Sister's residential area, with homes scattered about on large lots shaded with tall pines, all with plenty of elbow room.

Although Sisters projects a flavor of living high in the mountains, it actually has a 500-foot-lower elevation than Bend. Its 3,100-foot elevation helps it escape the rigorous winters suffered by high-altitude sites just a few miles to the west. This gives the area slightly milder weather and a bit more annual precipitation than either Bend and Redmond. Snowfall can be rather erratic around the Sisters area. Sometimes a winter is relatively free of snow much of the season, yet it can occasionally pile up to astounding depths. The winter of 1992-93 dumped a total snowfall of 100 inches on the town! Local residents are quick to point out that this was a most unusual winter, and that some places in the Eastern United States expect this much snow every winter.

Sisters has no formal senior center; the community center building serves the purpose. But this doesn't stop folks here from working together and socializing on an organized, as well as ad-hoc basis. An office of COCOA (Central Oregon Council on Aging) coordinates activities and handles services that a senior center normally supplies to a community. Retirees participate enthusiastically; in fact, 75 percent of the office's volunteers are retirees. They contribute weekly time to chores like delivering meals to homebound elderly, providing transportation, assisting with minor home repair and yard work, and just visiting or giving telephone reassurance. COCOA also administers the Oregon Project Independence (OPI). This excellent program provides in-home care for ailing seniors who choose to live independently in their own homes. Clients are charged according to a sliding fee scale that determines how much, if any, the services will cost.

Recreation and Culture The Deschutes National Forest at the edge of town is a 1.6-million-acre forest with miles of trails for the hiker and horseback rider, many streams and lakes for fishing, boating and whitewater rafting, and countless miles of forest roads for sightseeing. The McKenzie Pass-Santiam Pass National Scenic Byway is an 81-mile loop that touches Sisters at the west edge of town. Golfers will find great courses at nearby Black Butte Resort and Eagle Crest Resort. The Metolius River area, only a few miles to the northwest, is another popular vacation area for fishing, rafting, and camping. In the winter, skiers travel just a few miles west to Hoodoo Ski Area for both downhill and cross-country skiing at the Santiam Pass. Oregon snowmobilers have chosen the Sisters area as Oregon's best snowmobiling region, with many miles of groomed trails.

Central Oregon Community College operates an extension here, offering 30 classes and workshops in Sisters each fall, winter and spring. Residents join classes to learn pine needle basketry, oil painting or jewelry making, to be introduced to the wide world of the Internet, or to begin writing their life stories to pass along to family or friends.

Housing Costs   Homes here are an interesting juxtaposition of large and small, with cabins and two-story places on adjoining lots and huge Douglas pines looming high overhead. Since most homes here are single family and owner occupied, few rentals are usually available. Average price comparisons really aren't meaningful when the turnover in housing is so small. Land is plentiful, however, and newcomers are often tempted to build rather than buy an existing home. Listed properties at the time of our visit ranged from $78,500 for a two-bedroom, two-bath condo to $179,000 for a four-bedroom place on one acre of Ponderosa pines.

Medical Care   Obviously Sisters is too small to support a hospital, however it does have a clinic for minor ailments (it's located conveniently in the town pharmacy). An air ambulance service is available for emergencies the clinic can't handle; it flies to hospitals in either Redmond or Bend, each a few minutes away by air.

When Grandkids Visit   Sisters has two llama ranches and a domestic elk ranch. There's even a reindeer farm where you can show the grandkids where Santa parks his animals between gift lifts on Christmas Eve.

Important Addresses and Connections

Chamber of Commerce: P.O. Box 430, Sisters, OR 97759.
Senior Services: 231 E. Hood St., Suite D, Sisters, OR 97759.
Newspaper: *The Nugget*, 385 E. Main, Sisters, OR 97759.
Airport: Redmond.
Bus/Train: A Dial-a-Ride van transports seniors as well as other community groups. The Retriever, a small bus, connects with the Willamette Valley to the west.

SISTERS	Jan.	Apr.	July	Oct.	Rain	Snow
Daily Highs	38	57	85	63	12	30
Daily Lows	20	30	55	34	in.	in.

Klamath Falls

I like the peoples' attitude here, and all the things to do, like hiking, swimming, fishing, museums. My kids say they will never move.
                                                              —Vicky Meyer

Fur traders from the Hudson Bay Company were the first visitors to the Klamath Falls area, coming here to trap beaver in the lakes and slow-moving streams. A few years later, pioneers traveling the Oregon Trail pushed through here in search of an alternate route that didn't require traveling north to the Columbia River. This became the Applegate Trail, passing through what is now Klamath Falls. Since the string of lakes were linked by the Klamath River, the settlement first became known as Linkville. When the town grew into a small city, the residents decided Linkville wasn't adequately descriptive of the beauty of the area, so the name was changed to Klamath Falls. Later, the river was dammed to form Klamath Lake, the largest body of fresh water in the Pacific Northwest.

At an elevation of 4,100 feet, Klamath County enjoys a high, dry climate with four distinct seasons. Winters are cold, with heavy snowfall (about 39 inches a year), and are balanced by mild and sunny summers with light rainfall (only 13 inches a year), which accounts for the 290 days of sunshine each year. Utility costs are unusually low here, more than 25 percent below national average. This offsets higher heating requirements during Klamath Falls winters, and you save further by not needing air conditioning in the summer. One of Klamath Falls' unique features is an underground supply of geothermally heated water that's used to heat many homes and businesses, including the hospital and the Oregon Institute of Technology college campus. This heating source is completely sustainable, non-polluting, and inexpensive; it's even used to heat downtown sidewalks and bridges to keep them snow-free in the winter.

Although Klamath Falls is the major shopping and business hub for a regional population of more than 100,000, its city center is old-fashioned and low-key. During the summer, a quaint trolley rumbles through the downtown section of town, accenting the yesteryear theme. Shopping centers on the edges of town have become the mainstay of area consumers.

Recreation and Culture Fishing, hunting, camping, nature trails and sailing on the 133-square-mile Klamath Lake provide a full range of outdoor activities. Landlocked salmon and steelhead grow to astounding sizes (I've barbecued a few myself). Local fishermen claim that the average trout taken from the 82 lakes and streams in Klamath County measures 21 inches. And fishermen don't lie.

Three downhill skiing facilities are within two hours of here: Mt. Shasta to the south, Willamette Pass to the northwest, and Mt. Ashland in the west. The area also has racquetball and tennis facilities and a variety of health clubs. Three public golf courses are open for play at Harbor Links (18 holes, par 72), Round Lake (9 holes, par 29) and Shields Crest (18 holes, par 72).

The 800-seat Ross Ragland Theater hosts performers of various musical genres from around the world, as well as touring and local plays. The Linkville Players, an acclaimed theatrical troupe, produces four plays and a musical each year at the Linkville Playhouse. The Klamath Chorale, Klamath Art Association, and many other cultural groups have seasonal performances and shows. An upcoming vote is scheduled as to whether or not a community college should be formed here.

Housing and Other Costs The big drawing card for many retirees is affordable real estate. Housing is as low-priced as almost any city we've investigated in Oregon. In 1995, the average sales price for homes of all types in Klamath County was less than $80,000. A new three-bedroom, two-bath home (1,800 square feet) typically sold for under $125,000. Rent for a small home started at $437, and a two-bedroom apartment rented for about $375. Property taxes in Klamath Falls were $15 per $1,000, and less in unincorporated neighborhoods. According to statistics, this area has the lowest cost of living in the state, at two percent below national average.

Medical Care Merle West Medical Center in Klamath Falls is the largest health care facility in the area. It has 176 beds, over 85 physicians and 1039 employees. It also has cancer and heart clinics, a center for occupational health, and a Family Practice

Residency Program. The Klamath Basin is also served by a number of smaller clinics, home health care operations, nursing homes, and several ambulance/rescue services.

Crime and Safety Klamath Falls is an exceptionally safe area, according to FBI statistics, ranking in the top ten percent of cities nationally.

When Grandkids Visit Drive about 30 miles south to the Tule Lake Lava Beds and investigate the weird formations, caves and lava tubes. These caves were formed when molten lava encountered running water; the resulting high-pressure steam created hollow tubes and cavities.

Important Addresses and Connections

Chamber of Commerce: 507 Main St., Klamath Falls, OR 97601.
Senior Services: 2045 Arthur St., Klamath Falls, OR 97603.
Daily Newspaper: *Herald and News,* P.O. Box 788, Klamath Falls, OR 97601.
Airport: The local airport is served by two commuter lines.
Bus/Train: Local transit bus service, Amtrak and Greyhound.

KLAMATH FALLS	Jan.	Apr.	July	Oct.	Rain	Snow
Daily Highs	38	58	82	62	13	39
Daily Lows	20	32	49	35	in.	in.

Redmond

We're golf nuts, but we also wanted to do other outdoor sports. Here we also get to ski, fish and do whitewater rafting.

—G.A. Swift

North of Bend, toward the upper portion of Oregon's high desert country, several small towns have a strong potential as good retirement destinations. This could be a place for those who like to be near wilderness and the rugged outdoors, yet don't want to put up with severe weather and lack of services. Set in a wide valley, with half a dozen streams working their way north toward the nearby Columbia River, the area is bordered on the west by the magnificent Cascade Mountains and the beautiful Deschutes River—one of Oregon's designated Scenic Waterways. Tall, rugged mountain summits loom in the distance, most of the year blanketed with deep snow. The mountainous areas within eyesight expect 40 inches of precipitation as the yearly norm, yet this area catches as little as nine inches of moisture—much of which falls as snow. Since the elevation in the valley is from 300 to 1,400 feet lower than Bend, the weather is just a tad warmer and has less snowfall.

One reason for considering retirement here is that the population boom and resulting high real estate prices haven't hit here as they have in nearby Bend. In many ways, the small towns here remind us of Bend 20 years ago, before progress and automobile congestion caught up with it.

Redmond is the first town encountered north of Bend, sitting at the western edge of Oregon's high desert, just four miles from the Deschutes River, a half-hour drive from the Cascade Mountains and within minutes of several lakes. Beautiful panoramas make a dramatic backdrop, featuring the spires and craggy palisades of Smith Rock State Park just north of Redmond. The Ogden Wayside Rest Area, also north of Redmond, allows visitors to view the 500-foot-deep Crooked River Gorge, as well as breathtaking vistas of two of Oregon's highest mountains, Mt. Hood and Mt. Jefferson. This high-desert community rests on a flat plateau at an elevation of 3,077 feet above sea level.

While other towns and cities developed in natural stopping places on rivers and ocean bays, Redmond, with a population of 7,200, owes its existence to man-made water courses and its development to the coming of the railroad, major highways and an airport. The development of Redmond began in 1894 when Congress passed the Carey Desert Land Act. This act turned federally owned arid land over to individual states. The states were instructed to undertake reclamation and irrigation, then to encourage settlement. As a result of the Carey Act, the Central Oregon Irrigation Company, which built the main canal and laterals leading into Redmond, was formed in 1900.

Redmond prospered during World War II. Local businesses were full of soldiers in the area for maneuvers and airmen stationed at Redmond Army Air Base. After the war the city gained title to the air base with its improved runways. Development of the airport has continued, making it central Oregon's regional air facility.

Nearby Retirement Possibilities A resort development that grew into a thriving community of 3,000, Crooked River Ranch sits on a plateau with steep canyon walls plummeting to the waters of the Crooked River on one side and to the Deschutes River on the other. Although it's closer to Madras "as the crow flies," it's a half-hour drive to that town, while Redmond is only a 15-minute drive. Building lots here start at $6,000 and go to $65,000 for a view lot on the rim. Homes range from $70,000 to $250,000. The Rural Fire Protection District provides ambulance service.

Besides its golf course—one of the few open year-round in central Oregon—Crooked River Ranch boasts two heated swimming pools, hiking in surrounding gorges and at neighboring Smith Rock Park as well as bicycling on the many miles of trails that wind through the 12,000 acres in this development. Like Sunriver, the community is self-governed by an owners' association, and most facilities, except for the golf course, are for members' and guests' use only. An additional 9,000 acres of public land are adjacent to the ranch and accessible for hiking, fishing and hunting.

Recreation and Culture   Outdoor enthusiasts will love Redmond and the other towns in this area because of bountiful recreational opportunities. Nearby lakes include Billy Chinook, Suttle and Blue, as well as the Ochoco, Haystack and Prineville reservoirs. Rafting is always a thrill on the Deschutes River, along with swimming and fishing for summer steelhead and rainbow trout. Along the Cascade Lakes Highway, there are many lakes available for fishing for brook, brown and rainbow trout. Seven miles of hiking trails follow the Crooked River and wind up the canyon walls to the top of the ridges. The area's public golf courses are Eagle Crest Resort (18 holes, par 72) and Juniper Golf Club (18 holes, par 72). Since Redmond is only 14 miles north of Bend, you can participate in all of the amenities it has to offer, while still enjoying the small-town feel of Redmond.

Medical Care   The Redmond area is served by the Central Oregon District Hospital. This is a 48-bed facility that offers personalized family care with specialists on hand. It is also part of the Central Oregon Hospital network. Even more medical facilities are available in Bend, only 16 miles away.

When Grandkids Visit   Operation Santa Claus, two miles west of Redmond, has the largest herd of domesticated reindeer in the U.S. As a Christmas-theme working reindeer park, the reindeer travel the nation during Christmas time for all to see. Kids will love visiting Rudolph!

Important Addresses and Connections

Chamber of Commerce: 106 S.W. 7th Redmond, OR 97756.
Senior Services: 325 N.W. Dogwood, Redmond, OR 97756.
Newspaper: *The Spokesman*, 226 N.W. 6th St., Redmond, OR 97756.
Airport: Redmond airport is the air hub for central Oregon.
Bus/Train: Greyhound.

REDMOND	Jan.	Apr.	July	Oct.	Rain	Snow
Daily Highs	47	57	85	64	9	16
Daily Lows	20	36	50	35	in.	in.

Prineville

We are a pretty little town with lots of parks and campgrounds. I can remember when we had board sidewalks. We've made a lot of changes, but we're still a hometown—family oriented, a wholesome place.
                                                        —Kay Puckett

Prineville got its start in 1868 when Barnett Francis (Barney) Prine decided to build his cabin in a meadow between Ochoco Creek and Crooked River. His homesite was overshadowed by spectacular geological formations, straight-sided cliffs and towering Ponderosas. Others liked the location, too, and before long the town of Prineville was established.

Actually, the town resembles its neighbors, Redmond and Madras, in that it has a utilitarian downtown with a mixture of 1920s architecture and postwar modern. Ditto the residential neighborhoods: quiet, wide streets with comfortable-looking homes—neither expensive places nor run-down areas. Prineville is a solid, middle-class town with just about anything retirees need—especially if what they need is outdoor recreation. Prineville's population is about 6,000, mid-way between Redmond and Madras. The elevation is mid-range, too, at a comfortable 2,868 feet.

Prineville might have become the largest city in central Oregon had the Union Pacific Railroad not bypassed the town in favor of Redmond. Snubbed, the voters of Prineville elected to lay their own tracks to join the main line near Redmond. Thus Prineville became the only town in the nation to have its own railroad. They called it the Crooked River Railroad Company, named after the river canyon the train followed. Back then it was crucial for shipping timber. Today, while it still serves commercial ends, important for the town's strong industrial base, the tracks also carry passenger trains—not only for entertainment of tourists, but as a source of recreation for the entire community.

Situated on the edge of the Ochoco National Forest and other marvels to the east, Prineville acts as the gateway to one of the most scenic areas in the country. This vast region is undeveloped, its marvels practically unknown to outsiders. You can drive from Prineville to Baker City (east along highways 26 and 7) and encounter almost no other automobiles, while passing through astounding dimensions of pine forests, unbelievable rock formations and eye-pleasing, wide-open country. For us, Prineville's biggest advantage is its proximity to this secret wonderland.

An active senior center is sponsored by the Soroptimists and receives bountiful volunteer help. Their home-delivered meals program provides 65 to 70 hot meals per day to seniors who are unable to leave their homes. A minibus service provides transportation for elderly and disabled residents; this is owned and operated by the Soroptimists and driven by volunteers.

Recreation and Culture The city-owned 18-hole golf course, Meadow Lakes, is bordered by the Crooked River and is said to rival the best public courses in the state. Alternative public golfing can be found 20 miles away in Redmond.

The amazingly active Central Oregon Community College also has a learning center in Prineville. They offer 25 to 30 classes each term, some of which could be of interest to seniors. And, believe it or not, the Crooked River Railroad is the source of a certain amount of cultural diversion, with regular presentations of theatrical and musical entertainment. Every Saturday afternoon, a "dinner train" leaves Prineville for a 38-mile dining car trip. On Fridays, a Western hoe-down dinner train makes the run. Sundays are for "champagne brunch," and weekly "Western Murder Mystery Theater" productions entertain locals and tourists, as well as the Prineville city treasurer who stuffs profits into city coffers. At Christmastime the equipment is dolled up with seasonal greetings and blinking lights, thus substituting a Christmas Train for the more traditional Christmas Tree.

Housing Costs   Like the other towns grouped in this north-central Oregon retirement area, real estate is affordable. A Prineville contractor advertises new three-bedroom, two-bath homes (with two-car garages) for $85,200. Many older homes were on the market in the $65,000 to $85,000 range, and luxury places on several acres were priced at $185,000. Apartments and condos are not plentiful in Prineville, as is the case with most towns of this size.

Medical Care   Pioneer Memorial Hospital recently added two operating suites, a procedure room, a recovery room and a state-of-the-art emergency unit. Now a full-service hospital with 35 beds, the facility has a trauma team on call 24 hours a day. An ambulance service serves all the surrounding area and provides advanced cardiac life support and transport to hospitals for medical emergencies. Air Life, the aerial ambulance, also handles emergencies, and a person needn't be a member to receive the service; still, for $45 a year, members are covered.

When Grandkids Visit   Pick up a rock-collecting map from the chamber of commerce and head for the rimrocks that almost encircle the town. You can find petrified wood, agate and thundereggs (you may have to dig a little for the latter).

Important Addresses and Connections

Chamber of Commerce: 390 N. Fairview St., Prineville, OR 97754.
Senior Services: 180 N. Belknap, Prineville, OR 97754.
Bi-Weekly Newspaper: *Central Oregonian*, 558 N. Main St., Prineville, OR 97754.
Airport: Redmond.
Bus: A minibus transports the elderly or disabled. County buses operate between John Day and Bend; Greyhound also stops in town.

PRINEVILLE	Jan.	Apr.	July	Oct.	Rain	Snow
Daily Highs	42	56	87	63	9	18
Daily Lows	22	36	50	36	in.	in.

Madras

We moved here from Montana because the countryside around here reminds us of home. In a way, our new home is a glorified Montana—without the severe cold and terrible winters.
—Ginger Morrison

A town of approximately 4,500 inhabitants, Madras sits near the junction where the Deschutes River, the Crooked River and the exquisitely beautiful Metolius River join to form a long, three-fingered lake. With the lake and major rivers sweeping through the county, many outdoor activities naturally center around water. Immediately surrounding Madras is rich farming country, yielding bumper crops of potatoes, grains, peppermint, seed, and specialty crops—growing in fields against a backdrop of snow-covered mountain peaks in the distance.

The Madras town center is similar to the other two towns in this area: Redmond and Prineville. Modern amenities and old-fashioned businesses are hallmarks of all three communities, very much in keeping with the low-keyed, down-to-earth pace. Residential neighborhoods are comfortable, neat and well-kept, predominantly single-family homes.

Nearby Warm Springs Indian Reservation is the homeland for over 3,400 tribal members, most of whom live in the community of Warm Springs. Tourism and recreation are important economically to the three tribes on this reservation. Over half the reservation is forested, and includes alpine lakes, pristine rivers, deep canyons and vistas of high desert and volcanic peaks. The Metolius River and Lake Billy Chinook form the southern boundary. Golfers from the area travel to Warm Springs for the Kah-Nee-Ta Hot Springs Resort for golfing and good restaurant food.

Recreation and Culture Outdoor recreational opportunities include whitewater rafting, fishing, rockhounding and more. Since this area enjoys 300 days of sunshine every year, golf is popular. Three golf courses provide exercise for hackers: Nine Peaks Golf Course (18 holes, par 72) in Madras; Kah-Nee-Ta Resort Golf Course in nearby Warm Springs Indian Reservation (18 holes), and a nine-hole course at Crooked River Ranch, a half-hour drive from Madras. The city of Madras provides eight tennis courts (four of which are illuminated for night play), more than three miles of paved walking/bike paths and six parks.

Madras is fortunate to host a branch of Central Oregon Community College, which brings a variety of educational services to residents. A community education program offers 20 to 25 courses during fall, winter and spring sessions, for self-enrichment and art classes.

Medical Care The Mountain View Hospital, a 38-bed facility, offers a variety of services including general medical, surgical, orthopedic and emergency care. An emergency medical service team is on 24-hour assignment with four full-time employees, 19 volunteers and four ambulances. When air transport is necessary, Air Life of Oregon is the primary provider, although Life Flight of Portland is used, too, depending upon the situation.

When Grandkids Visit The lake at Cove Palisades State Park is a great place for boating. You can rent everything from canoes to houseboats, even something to do some water skiing or jet skiing, if that's your thing. If not, try Richardson's Recreation Area agate beds for rockhounding and hiking.

Important Addresses and Connections

Chamber of Commerce: 197 S.E. 5th St., Madras, OR 97741.
Senior Services: 860 S.W. Madison, Madras, OR 97741.
Weekly Newspaper: *The Pioneer,* 241 S.E. 6th St., Madras, OR 97741.
Airport: Redmond Airport.
Bus/Train: Dial-a-Ride (to Bend) and Greyhound serve the community.

MADRAS	Jan.	Apr.	July	Oct.	Rain	Snow
Daily Highs	49	58	88	63	11	18
Daily Lows	31	40	53	41	in.	in.

The Oregon Trail

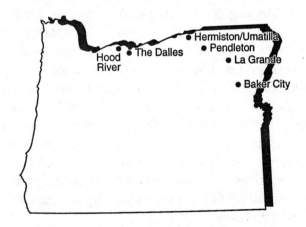

Between 1840 and the late 1860s, an estimated 350,000 to 500,000 emigrants journeyed from Independence, Missouri, to Independence, Oregon, and the Willamette Valley. This was the largest voluntary migration in U.S. history. The adventurers' route led them through present-day Baker City, La Grande, Pendleton, Hermiston, The Dalles, and Hood River, before reaching Multnomah Falls (at Portland) and branching out toward various Oregon and Washington destinations.

The first trailbreakers came in 1840, but the migration started in earnest in 1843, when one thousand pioneers started by wagon train from Independence, Missouri, and headed for the promised land of Oregon. Their route was known as the Oregon Trail, and 1843 became known as the year of the Great Migration. Because of frequent deaths from sickness, accident and starvation, this route was often called the "2,000-mile graveyard." The trip to Oregon required four to six months of trudging beside oxen-drawn wagons and herds of cattle, over muddy hills, through dusty ruts and over rocky and steep mountain trails.

Contrary to common belief, travelers encountered few problems with Indians, who were often friendly and helpful. By the time the wagons reached what today is Oregon, the pioneers were exhausted, out of food, and often out of money. So they were delighted to meet the Paiute, Nez Perce, Cayuse, Umatilla and Walla Walla Indians who did a brisk business trading food and supplies to the half-starved travelers for fish hooks, frying pans and other household goods. Indians often helped the pioneers' wagons and livestock ford the dangerous river crossings. Cholera and diptheria were by far the biggest killers of travelers.

But those who made it as far as Eastern Oregon were rewarded by the spectacular beauty of the land they risked so much to see. For them, this was the beginning of the end of a long, long journey. Many pioneer diaries waxed poetic at their first glimpse of green trees in what must have seemed an eternity. Thomas Farnham, in 1839, wrote the following: "Nature stretched her bare and mighty arms around us! We looked upon the beautiful heights of the Blue Mountains and ate among its spring blossoms, its singing pines and holy battlements, ten thousand feet above the sea."

Today, you can retrace the route, observing deep marks of wagon wheels still tracing the way. You can feast your eyes on the same snowcapped crags and lush valleys that delighted the weary vanguard. From the river crossings into Oregon, near Nyssa and Vale, the trail moved north following or paralleling the route of Interstate 84. Interpretive sites and historic markers guide you along your journey as you trace the pioneers' itinerary.

In this chapter, we'll follow the Oregon Trail's wagon ruts as we search for our own "promised land" and investigate suitable locations for a new start, just as pioneers did 150 years ago. Only this time we'll travel on smooth pavement, thank you. Now, this country may not be your style; it could contain too much wilderness, empty space or solitude. On the other hand, you may be looking for just such a place. We'll start at Baker City and work our way toward the Pacific along the Oregon Trail.

Baker City

This is a wonderful place to raise kids and to retire. It's a safe area; everyone takes pride in their yards; people look out for each other. And the natural beauty takes your breath away.
—Debbie Wood

Baker Valley—originally known as Lone Pine Valley—gave Oregon Trail travelers their first taste of the Oregon Territory's potential. Located on the Powder River, the settlement of Baker was a just stopover on the Oregon Trail until 1861, when gold was discovered in nearby mountains. Baker City soon became a supply center and farms sprang up around the settlement. Before long, Baker became known as the "Queen City" of the region. An amazing 110 buildings on the National Historic Register in Baker City recall those early gold rush days. The U.S. National Bank has a display of nuggets and natural gold taken from the local mines, including one nugget weighing five pounds. A horse-drawn trolley rolls through the city, guiding visitors to historic homes and buildings.

Today Baker City is a bustling town of 9,500 inhabitants, with another 5,000 in the county. Our first impression was one of pleasant surprise at the modern, prosperous look and the thriving business district. Part of this impression is due to the town's wide streets, an early instance of city planning by the town's founders who shunned the ordinary two-lane throughways typically found in unplanned pioneer towns. This lends an air of spaciousness and eases traffic.

The residential areas show the occupants' pride in owner-ship, with nicely kept lawns and well-maintained homes. Condominiums aren't too plentiful, but there are some apartment complexes. A downtown hotel was recently converted to apart-ment rentals and the old St. Elizabeth's Hospital was also turned into living units.

Recreation and Culture Just 55 miles away is the famous Hell's Canyon, even deeper than the Grand Canyon and almost as long. At one point the canyon rim is 8,000 feet above the Snake River far below. Whitewater raft trips and powerboat excursions run over this river, and several species of fish thrive. The mountains' lush forests harbor animals that range from the tiny pika to bobcats, cougars, deer, elk and even the elusive bighorn sheep. But fishermen don't have to drive all the way to the mountains for fishing, they can fish right in town in the Powder River. Also, the Baker Golf Course (nine 9 holes, par 35) is open for public play.

Continuing education programs are presented locally through Eastern Oregon State, with the main school facility at La Grande, about 45 minutes away by interstate. A local theater group, the Crossroads, presents dramatic productions throughout the year.

Housing and Other Costs According to local real estate people, prices of three-bedroom homes range between $70,000 and $100,000. A very limited number of condos sell from $55,000 to $75,000. Two-bedroom apartments start at $500 a month. Taxes are about $12 per $1,000 valuation. Cost of living statistics aren't available for any of the Oregon Trail towns, but from what we can tell, in most places living costs are about as low as any-where in the state.

Medical Care St. Elizabeth Hospital is now in a new build-ing, offering up-to-date services and medical care with a 24-hour emergency clinic and a coronary-care unit. Several medical clin-ics and an ambulance service supplement the hospital.

When Grandkids Visit Take them to the National Historic Oregon Trail Interpretive Center, operated by the Bureau of Land Management at Flagstaff Hill, five miles east of Baker City. Permanent exhibits with audio, video, dioramas and artifacts recreate the experiences of Oregon Trail emigrants.

Important Addresses and Connections

Chamber of Commerce: 490 Campbell St., Baker City, OR 97814.
Senior Services: 2610 Grove St., Baker City, OR 97814.
Weekly Newspaper: *The Herald*, 1915 First St., Baker City, OR 97814.
Airport: Pendleton.
Bus/Train: Greyhound Bus Stop, no local transit system, but Dial-a-Ride for seniors.

BAKER CITY	Jan.	Apr.	July	Oct.	Rain	Snow
Daily Highs	34	58	86	63	11	26
Daily Lows	17	31	48	30	in.	in.

La Grande

This is a place—one of the few we have seen in our journey so far—where a farmer would delight himself to establish [his farm].
—John C. Fremont (when he entered the valley in 1843)

La Grande was the next stopping place on the Oregon Trail that eventually became a city. The Grande Ronde Valley's name was bestowed by French Canadian Voyagers to describe the way the river loops about to form the oval-shaped valley. This is one of the few towns where the old Oregon Trail passes right through a modern-day town, running along present-day Avenue B. In La Grande, pioneers rested, fed their livestock, and gathered courage to abandon the green beauty of the Grande Ronde valley. Ahead they were challenged by steep and rocky trails through the Blue Mountains, the most grueling leg of the trip—even worse than the Rockies. Some families decided they had gone far enough; they stayed to swell the population of La Grande. Today, it's grown into a small city with a respectable population of over 12,000.

The river valley is a fertile plain 20 miles long and 12 miles wide, with mountains rising some 3,500 feet above the valley floor in the distance, and the high peaks of the Blue Mountains towering between 6,000 and 7,000 feet in the north. On the western horizon, the Wallowa Mountains form a greenish-blue backdrop. In some ways La Grande reminds me of Prescott, Arizona, because of the large pines and rocky formations overlooking the town. The Grande Ronde River winds through town, adding to La Grande's attractiveness.

The downtown is pedestrian-friendly, comfortable and sleepy, with tree-lined streets exhibiting wonderful examples of turn-of-the-century architecture. Parking is seldom a problem in downtown La Grande. There's an assortment of specialty shops and restaurants, while major shopping is transacted at the shopping mall and chain discount stores on the edges of town. Actually, this is a college town (Eastern Oregon State), yet for some reason, students appear to blend in here rather than making significant differences in shopping, restaurants and the like. In short, we feel that La Grande offers retirement possibilities for those who enjoy small-city living with lots of outdoor recreation.

Recreation and Culture   The Wallowa Mountains and Eagle Cap wilderness areas provide numerous opportunities for outdoor activities, such as downhill and cross-country skiing, rafting, hunting and fishing, backpacking and water-skiing. There aren't many outdoor sports that aren't covered here.

La Grande is the home of Eastern Oregon State College. It's motto is: "Large enough for quality, small enough to care." The college serves as the cultural center for Union County, providing facilities for Oregon's oldest continuous symphony orchestra, musical performances, art exhibits and outstanding theater productions. The nearby Elgin Opera House is another major performing arts center. The Grande Ronde Symphony, a college/community orchestra, presents regular concerts for the entertainment of the community.

Housing Costs   Three-bedroom homes average between $80,000 and $90,000 in comfortable neighborhoods. Condos seem to be scarce, probably non-existent. There are some apartments, with rents for a two-bedroom place beginning at $450. The city property tax rate is $17.10 per $1,000.

Medical Care   Health care is provided by Grande Ronde Hospital in La Grande. A private, not-for-profit institution, the hospital has 40 active and associate physicians, and a 24-hour emergency room.

When Grandkids Visit   Take them to the Oregon Trail Interpretive Park at Blue Mountain crossing, 12 miles from La Grande, westbound on Interstate 84. An easily accessible path takes you alongside some of the best preserved traces of the

Oregon Trail, with original wagon ruts clearly evident. Illustrated panels depict the pioneers' struggle through the Blue Mountains.

Important Addresses and Connections

Chamber of Commerce: 2111 Adams Ave., La Grande, OR 97850.
Senior Services: 1901 Adams Ave., La Grande, OR 97850.
Newspaper: *The Observer*, 1406 5th St., La Grande, OR 97850.
Airport: Pendleton.
Bus/Train: The Senior Center operates a bus for senior rides in town. Greyhound provides out-of-town service.

LE GRANDE	Jan.	Apr.	July	Oct.	Rain	Snow
Daily Highs	38	60	87	66	19	31
Daily Lows	23	35	58	38	in.	in.

Pendleton

We moved away from here for a while. But after spending seven years in rain, traffic and confusion, we couldn't wait to get back to Pendleton!
—Pat Smootz

Once the prairie schooners crossed over Blue Mountain Summit, the toughest part of the journey was over. But there was more to come, with 200 miles of slow travel ahead. The next way station along the Oregon Trail was Pendleton. Here travelers could look forward to plenty of clear, fresh water from the Umatilla River and abundant feed for the animals. After a respite, the emigrants were ready to face a relatively short trek to the Columbia River and from there, the final, downriver portion of the journey.

Touches of the past are still evident in the old-fashioned downtown area, where many buildings display intricate brick-work designs and fancy architectural touches in the style of a bygone era. Pendleton's downtown has been designated a National Historic District, and it continues to serve as the city's center despite competition from shopping malls on the edge of town. Pendleton's 16,000 residents join with many more thousands in the surrounding area to support more than adequate shopping facilities.

North of downtown is an area famous for Victorian and early 1900s architecture. Some truly regal homes perch on these elevations and overlook the town below. Interspersed between large homes, smaller houses display the same grandeur but on a smaller scale and at diminished prices.

While some might classify Pendleton as high desert, the elevation here is just a little over 1,000 feet. Furthermore, the 13 inches of rain and 17 inches of annual snowfall keep the area from falling within the definition of "desert." Consequently, winters are fairly mild, and summers rarely hot.

The town is unusually blessed by intercity transportation. Not only is it situated on an interstate, Pendleton is one of the few cities of its small size that is served by Greyhound buses and Amtrak and has its own airport with commuter connections to the outside world. The grandkids will have no problems visiting.

While you're investigating Pendleton, take a tour of the famous Pendleton Woolen Mills, with its local tradition of 100-percent virgin wool shirts, blankets and famous brand clothing. This could be your last opportunity to visit a genuine United States fabric mill; the ones that haven't skipped off to Mexico or the Orient in search of cheap labor are poised and ready to go. Pendleton continues six generations of operation here and promises to continue the tradition. (Pause for cheers.)

Recreation and Culture The deep-cut river valley that shelters Pendleton is overshadowed by the majestic Blue Mountains in the distance giving the town a picturesque setting. These mountains are the site of winter sports such as skiing or snowmobiling, and such warm-weather sports as fishing, hunting or hiking the acres and acres of wide-open spaces.

Another form of diversion available to Pendleton folks is a gambling casino on the Umatilla Indian Reservation, just a few miles west of town. If your idea of entertainment is throwing your money away, you can have a great time at the Wildhorse Gaming Resort.

The Blue Mountain Community College brings seniors into the academic current by offering them evening courses free of charge. But the entertainment highlight of the entire region is the Pendleton Round-Up and Happy Canyon Pageant. This is America's classic rodeo, drawing crowds of up to 50,000, coming from all over the country to see real cowboys do their thing. Spread over several days, the celebration treats you to daily competitions, portrayals of Native American and frontier life, and a major country music concert.

Housing Costs Pendleton's major era of growth and expansion is long past, therefore most homes are old—dating from before or just after World War II. However, several areas offer more modern homes and lots for building, should that be your goal. Most are on the southern edge of town, sitting on steep hills, with lovely views of the town and the snow-covered Blue Mountains in the distance.

Real estate prices seem to be stuck in the 1970s. We looked at three-bedroom homes from as low as $65,000 and one five-bedroom home for $118,000. Since most housing is single family, and condos and apartment buildings scarce to non-existent, the rental market is understandably tight.

Medical Care St. Anthony's hospital has two locations with both primary care and outpatient appointments accepted. They offer 24-hour emergency service. As in many areas of Oregon, doctors may be reluctant to take on new patients.

Crime and Safety Pendleton isn't included in the FBI's Uniform Crime Report, so statistics aren't available, but local people assure us that the city is as safe as any in the state. Our observations would confirm this; Pendleton appears to be peaceful and tranquil.

When Grandkids Visit Take 'em on a trip back to Pendleton's wild past. Tours start in the Shamrock Cardroom, a turn-of-the-century honky-tonk, and go on to visit an interesting underground Chinese settlement, complete with homes and stores constructed in tunnels under the town.

Important Addresses and Connections
Chamber of Commerce: 25 S.E. Dorion Ave., Pendleton, OR 97801.
Senior Services: 510 S.W. 10th Street, Pendleton, OR 97801.
Newspaper: *The Record*, 809 S.E. Court Ave., Pendleton, OR 97801.
Airport: Local regional airport with commuter connections.
Bus/Train: No local bus, but both Amtrak and Greyhound stop in town.

Hermiston/Umatilla

We were used to a big city, but we found no problem fitting in here. It's small, quiet, and we like it.

—Nicole Shubin

When wagon trains reached the Echo way station, some wagons continued on across the dry Columbia Plateau toward The Dalles, while some went north to the Columbia Rivers. The choice was, either continue on the land portion of the trail, go to Umatilla and follow a trail along the river, or rent rafts and float down as far as The Dalles. To get to Umatilla, the trail passed through what today is Hermiston, which got its start as an overnight stop for trail-weary travelers and freighters. In the 1850s it was known as "Six Mile House," consisting of a sturdy Old West hotel with a deep well, curbed with lava rock, and a feed barn for mules and horses. Inside, the hotel featured a bar with a genuine brass rail.

A hundred years later—in the late 1950s—I became acquainted with Umatilla and Hermiston when I was working on the Columbia Basin News in Pasco, Washington. It turned out that since Umatilla was in Oregon, this was the nearest place to buy imported beer. (In those days, Washington permitted the sale of only domestic, 3.2 percent beer, while Oregon stores could sell stronger—and better—Canadian and European beers.) During the year we lived in Washington, I became well acquainted with the highway to Umatilla and Hermiston.

Today Hermiston is a small city of 10,600 inhabitants, and Umatilla, six miles away, has 3,300. The towns are only five miles apart, but residents say they are separate when it comes to socializing except for special events like traditional celebrations. Each has its own senior center and local organizations. This is rich farm country under irrigation, producing potatoes, asparagus, peppers and regionally famous Hermiston watermelon.

I personally have mixed feelings about this particular area as a place for retirement. The surrounding country is flat, with few trees, and arid in the summer. On the other hand, the Columbia River makes up for the lack of mountains, and the mild climate and low rainfall compensates for the landscape.

Recreation and Culture Local fishermen call this part of the Columbia River "the walleye capital of the world." They claim that you'll find great fishing for not only walleye, but bass, salmon, sturgeon, steelhead, shad and panfish. The Umatilla River also conceals huge sturgeon, waiting to grab your hook. The nearby Blue Mountains are known for big-game hunting, such as deer, elk and bear. Snow skiing is also available in the Blue Mountains.

Hermiston is proud of its 75 acres of city parks, containing lighted tennis and volleyball courts, jogging paths and horseshoe pits, as well as picnic and barbecue areas. Umatilla has a public golf course, an 18-hole layout, par 70.

The Blue Mountain Community College in Pendleton (30 miles away) operates a branch campus in Hermiston, with some classes of interest to seniors. The school's performing arts department provides dramatic presentations throughout the year. Community sponsored cultural events are the Desert Arts Council, the Community Concert Association, the Oregon East Symphony, Stage Struck Theatre and many concerts and outdoor music productions.

Housing and Other Costs Recent sales prices for homes range from $50,000 to a high of $175,000. At one time, the military presence was all important, and lots of rentals were made available for the floating population. Now that the military has downsized, rentals are plentiful, with rents for apartments or duplexes from $300 to $500 per month and homes from $400 to $900. About five apartment complexes have subsidized housing for those who qualify. There are also 12 mobile home parks, an unusually large number for the size of the town. Because this is not a tourist area, and because the housing market is low, the cost of living seems to be quite favorable here.

Medical Care Hermiston is served by the 74-bed Good Shepherd Community Hospital, boasting modern diagnostic and surgical facilities. Seven other hospitals are located within a 60-mile radius of the city. Ambulance service is provided by the city Fire Department; the city also operates an emergency care unit.

When Grandkids Visit Two miles from downtown Hermiston is a small museum that ought to appeal to the enthusiastic young and nostalgic old, with toys dating back to the 1850s. The Doll and Toy Museum displays very old cap pistols, Teddy bears, doll carriages and 2,000 dolls of every description. An alternative is the Pacific Salmon Information Center at McNary Dam. There, you'll learn about the life cycle of the salmon and the struggle to ensure their survival.

Important Addresses and Connections
Chamber of Commerce: 540 S Highway 395, Hermiston, OR 97838.
Senior Services: 100 Van Buren, Umatilla, OR 97882.

Weekly Newspaper: *The Herald*, 193 E. Main St., Hermiston, OR 97838.
Airport: Connector airlines stop less than an hour away at Pasco or Pendleton.
Bus/Train: Pendleton is the closest town that Greyhound and Amtrak serve.

HERMISTON	Jan.	Apr.	July	Oct.	Rain	Snow
Daily Highs	53	66	83	65	12	8
Daily Lows	32	46	52	45	in.	in.

The Dalles

Retirement in The Dalles is important for our city, because folks living here don't want industry. We prefer to see lots of retirees instead of factories. I especially like it here because everybody is so friendly.　　　　　　　　　　　　　　　　—Hilda Duran

Most pioneers followed the inland route, across the dry Columbia Plateau, to The Dalles. The ones who floated downriver tied up when they reached the place where the Columbia raged through the canyon below and, in the background, Mt. Hood towered ominously. Now the promised land was drawing closer, but another agonizing choice had to be made. The emigrants could either hire rafts, expensive and dangerous through the river's treacherous currents, or they could turn inward to detour around Mt. Hood. This meant traversing the steep Barlow Toll Road and unpredictable weather around the dormant volcano of Mt. Hood.

Today the drive is along a high-speed, divided interstate highway. You can speed past huge basalt cliffs rising as high as 3,000 feet, cascading waterfalls and snowcapped volcano cones in the distance. A half-dozen historic little towns space themselves along the way, with the broad river flowing past carrying fishing boats, cargo barges and windsurfers. Two places in particular make for excellent retirement locations: Hood River and The Dalles. Traveling downriver, The Dalles comes first.

The Dalles received its name from French-Canadian voyagers who used to "shoot the rapids" here instead of tediously unloading their boats and dragging them around the narrow rapids (which are now buried beneath the dam). The French used the word *dalle* to refer to a place where waters were constrained between high rock walls. They called this exciting stretch of river *la grande dalle de la Columbia,* "the great rapid of the Columbia." Those traveling the Oregon Trail who floated downriver to this point had to portage around the rapids for the final leg of the trim. Others arrived with their wagons and either had to build rafts and float their belongings downriver from this point or detour inland around Mount Hood. Some weary travelers decided to give it up and settle in The Dalles, making it one of the earliest towns in the state.

Today The Dalles has an 11,200 population and is the center of a thriving agricultural region, with wheat fields and orchards fringing the town limits. It's definitely dry here, with less than half the rainfall of Portland, just 100 miles downriver. The Dalles catches about 14 inches of rain (about the same as Los Angeles) and a couple of inches of snow, two or three times each year. Summers are warm, often in the 90s, but it's a dry heat, with lots of wind off the river, and almost no rain during July and August.

In the historic downtown shopping district, streets run parallel with the river, full of substantial brick buildings of a late 1800s vintage. The town center seems to be active and spared from traffic by the interstate that bypasses The Dalles. Most major shopping retailers are represented on the edge of town. Residential neighborhoods climb the rather steep hillside behind the town, each street enjoying panoramic views of the Columbia River Gorge and Dallesport Peninsula. The Columbia Gorge Community College and the large Sorosis Park command the final view across the river into the state of Washington.

Residential neighborhoods are almost sitting on streets that stairstep up the steep hillside. Most homes therefore, enjoy great views of the river and of the state of Washington in the distance. Residential neighborhoods vary from elegant to economical, something for every pocketbook.

Recreation and Culture Skiing at Mt. Hood Meadows is just over an hour's drive, with national forest campgrounds for hiking and camping about the same distance. Most outdoor recreation here involves the Columbia River. Boating and fishing for salmon, steelhead trout and many other species are popular here, with different conditions above and below the dam. Golfing usually requires a 22-mile drive downriver to Hood River at an 18-hole public course. There is also a private course in the Dalles that is open to the pubic during the winter.

The Columbia Gorge Community College occupies a 60-acre campus in The Dalles and offers many classes of interest to retirees, as well as regular degrees and coursework. The school's extensive library is open to the public, with more than 10,000 books and 100 periodical titles, plus CD-ROM databases.

The Civic Auditorium, a historic center for the performing arts, is presently under renovation downtown. Access to Portland's many cultural events requires an hour-and-a-half-drive along fast-moving Interstate 84.

Housing and Other Costs   Higher prices don't seem to have reached The Dalles, because the average market price for a three-bedroom home in 1995 was only $77,000. Numerous homes were listed below $70,000, a few in the $50s and $60s. We looked at a three-bedroom home situated on a bluff overlooking the river and the Columbia Gorge for $59,000. From one side of the property, we could see the top of Mt. Hood. There are no condos here, and the rental market is tight, with two-bedroom apartments going for about $450 to $600. The cost of living here is slightly higher than in most other Oregon Trail towns, partly because The Dalles is closer to Portland and shares its above-average price structure.

Medical Care   The region's largest hospital, Mid-Columbia Medical Center, is located here with complete emergency service and diagnostic care. The hospital is proud of its technical support equipment and patient care. Also, The Dalles has several medical clinics and is building Oregon's first Veterans Home/Hospital.

When Grandkids Visit   Try a guided tour through The Dalles Dam, the largest hydroelectric dam on the lower Columbia, and a train ride to the powerhouse, fish ladder and lock.

Important Addresses and Connections

Chamber of Commerce: 404 W. 2nd St., The Dalles, OR 97058.
Senior Services: 700 Union St., The Dalles, OR 97058.
Newspapers: *Chronicle* (daily), 414 Federal St., The Dalles, OR 97058;
    Reminder (weekly), 723 E. 2nd St., The Dalles, OR 97058.
Airport: Portland.
Bus: City bus, Senior Caravan service and Greyhound serve the area.

THE DALLES	Jan.	Apr.	July	Oct.	Rain	Snow
Daily Highs	50	64	86	65	17	7
Daily Lows	35	41	57	48	in.	in.

Hood River

*When we moved here, we were just passing through, only plan-
ning to stay six months or so. Once here, we fell in love with the
area. This is the greatest place on earth.* —Linda Baker

When it was settled in 1854, early residents called the community "Dog River," but under pressure by housewives the name
was changed to "Hood Vale" and later to "Hood River." This was
one of the first places along the Oregon Trail where pioneers
found enough rain to grow some of the same kinds of crops they
were used to back East. Some of the first things planted were
apple trees and strawberries. Today the region is famous for pear
and apple orchards.

It's interesting how just a little distance between The Dalles
and Hood River (22 miles) makes a real difference in the climate.
Hood River gets 30 inches of rain and lots more snow than The
Dalles. This extra precipitation makes a big difference in the vegetation as well. Everything is green, even through the summer,
and more lush. Still, Hood River gets less precipitation than
Portland—or about the same as Des Moines or Detroit.

Today a town of 4,700, Hood River is only about an hour's
drive from Portland. The downtown business center, varying
from one to three blocks wide, follows along the river. It seems
to be holding up well against the heavy shopping competition
on the highway leading out of town. Several interesting restaurants and historic buildings with specialty stores draw downtown
shoppers. Residential neighborhoods close to the town center
vary from comfortable to not-quite-elegant, and most older
homes are shaded by large trees. The newer homes away from
downtown can be quite upscale and command great views of the
Columbia River. Many places, either up or down the river, combine views and acreage. Behind Hood River, ascending the
mountain slopes toward Mt. Hood, a series of small communities
and towns add to Hood River's regional population—such places
as Odell, Dee and Parkdale.

Hood River has one of the higher senior populations (per-
centage-wise) in the state, and retirees account in part for the
region's prosperity. Two retirement living/senior apartment complexes are found here. The senior center is said to be bustling
with activities.

Recreation and Culture Mt. Hood, an ancient volcano and Oregon's highest mountain, sits just a few miles to the south of here, offering a variety of downhill and cross-country skiing in the winter. Summer is for hiking and camping. Fishing in the Columbia River is augmented by fly casting for rainbow trout and steelhead in the Hood River. Two public golf courses provide year-round play at Indian Creek (18 holes, par 72) and Hood River Golf (nine holes, par 34).

With the 55-mile-per-hour speed limits removed from the interstate, zipping into Portland to participate in its multitude of cultural activities is no problem, a matter of 45 minutes or so. And just 22 miles to the east, the community college at The Dalles accommodates Hood River residents. The local calendar of events ranges from blossom and harvest festivals to windsurf races and even a rodeo.

Housing Costs Real estate is a little more expensive here than in the Dalles, but as one broker put it, "If you come here and see how beautiful it is, you would understand." We have to admit that Hood River is inviting as a retirement location. Although satisfactory three-bedroom homes can be found for well under $100,000, typically they'll start above that figure. Hood River has one condominium complex, and when available, the units sell for between $70,000 and $90,000. There were several two-bedroom apartments renting for $450 and up. Property taxes vary depending upon the district, but are mostly under $15 per $1,000 valuation.

Medical Care Residents seem to like the local medical services, with a high ratio of doctors to patients. The Hood River Memorial Hospital recently added a new patient services wing. The facility offers 24-hour emergency care and a large staff of participating physicians. Hood River also has three medical clinics as well as an ambulance service.

When Grandkids Visit Take in the Hood River Historical Museum in Port Marina Park. Exhibits include artifacts from Oregon Trail days and early pioneer history. An alternative might be a train ride on the Mt. Hood Railroad, which climbs impressive grades through steep canyons and rolls through lush fruit orchards to nearby Parkdale and back.

Important Addresses and Connections
Chamber of Commerce: Port Marina Park, Hood River, OR 97031.
Senior Services: 2010 Sterling Place, Hood River, OR 97031.
Bi-Weekly Newspaper: *The News,* 409 Oak St., Hood River, OR 97031.
Airport: Portland.
Bus/Train: Local Transit Bus, Senior Bus, Greyhound.

HOOD RIVER	Jan.	Apr.	July	Oct.	Rain	Snow
Daily Highs	49	64	85	63	30	9
Daily Lows	34	42	56	78	in.	in.

The Oregon Coast

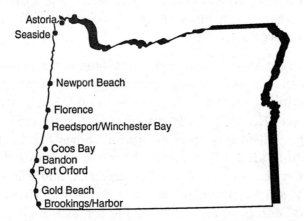

North from California, along scenic Highway 101, an inviting string of small towns await your visit and consideration as retirement locations. Sandy beaches interspersed with rocky headlands mark the Oregon coast all the way from its start at the California border to the mouth of the Columbia River north of Astoria. For over three hundred miles, the Oregon coast presents ever-changing scenes of beauty and tranquility. Offshore rocks shelter marine mammals, and coastal rivers end in estuaries that are among the biologically richest places on earth. Most coastal towns have a large percentage of retired residents.

When we asked a retiree why he chose the Oregon coast for his retreat, he invited us into his mobile home for coffee, to talk it over. "This is my home," he said proudly. "Not very big, but it's all I need as a bachelor and fisherman. My [space] rent is $200 a month, and this trailer cost me $2,800. Paid more than that for my boat. So here I am, gettin' by on my Social Security money and goin' fishin' anytime I care to, which is almost every day." He explained that after working for years in the Midwest, roasting in the summer and freezing in the winter, he wanted someplace where he didn't have to stay indoors because it was too hot or too cold to go outside. "Also, I wanted a place by the ocean I could afford. This was it." In short, pleasantly cool weather and outdoor recreation are the drawing cards here.

Since temperatures rarely drop to freezing, even in the depths of winter, sweaters or windbreakers are the heaviest winter clothing required. Because mid-day temperatures rarely top 75 degrees, folks here sleep under electric blankets year-round. A number of part-time retirees come here every summer from Southwest locations like Phoenix; they cherish their cool summers here and love their warm Arizona winters.

This cool weather isn't for everyone, however. It takes a love for sweaters and a hatred of sweltering and air-conditioning to enjoy living on the coast. And this is not the place for those who can't stand a little rain now and then. Actually, it's the Pacific Coast that earns Oregon its reputation for being rainy. Between 60 and 80 inches of rain fall on the coastal towns each year, most of it in the winter. However, the up side of the picture is that it can't snow while it's raining. One lady who retired from New York state said, "We used to get 80 inches of snow back there. I'll take the rain any time!"

Since weather here is governed by the Pacific Ocean, which is remarkably constant in temperature, one weather chart is just about adequate to describe all Oregon coast towns. There may be a little more snow in the more northern locations, but nothing really significant. Having said this, I must also point out that the Brookings/Harbor area is a bit different from other coastal towns, as will be explained later.

Oregon coast residents have plenty of elbow room. There's only a scattering of small towns, each separated from the others by long stretches of sandy beaches, forested hills and fish-laden rivers. The only places large enough to earn the title of "city" are Coos Bay and Astoria, and they just barely qualify. Florence and Lincoln City are growing fast, and probably some day they'll fit into the category of "city," too. Most beaches are all but deserted, with unrestricted public access guaranteed by state law. Five or ten minutes' drive inland takes you to a low mountain range, the Cascades, with thousands of square miles of wilderness—almost all publicly owned, much of it in national forest.

Good fishing is another plus—both ocean and river. Steelhead, chinook salmon, and rainbow trout lurk in streams flowing from nearby mountains. Clamming, crabbing and whale watching are popular activities. The open countryside is perfect for camping, picnicking or beachcombing, as well as golf and horseback riding. Whitetail deer are plentiful, plus an occasional black bear or cougar. A large proportion of beachfront is dedicated to public parks and campgrounds, in the midst of the most beautiful seascapes to be found anywhere in the world.

With few exceptions, the real estate market along Oregon's coast has boomed over the past few years. During our first research trip we found some of the best bargains imaginable among the quiet little beach towns here. I reported this in earlier writings, predicting that prices had no place to go but up. Time has fulfilled this prophecy, but I still see a healthy market here.

You might expect the cost of living to be a bit higher along Oregon's Pacific Coast. This shouldn't be surprising, since the major economic force hereabouts is tourism. However, higher prices of some consumer goods are offset by lower utility bills because of the mild summers and gentle winters.

OREGON COAST	Jan.	Apr.	July	Oct.	Rain	Snow
Daily Highs	53	54	62	58	65	1
Daily Lows	41	44	51	48	in.	in.

Brookings/Harbor

This place has a small-town feeling, where things today are like they used to be: with a low crime rate and lots of community minded individuals.
                                                            —Rosemary D'Amato

Just across the California line, the twin towns of Brookings and Harbor sit on opposite banks of the Chetco River. Of their combined population of 12,500, an estimated 30 percent are retirees. As you can see, retirement is big business along this coast. Seniors take an active part in the political, social and economic life of Brookings and Harbor, together one of the larger communities on the Oregon coast.

Encouraged by mild, ice-free winters, flowers bloom all year along Oregon's coast. But for years, Brookings residents have been boasting that their climate has even warmer winters, claiming the title of "banana belt" of the coast. Quite frankly, I always smiled indulgently when hearing this as I tried to imagine banana plants swaying in the Pacific breezes. However, when I looked into it, their claims were somewhat vindicated. No, bananas don't really grow in the Brookings-Harbor area, but their bragging isn't just propaganda created to get tourists here; it really is warmer here, as much as five degrees warmer—for what that's worth to you. Compare the figures for Brookings-Harbor with the weather chart above and see for yourself.

The explanation given me is as follows: "The banana belt phenomenon is the result of high pressure systems that move inland over southwestern Washington and northwestern Oregon. The system circles around toward Brookings, where air is compressed and heated as it moves down, pulled south by low pressure systems from California's San Joaquin Valley." There you have it. I don't pretend to understand it exactly, but statistically it is a bit warmer here. The down side is that the area catches about five inches more rain each year, but that's comparatively little when you consider that this is a rainy coast anyway.

This slightly warmer weather accounts for all the flower farms here, producing 90 percent of the country's Easter lilies. Rhododendrons and azaleas bloom wildly in the late spring, and an Azalea Festival is held every Memorial Day.

Recreation and Culture About 90 percent of Curry County is National Forest, Bureau of Land Management or lumber companies' property—almost all open to the public. This means plenty of room for hiking, camping, hunting and fishing. The Chetco River is said to be good salmon and steelhead domain. Its headwaters originate in the Klamiopis Wilderness east of town. Of course, the main focus for most sports-minded folks here is the ocean. The river mouth and jetties shelter boats, and it seems as though every other person here owns one. Fishing, clamming, crabbing and whale watching are "in" things to do. There are two tennis courts, but golfers have to go to either Crescent City or Gold Beach.

The Southwestern Oregon Community College has a branch here for continuing education. And, like most places along the coast, Brookings and Harbor have plenty of things for retired folks to do, both organized and do-it-yourself. As one lady put it, "The senior center is incredible."

Housing Costs Home prices vary along the Oregon coast, from town to town, but not as much as in the interior. This is because all coastal communities partake in the same climate, ocean views, cultural and recreational aspects. So, the old adage of "location, location, location" doesn't apply here. Therefore, while real estate in one area might be a bit higher than another location, the differences aren't dramatic.

Older homes in acceptable neighborhoods sell for between $70,000 and $110,000. New houses in new subdivisions start at $115,000 and often top $250,000—depending on location. Homes with a view will add $50,000 to the price, but many people will agree that it's worth it. Ocean front properties can go sky-high or be surprisingly affordable, depending on circumstances. Mobile homes on residential lots or acreage can be found for as little as $50,000 or as high as $150,000.

In towns like Brookings and Harbor, and most small towns, apartments and condos are not plentiful; most people prefer single-family living units. When condominiums are around, they tend to be expensive, being sold as vacation places and rented out to tourists while owners are not there. During our last visit to Brookings the only unit that was for sale was over-priced at $160,000. Property taxes are said to be low here, less than anywhere in the state—at $11 per $1,000 valuation—but you should verify this for yourself. We've heard this boast about "lowest taxes in the state" coming from several other places.

Medical Care It seems odd that a community as large as Brookings and Harbor would have no hospital. They have three medical clinics, but for surgery or specialized treatment, residents depend on the Curry General Hospital in Gold Beach or the Sutter Coast Hospital in Crescent City, California. Both are about 27 miles away, one north and one south. This is said to be a 30-minute drive, either direction. An ambulance service and 20 doctors complete the medical picture here.

When Grandkids Visit Do a picnic at Loeb Park, up the Chetco River about seven miles. Located in a grove of huge

Myrtlewood trees, the park features a good old-fashioned swimming hole. The water is crystal clear and pure as it flows out of the wilderness on its way to the ocean.

Important Addresses and Connections

Chamber of Commerce: 16630 Lower Harbor Rd., Brookings, OR 97415.

Senior Services: P.O. Box 214, Brookings, OR, 97415.

Weekly Newspaper: *Curry County Coastal Pilot,* 507 Chetco Lane, Brookings, OR 97415.

Airport: Medford.

Bus/Train: Dial-a-Ride for seniors and Greyhound serve the area.

BROOKINGS	Jan.	Apr.	July	Oct.	Rain	Snow
Daily Highs	55	59	68	65	73	1
Daily Lows	41	43	50	48	in.	in.

Gold Beach

Our senior center is nearly full every day: music, cards, lunch, lots of activities. Gold Beach has lots of good restaurants in town—and we seniors love to eat well!   —Richard Stephens

Gold Beach is where the legendary Rogue River empties into the powerful and scenic Pacific Ocean. This is a small town, with only 2,100 residents, but it has all the necessary shopping conveniences. From the Rogue's mouth, a road follows the river's course upstream, past retirement homes of devout fishermen who prize the steelhead and salmon that pass their doors every day. When the fish decide not to bite, the anglers simply head their boats downriver for some ocean fishing. The country behind Gold Beach is mile after mile of forested wilderness, with trout, steelhead and salmon streams and deer hunting.

Gold Beach has an interesting history. It derived its name from an incident that started a frantic gold rush back in the '49er days. A prospector passing through the area discovered a small quantity of gold mixed in with beach sands. He panned a tiny bit of color and casually mentioned the fact to some other miners. As the word spread, the story expanded until gold mining camps all over California and Oregon blazed with news of a beach where the ocean's waves placered nuggets of gold from the sand. "Why, the beach is strewn with riches, there for the gathering." Mining camps in California's Mother Lode all but emptied as miners frantically rushed to the "gold beach."

Actually, gold is rather common on Oregon and California beaches, usually found in black streaks of magnetite sand mixed in with beach terraces. The problem is that it is very fine and difficult to separate from the coarser sand. Back during depression days, when many people had nothing else to do, a large quantity of gold was gleaned from the beaches, but it was tedious work.

Gold Beach's stampede was short lived, but some miners, tired of moving from place to place in search of riches, decided to retire from gold panning and settle down. They started the first retirement community on the Oregon coast. The tradition continues today, with retirement a more significant industry than fishing or lumbering.

Gold Beach is the county seat for Curry County, and it has one of the larger commercial districts in the area. The downtown shopping area clearly reflects the prosperity that comes with being a tourist center.

Recreation and Culture   Describing the outdoor activities available to Gold Beach retirees is like reciting the highlights of most of the other coast towns. All of them have pretty much the same recreational opportunities available. Outdoor enthusiasts enjoy the spectacular scenery of the Oregon Coast Trail. A combination of beach, grassy and wooded paths, the trail is easy walking and can be accessed just a few minutes away from Gold Beach's town center. Some trail sections intersect with Highway 101 frequently, so short hikes of one-half to three miles can be planned, or you can travel several sections in one day and be home in time for supper.

Gold Beach is a year-round angler's paradise, with the Rogue River and seven smaller nearby streams famed for steelhead and salmon. You can charter a deep-sea ocean trip or try your luck from shore. An almost limitless trail follows the banks of the Rogue into the designated Wild and Scenic wilderness area where you can explore the scenery, and when the sun sets you can spend the night at one of several luxury lodges or in a wilderness campsite. You can also golf year-round at Cedar Bend, 10 miles north of Gold Beach, just east of Cedar Fork Creek.

The Gold Beach Calendar of Events is filled with cultural and entertainment events the year-round, from summer theater presentations to power boat races.

Housing Costs   Single-family homes, cottages and mobile homes are the general rule in Gold Beach, with people living in multi-generational communities rather than strictly adult developments. Prices have risen over the past four years, with few homes priced under $90,000. View homes can run $175,000 and up. There are a few luxury condos which start around $130,000. Property taxes are $13.50 per $1,000 valuation, but there could be bonds and assessments on top of that, depending on where you choose to live.

Medical Care   Curry General Hospital provides medical care for the surrounding area. A 24-bed, certified trauma facility with 24-hour emergency service, the hospital is served by physicians in many specialties. In addition to the hospital, there are three independent medical clinics and an ambulance service.

When Grandkids Visit   The Mail Boat, a powerful hydro-jet, takes you on an exhilarating trip up the river—through the narrow canyons and swift rapids of the Wild and Scenic section of the Rogue. You'll view eagles, osprey and deer, and you'll scare the bejazzles out of wide-eyed fishermen as your roaring boat splashes foam and water into their boats while you go soaring up the river as far as Blossom Bar.

Important Addresses and Connections

Chamber of Commerce: 1225 S Ellensburg Av., Gold Beach, OR 97444.
Senior Services: 410 Airport Way, Gold Beach, OR 97444.
Newspaper: *Curry County Reporter,* 510 N Ellensburg, Gold Beach, OR 97444.
Airport: Eugene or Medford.
Bus/Train: No local bus system, but Greyhound stops in town.

Port Orford

We used to come here to visit, and I always thought someday I'm going to retire there, and here I am! And I've never regretted it!
—Lillian Poland

As you drive north from Gold Beach, in about 40 minutes you'll catch a glimpse of one of the Oregon coast's prettiest sights. The beach at Port Orford is the ultimate picture-postcard scene. Dramatic rock formations jut from the sea, catching the force of waves, sending spray flying, and then the swells continue on to become gentle breakers on the sandy beach. Beaches here are also known for semi-precious stones such as agate, jasper and jade, as well as being good places to look for redwood burls. Both Port Orford and Bandon (27 miles up the road) are truly retirement communities. A local real estate broker claims that 68 percent of his new clients are retired.

The population of Port Orford is only about 1,100, so real estate choices are limited. During our last visit we noticed that prices had climbed a bit in the past two years. Local real estate people say three-bedroom homes are selling in the range of $80,000 to 120,000, while a two-bedroom apartment rents for about $450. Taxes are about $12 per $1,000 valuation.

A Senior Van provides transportation around town, and there's Greyhound bus service through town. Port Orford is too small to support its own hospital—it depends upon the hospital in Gold Beach, but it does have a medical center with two doctors, an ambulance service and one dentist. Much of the description of Bandon (see below) fits Port Orford. The local senior center serves lunches twice a month, dinners once a week, and has card games, a pool table, and other activities for the entertainment of residents.

Important Addresses and Connections

Chamber of Commerce: 520 Deady, Port Orford, OR 97465.
Senior Services: 1536 Jackson, Port Orford, OR 97465.
Newspaper: *Port Orford News*, 519 W. 10th., Port Orford, OR 97465.
Airport: Eugene or Medford.
Bus/Train: Greyhound, senior van service in town.

Bandon

I just wanted a small coastal town like Newport Beach, California, used to be. I love things like the Cranberry festival, holiday celebrations and the seafood. Would I move back to California? Not in my worst nightmare! —Roberta Taylor

Forty-four miles north of Port Orford and 51 miles south of Coos Bay, the town of Bandon, with about 2,500 inhabitants, is quite dependent on tourism. Local residents derive the benefits of tourist business because Bandon deliberately cultivates a "quaint" atmosphere, with period restaurants, art galleries, ceramic studios and small shops of every description. The rejuvenated Oldtown Harbor District is a major location of art galleries and helps create Bandon's artists' colony reputation. The local chamber of commerce coordinates activities for retirees, with monthly dinners, art shows, and an annual cranberry festival.

Housing Costs Because views are so spectacular here, ocean-front property has become scarce and expensive, with view homes commonly selling for as high as $300,000. However, if a seascape is not essential in your choice of homes, away from the ocean's edge and up nearby rivers you'll find three-bedroom homes starting at $90,000. Two-bedroom apartments are not too high, going for $400 to 500 a month. Property taxes are about $15 per $1,000 valuation.

Recreation and Culture When my wife and I lived in Oregon, we enjoyed driving to the coast to try for our limit of Dungeness crab. Bandon is a convenient place for first-time crabbers. A series of floating docks extend out into the water, and you catch the tasty crustaceans by lowering a crab net loaded with bait to the bottom and waiting for the creatures to visit. Then, with quick hand-over-hand pulls, up comes the trap, often with half a dozen hefty, so tasty, morsels, each weighing a pound or more. The market price, last time we went crabbing, was $3.85 a pound! You can rent crab nets, bait and everything you need for an afternoon's fun.

There is one local public golf course, Face Rock Golf Course, for those who can't stand to do without a little putting now and then. For continuing education, Southwestern Oregon Community College is located in nearby Coos Bay (23 miles).

When Grandkids Visit The West Coast Game Park Walk-Thru Safari, just south of Bandon on Highway 101, has more than 450 animals on its 20 acres of grounds, including cougars, snow leopards, zebras, African lions and tiger cubs. You can walk among the animals and even feed some of them. If the grandkids are obstreperous, this might sober them up a little.

Important Addresses and Connections
Chamber of Commerce: 300 Second, Bandon, OR 97411.

Senior Services: 1100 W. 11th, Bandon, OR 97411.
Weekly Newspaper: *Western World,* 1185 Baltimore Ave. S.E., Bandon, OR 97411.
Airport: Eugene, Medford.
Bus/Train: Dial-a-Ride for seniors and Greyhound serve the area.

Coos Bay

I like it here because of reasonable property prices and the mild climate. —Al Charamza

Three cities comprise the Coos Bay complex: Charleston, North Bend and Coos Bay itself, combining to form the major population center of the Oregon coast, with a combined population of 32,000. Since the municipality of Coos Bay is the largest, people refer to all three towns as Coos Bay. The cities truly approach being metropolitan, because this is a major trading center for an area extending 50 miles north to Florence and 100 miles south to Brookings.

You can quickly tell the difference between an industry-oriented city like Coos Bay and other tourist-driven places on the coast by their downtown centers. Those without the driving force of tourism just aren't as vibrant or prosperous looking. The downtowns are like many in the United States, left behind by the strip malls and shopping centers on the fringes of the city. This doesn't detract from the residential areas, which range from nice to modest.

Coos Bay-North Bend is situated on the blunt end of a peninsula, with Pacific beaches on one side and the waters of Coos Bay on the other. The mountains of the Coast Range, heavily timbered and colored a shadowy blue-green, make a pretty background for the town. The mouth of the bay is crossed by graceful McCullough Bridge where the third small city, Charleston, completes the Coos Bay area. Fishing and lumber are the major industries, with fine harvests of salmon, tuna, crab, shrimp, oysters and clams. Because the well-protected harbor is navigable by ocean-going vessels, Coos Bay is perhaps one of the world's largest ports for forest products. But since lumber isn't the hottest item going nowadays, things are rather slow. I have to admit that the Coos Bay area lacks the charm of some of the more attractive, smaller towns, but the real estate prices compensate for this.

Recreation and Culture   This part of the Oregon coast is big on parks. Within a six-mile drive of Coos Bay are four exceptional ones, including Cape Arago, the site where (according to local history buffs) Sir Francis Drake first set foot on the North American continent. Just north is the lower entrance to the famous Oregon Dunes National Recreation Area, with 50 miles of unspoiled beaches, woods and marvelous sand dunes. This is a great place for picnicking, camping and beachcombing. A current sweeps ashore, bringing all sorts of treasures, some from as far away as Japan. Among the prizes are weathered redwood burls, which make marvelous natural sculptures. The smaller ones are made into lamps; larger pieces are cut into slabs, polished and turned into table tops. Some retirees have turned collecting and woodworking into a small business sideline. One man said, "I sell all the redwood sculptures I can make. Problem is, I keep too busy making things to go out and look for burls—have to buy 'em nowadays."

The region has two public golf courses: Sunset Bay and Kentucky Golf and Country Club in North Bend. Coos Bay is the home of Southwestern Oregon Community College, which is located on a 125-acre site near Empire Lakes. SWOCC offers accredited certificate and associate-degree programs, as well as a wide range of adult enrichment courses.

Housing Costs   This is one coastal area where real estate has remained more or less at an affordable level. Typical three-bedroom, two-bath homes sell for an average of $90,000, many for much less. Rentals seem to be plentiful and at competitive rates, with $500 to $800 for homes and $400 to $600 for two-bedroom apartments. Property taxes are at the usual $15 per $1,000 valuation, however there are areas with bonded debt which elevates the outlay.

Medical Care   Health care is excellent here, with the publicly owned, not-for-profit Bay Area Hospital serving all three communities. As you might expect, it's the largest medical facility on the entire Oregon Coast, with 175 beds, and is responsible for more than 90,000 residents of the South Coast in a 175-mile area. The facility is proud of its state-of-the-art equipment for diagnostic and therapeutic services.

Crime and Safety As with the other Oregon coast towns, Coos Bay is quite a safe place to make your home. It ranks in the top third of U.S. cities for safety, according to FBI crime statistics.

When Grandkids Visit The Charleston Fishing Dock is a great place for crabbing. You can get crab rings and bait there and have a great time snatching succulent crustaceans from the ocean. If you would rather go clamming, you can obtain information and directions for the best beach locations from the chamber of commerce.

Important Addresses and Connections
Chamber of Commerce: 50 E. Central, Coos Bay, OR 97420.
Senior Services: 888 S. Fourth St., Coos Bay, OR 97423.
Daily Newspaper: *The World*, 350 Commercial Ave., Coos Bay, OR 97420.
Airport: Eugene or Medford.
Bus/Train: Dial-a-Ride for seniors and Greyhound serve the area.

Reedsport/Winchester Bay

Coming from the Midwest, we decided we wanted someplace where we'd never have to shovel snow in the winter or bake in the summer. When we found the Oregon coast, we knew we were home.
—Marianne Landers

Twenty-three miles north of Coos Bay—a short drive for heavy shopping—the town of Winchester Bay (pop. 1,000) is the "suburb" of Reedsport, another four miles to the north, with 5,000 inhabitants. This is the center of the 50-mile long Oregon Dunes National Recreation Area, renowned for wild and virtually empty beaches and scenic oceanscapes.

Reedsport is another place where the economic woes of the lumber industry have impeded higher real estate prices. That is the up side, but the down side is that the town center reflects the industry-based economy. The major shopping is consummated in the strip malls and shopping centers on the edges of town. The city has a growing waterfront development centered around the Umpqua Discovery Center. Property taxes in Reedsport are about $17.50, and in Winchester Bay, $12 per $1,000 valuation.

Despite the excellent medical facilities of nearby Coos Bay, Reedsport has its own, the Lower Umpqua Hospital, with 18 acute-care beds and 25 extended-care beds. Also, there are two medical clinics serving the area and sufficient dentists and private doctors.

Recreation and Culture

The area abounds in Oregon's natural wonders. The Umpqua River is navigable for miles both upstream and downstream from Reedsport and is very popular with salmon and steelhead fishermen. They have a good chance of picking the fish off before they start their upstream breeding missions. The Dunes National Recreation Area headquarters and visitors information center is here, just a few feet from the chamber of commerce visitor center. Forest Hills (9 holes, par 36) is the public golf course locally.

Important Addresses and Connections

Chamber of Commerce: 805 Highway Ave., Reedsport, OR 97467.
Senior Services: 460 Winchester Ave., Reedsport OR 97467.
Weekly Newspaper: *The Courier*, 174 N. 16th St., Reedsport, OR 97467.
Airport: Eugene, Medford.
Bus/Train: No local transit but there's Dial-a-Ride for seniors and a Greyhound bus stop.

REEDSPORT	Jan.	Apr.	July	Oct.	Rain	Snow
Daily Highs	51	57	71	63	73	2
Daily Lows	37	43	53	46	in.	in.

Florence

We decided to move back to Florence after 20 years away. This is more like home than any place we've lived, partly because of the friendly folks who live here. —Doris Slonecker

Along the drive north from the California border, heading for Washington, Florence stands out as one of the higher quality communities. With 6,400 inhabitants, the town is the shopping area for 15,000 people living nearby, and you therefore find far better than average shopping for the town's size. Also, it's only 60 miles to Eugene, with its big-city shopping and all the amenities of a university town, including excellent cultural and entertainment opportunities.

Florence is an excellent example of how tourism can affect the appearance and composition of a town. Businesses look healthy, offering a broad spectrum of stores, shops and restaurants, with competition bringing out the best in service and quality. An abundance of viable enterprises obviously creates well-paying jobs, thus adding to the prosperity of the area. This is reflected in the higher-quality homes in residential areas and attractive neighborhoods. All of this can be contrasted to some similar-size towns along Oregon's coast and elsewhere, places that rely on one particular industry for economic support. When business falls off—as it has in so many towns that depend upon lumber, fishing or a single enterprise for paychecks—the town quickly appears to be on the verge of collapse. Store windows are boarded up and businesses close. A town can begin to look shabby, with neighborhoods going to seed. This in turn, discourages tourism, putting the town into a slow downward spiral.

None of the foregoing is meant to put down the less successful towns as not being good for retirement. You need to inspect each place with a view to your own particular needs. The nice thing about one of those slower towns is that real estate will obviously cost less for the kind of home you need, and rentals will usually be available—something that can be scarce or expensive in a more successful, tourist-oriented town.

Excellent senior services and a helpful chamber of commerce make Florence an easy place to settle into for retirement. In the late spring, thousands of rhododendrons bloom, and the event is celebrated with an annual Rhododendron Festival.

Recreation and Culture An interesting phenomenon along this part of the coast is the large number of freshwater lakes just a few hundred yards from the ocean. Groundwater flowing from the mountains tries to find its way to the ocean, but sand dunes—sometimes 300 feet high—trap the water in low-lying areas to form freshwater lakes. Within a few miles of Florence, the Oregon Fish and Wildlife Department stocks two dozen of these lakes with game fish. Some are loaded with cutthroat trout and restricted to barbless hooks, flies and lures—no bait permitted. Other lakes feature prize-winning bass, and still others are reserved for sailboats.

At the mouth of the Alsea River, Waldport is popular with saltwater and freshwater anglers. The coastline on both sides of Alsea Bay varies from smooth sandy beaches to rugged rocky formations. Several nearby state parks offer hiking, agate hunting, clamming and crabbing.

Public golf courses are Ocean Dunes (18 holes, par 70), Crestview Hills at Waldsport (9 holes, par 36) and Sand Pines Golf Links (18 holes, par 72), which was voted "Best New Public Golf Course in America" by *Golf Digest* in 1993.

The Oregon Coast Music Association was established in 1979 to present an annual classical music festival of the highest professional caliber and to support a varied range of year-round music performances and activities. Over the years Florence's Oregon Coast Music Festival has grown from a three-day Haydn Celebration to a two-week bonanza of music including classical, jazz, folk, dance, choral, concert band, blues, chamber, and some rather eclectic offerings. The centerpiece of the festival is the highly acclaimed Festival Orchestra which features internationally recognized soloists performing as special guest artists.

Lane Community College augments the community's cultural and social needs. Many classes are tailored for retirees with a thirst for more knowledge or who are simply looking for a place to meet with neighbors. Elderhostel programs at the college offer new worlds to explore with interesting, stimulating people from all walks of life.

Medical Care Doctors are said to be accepting new patients without problems, and all are connected with Florence's 20-bed hospital. The hospitals in Eugene are available for serious care.

When Grandkids Visit They'll enjoy a romp in the sand dunes, where they can wear themselves out sliding and tumbling down the steep sand knolls. There's also the Sea Lion Caves (11 miles north of Florence) for an adventurous descent to caves at the foot of a cliff, where sea lions like to cavort. At the right time of the year, you may see baby sea lions with their moms.

Important Addresses and Connections

Chamber of Commerce: 270 Hwy 101, Florence, OR 97439.
Senior Services: 1424 15th St., Florence, OR 97439.
Weekly Newspaper: *Siuslaw News,* 148 Maple St., Florence, OR 97439.
Airport: Eugene.
Bus/Train: Greyhound.

Newport Beach

I've made a lot of friends line dancing; the people are very friendly. Newport is an ideal place for a retired person.
                                                              —Pauline Shults

Newport is one of our own personal favorites among Oregon coast towns. One reason we like it here is the town's rich diversity of cultural interests and local arts that make it a stimulating place to visit, to live, and to explore your own creativity. With 9,500 inhabitants, Newport strikes a balance between small-town beach community and being large enough to provide all services. Nearby Yachats (pronounced *yah'hots*), a favorite place for fishing, picnicking or rockhounding on uncrowded beaches, also looks as if it might be a great place for retirement. Still, it's much smaller, and real estate is more costly in Yachats. Corvallis is a 52-mile drive, not too far to go shopping for the day and return, and Portland is 119 miles away.

Newport's homes are a curious mixture, from older cottage styles in the historic Nye Beach District, to beautiful custom-built homes with views; from condominiums to manufactured homes, from retirement villages to small acreages hidden away in the quiet rural countryside. An especially interesting part of Newport is the old port area, "below the bridge," where interesting restaurants, seafood markets and old buildings remind you of Newport's marine history. Every now and then a filmmaker utilizes the many colorful spots in and around Newport as a shooting location.

The cultural prize here is the Newport Performing Arts Center. A vibrant arts community of working artists, talented young people and senior citizens, exuberant volunteers and dedicated audiences have developed a year-round season of theater, music, dance, exhibitions, readings and lectures. With the Pacific Ocean as a backdrop, the center is itself a dramatic addition to Newport's historic Nye Beach District. In the 400-seat Alice Silverman Hall or the experimental Studio Theatre, a progression of actors, dancers and musicians present classic and experimental work. Red Octopus Theatre hosts an annual Original Scripts Workshop that entices playwrights from throughout the United States to develop new plays. A number of groups are able to rehearse here during the day, and these activities provide a full complement of opportunities for experienced and neophyte actors and technicians.

Recreation and Culture Yaquina Bay and the Pacific Ocean offer an endless array of recreational activities to revitalize and recharge your batteries. Fishing, crabbing, clamming, boating, canoeing, bike riding, kite flying, tidepooling or taking long walks on the beach are favorite activities and there's a public golf course at Agate Beach (nine holes, par 36).

The Yaquina Bay Family YMCA, an active Newport-based organization, offers a fitness center, swim club, racquetball club and a myriad of other special programs and activities to stimulate the health and well-being of citizens of all ages.

In addition to the Performing Arts Center, Oregon Coast Community College has its headquarters in Newport and provides adult education, personal enrichment and other courses. Its enrollment tops 1,500 students, and it has many courses of interest to retirees.

Housing Costs Because the economy here is booming, prices have risen in recent years, yet real estate prices still average below the national median, and some outstanding values can be found in Newport and the surrounding areas of Lincoln County. Newport living alternatives offer unique ocean, bay and river properties with dramatic sandy beaches, breathtaking rocky shorelines, and hillsides with colorful landscapes and magnificent views.

Medical Care Pacific Communities Hospital has been taking care of Newport's medical needs since 1952. With 42 licensed beds, this is one of the largest and most complete health care facilities on the Oregon Coast. The hospital offers a complete range of health and medical services, including 24-hour, physician-staffed emergency care, a full-service medical laboratory, physical therapy and rehabilitation, outpatient surgery and single-room maternity care. More than 30 doctors comprise the medical staff at Pacific Communities Hospital. Home health and hospice services are also offered by local providers, as are chiropractic, naturopathic and homeopathic care.

When Grandkids Visit Take them for a walk through the Oregon Coast Aquarium and the Hatfield Marine Science Center, where they can participate in one of the many marine discovery adventures such as whale watching and birdwatching or visiting the Undersea Gardens and Yaquina Head Outstanding Natural Area. The star attraction here is Keiko, of "Free Willy" fame, the orca who was rescued from an exhibit in Mexico. Malnourished and suffering from skin ailments, Keiko was rehabilitated in a large tank here. Keiko's story is one of life imitating art; the movie "Free Willy" is the story of a whale rescued from an amusement park. Today Keiko is very happy to be retired in Newport.

Important Addresses and Connections

Chamber of Commerce: 555 S.W. Coast Hwy, Newport, OR 97365.
Senior Services: 155 E. Olive St., Newport, OR 97365.
Newspaper: *Newport News Times*, 831 N.E. Avery St., Newport, OR 97365.
Airport: Portland or Eugene.
Bus/Train: Greyhound stops locally.

Seaside

We accidentally discovered this part of Oregon while on a vacation. We loved the weather and the people, but first and foremost was that first glimpse of the beautiful beach and surroundings.
—Jean Marote

Seaside lies 16 miles to the south of Astoria. Dramatically situated just north of Tillamook Head, this charming town of 5,600 people commands a stretch of miles and miles of wide and sandy beach—all accessible to the public. Seaside is the quintessential beach community, Oregon's oldest seaside resort. The town's focus is on its historic oceanfront promenade and its centerpiece—the famous Turnaround at the end of Broadway—a large, circular promenade at the center of beach activity.

Summer is the hectic tourist season, and one lady volunteered, "We love the state of peace and serenity during the winter months. We have plenty of fun activities, but we don't miss the excitement of families coming to enjoy the ocean and beaches as in the summer."

Seaside's Providence Hospital operates a 24-hour emergency clinic, and for major medical crises they fly patients to Portland by helicopter in less than 30 minutes. According to local people, the medical care here is excellent.

Important Addresses and Connections
Chamber of Commerce: None.
Senior Services: None.
Weekly Newspaper: *The Signal,* P.O. Box 848, Seaside, OR 97138.
Airports: Portland.
Bus: No local bus system, but the town is serviced by Greyhound.

Astoria

*Frank was stationed here with the Navy during the war, and we
always thought we'd retire here some day. And we did.*
—Harriet Halderman

Holding down Oregon's north edge is Astoria, a city of about
10,100 inhabitants about 16 miles north of Seaside. As the oldest
American settlement west of the Rockies, Astoria has a rich history. It was first visited by Captain Robert Gray in 1792, next by the
Lewis and Clark expedition in 1805. (That's Meriwether Lewis
and William Clark, not Jerry Lewis and Dick Clark!)

This was the site of John Jacob Astor's fur trading post back
in 1811; within a few decades, Astoria developed into a thriving
seaport. The affluence of that time shows today in the stately
Victorian homes scattered among the wooded hills, imparting a
formal, but comfortable visage to Astoria.

Astoria doesn't face the open ocean; it fronts a large bay
where the mighty Columbia River empties into the Pacific.
However, the water expanse is so large it seems like the ocean.
Nearby beaches are famous for long-neck clams (have to dig fast
to catch 'em) and dungeness crab for delicious cioppinos.
Portland is a two-hour drive for those who need a "big-city fix"
once in a while. Washington is reached by a drive across the
beautiful four-mile Astoria Bridge. An active senior citizen center
helps newcomers get settled.

A walk to explore the city's waterfront should include stops
at the 6th Street Viewing Dock, the 14th Street Riverpark, with its
interpretive panels of river activity, and the 17th Street Pier
where there's a chance to tour visiting ships. Astoria has a
bustling business district with many unique shops and galleries.

For some reason, Astoria has an unusual number of residents
of Scandinavian origin. The city celebrates this heritage with the
Scandinavian Midsummer Festival, held in mid-June. Local
Icelanders, Finns, Danes, Norwegians and Swedes join together

to celebrate their ancestry. People come from far and wide to enjoy the festivities and watch the costumed townspeople dance the midsummer pole dance, see the bonfire burn to destroy evil spirits, and witness the tugs-of-war pitting Scandinavian nationalities against each other. The festival features authentic Scandinavian musicians, a smorgasbord of Old World delicacies, ethnic entertainment, dancing, crafts and a parade.

This area is one of the reasons for the Oregon coast's reputation for wet weather. The average rainfall here can be as high as 70 inches a year, plus there are many overcast days when it isn't raining.

Recreation and Culture   Charter boats take fishing fans out for great salmon and sturgeon catches. The bay here has heavy fish traffic as they enter or leave the Columbia River. In addition to the natural attractions, within a 20-mile radius, one can see dozens of exciting, man-made attractions, including Fort Clatsop National Memorial, Fort Stevens State Park, Fort Astoria, Heritage Center Museum, Flavel House Museum, Uppertown Fire Fighters Museum, Astoria Column, and the Columbia River Maritime Museum, home to one of the nation's finest displays of model ships and nautical artifacts.

Housing Costs   Homes here are slightly below market rate for the Pacific coastal towns. According to local real estate brokers, three-bedroom homes range between $85,000 and $125,000. Total property taxes in the city are $15.40 per $1,000 valuation.

Medical Care   Health care is said to be adequate, with the Columbia Memorial Hospital supplemented by several medical clinics and a good ambulance service.

Crime and Safety   Astoria's small-town atmosphere is affirmed by an exceptionally low crime rate, falling in the top 15 percent of the nation's safe places.

When Grandkids Visit   Take them to climb Astoria Column, patterned after Trajan's Column in Rome and built in 1926. Once on top, you will have a breathtaking view of the Pacific Ocean, Columbia River and the volcanic cone of Mt. St. Helens, which erupted in May, 1980.

Important Addresses and Connections

Chamber of Commerce: 111 W. Marine Dr., Astoria, OR 97103.
Senior Center: 1512 Duane St., Astoria, OR 97103.
Newspaper: *Daily Astorian,* 949 Exchange St., Astoria, OR 97103.
Airport: Portland.
Bus/Train: Daily bus service to Portland and local bus service.

ASTORIA	Jan.	Apr.	July	Oct.	Rain	Snow
Daily Highs	47	56	68	61	70	5
Daily Lows	35	40	52	44	in.	in.

WASHINGTON

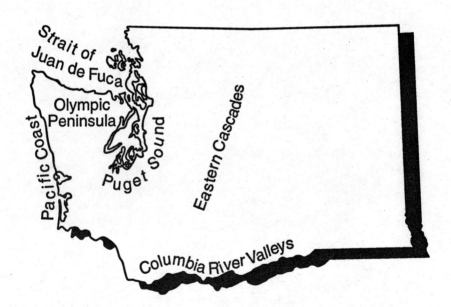

Strait of Juan de Fuca

Olympic Peninsula

Pacific Coast

Puget Sound

Eastern Cascades

Columbia River Valleys

W ashington's star is on the rise as a retirement destination. In 1990, Washington's over-65 population was 571,000—about 12 percent of the state total—and it is projected to grow to 1.2 million by the year 2020. While a large proportion of present retirees were Washington residents during their working years, the state has traditionally been a favorite among retired military personnel as well.

Much of the anticipated future growth will result from the population boom that has been taking place in western Washington since the late 1980s. The state's electronics and aerospace industries have brought workers from all parts of the country, and a steady stream of Californians have been immigrating to the area to trade in California's faltering economy for Washington's bullish one. Experience suggests that many of today's newcomers will become tomorrow's senior citizens of Washington. The word is spreading, and each year more retirees from around the United States discover the pleasant living conditions, mild climate and moderate housing costs that can be found in many parts of the state.

The defining feature of western Washington is Puget Sound, a 100-mile-long, island-studded, saltwater inlet that separates the Seattle metropolitan area from the wilderness of the Olympic Peninsula. Because so much land fronts on the sound, Washington's coastline is almost twice as long as Oregon's. Protected by the towering Olympic Mountains to the west, Puget Sound is a natural harbor on a huge scale, merging the prosperity of a major Pacific Rim seaport with the quiet dignity of forested islands and glacier-clad mountains in the distance. Nearly 8,000 feet high, Mount Olympus shelters Puget Sound communities from the winter storms that pour as much as 145 inches of rain a year on the rugged Pacific coastline. Meanwhile, the deep water moderates temperatures, which rarely drop below freezing or rise above 80 degrees.

It is the high-quality towns near Seattle and on Puget Sound's network of bays, coves, straits and inlets that make Washington such a great retirement choice. Places like Shelton, Sequim and Port Townsend share Seattle's climate and scenic beauty but also offer the benefits of small-town living. Equally charming are the communities set on islands, large and small, in and around the sound, among them Whidbey Island, Fidalgo Island, and the San

Juans. These quaint coastal towns nestled in forests of Douglas fir remind us of New England fishing villages.

The Olympic Peninsula and nearby islands are perhaps the most idyllic retirement spots Washington has to offer, and much of this chapter is devoted to them. Though these communities feel like a world apart from greater Seattle, ferries make getting to the big city relaxing and—usually—quick. One drawback is that both Olympic National Park and the San Juan Islands attract tourists by the thousands, which can mean waiting in line for several hours to board a ferry during the summer and on weekends year-round.

After a brief investigation of the greater Seattle area, much of this chapter focuses on the small towns of the Puget Sound area, where far more retirees choose to live than in any other part of Washington. Nearly two-thirds of Washington residents live in towns of fewer than 10,000 people or in unincorporated rural areas, and retired people, who do not need to commute to the city on a daily basis, have a distinct advantage in these places.

All around Puget Sound, however, the cost of living is relatively high. In some places, especially the San Juan Islands, it can be extremely high. More affordable living can be found farther south in seaside communities such as Grayland and Long Beach on the Pacific coast.

As in Oregon, the Cascade Range divides Washington into a western "wet side" and an eastern "dry side." If a low cost of living is a high priority, the best solution may be to head inland to the less populous dry side of the Cascades. Seattlites may cringe at the mention of Washington's eastern half, a semi-arid landscape famous for wheat, beef, rattlesnakes and spring duststorms. This image—fairly accurate in some parts of eastern Washington—makes for the lowest real estate prices in the state. Low prices, in turn, are a key factor in the ranking of certain eastern Washington communities among the fastest-growing towns in the state.

Not everywhere east of the Cascades fits this bleak description, though. The fruit-growing country at the foot of the mountains contains an assortment of very different, picture-perfect communities such as Leavenworth, Cashmere and Chelan. These places enjoy much more year-round sunshine than western Washington, but they also have what locals euphemistically refer to as "four seasons," by which they mean winter snow and long spells of freezing temperatures. Migratory "snowbirds" in search of a northerly home for the warm months, however, will find these towns well worth investigating.

History

Native Americans came to Washington at least 12,500 years ago, as evidenced by the discoveries in Sequim and Wenatchee of some of the oldest artifacts on the North American continent. Coastal civilizations developed permanent villages, complex mythologies and sophisticated artistic traditions spanning at least 2,000 years. Although hostilities between Indians and pioneers were few and minor, more than 90 percent of western Washington's indigenous population died from smallpox, measles and other diseases during the 19th century. Descendants of the survivors live on tiny reservations scattered throughout the Puget Sound area.

Sea captains representing Spain, Russia and England laid claim to Washington during the 1700s, but none succeeded in establishing a colonial settlement here. France also claimed it sight-unseen as part of the Louisiana Territory, which it sold to the United States in 1803. Two years later the Lewis and Clark expedition solidified the United States' claim to the region. Spain and Russia soon relinquished their claims, but the United States and England shared the territory under a unique Joint Occupancy Treaty until 1846. Still almost completely uninhabited, the area that is now Washington was part of the Oregon Territory until 1853.

Prosperity came suddenly as timber barons, salmon canners and cattle ranchers rushed to exploit the new territory's natural bounties. At first, all Washington products were exported to gold-rich northern California; Eastern markets were out of reach until

---

Washington
The Evergreen State
42nd state to enter the Union
November 11, 1889

State Capital: Olympia
Population (1990): 4,866,663; rank, 18th
Population Density: 71.6 per sq. mile; urban, 35%, rural: 65%.
Geography: 20th state in size, with 66,570 square miles, including 1,622 square miles of water surface and 12.7 million square acres of forested land. Highest elevation: Mount Rainier, 14,411 feet; lowest elevation: sea level on Pacific Ocean beaches. Average elevation: 1,700 feet.
State Flower: Coast Rhododendron
State Bird: Willow Goldfinch
State Tree: Western Hemlock
State Song: Washington My Home

WASHINGTON TAXES

Income Tax
State law prohibits net income taxes. Furthermore, other states are prohibited from placing liens on property located in Washington to collect taxes owed to them. Businesses and self-employed persons pay a business and occupation tax on their gross revenues, ranging from 0.484% for retailers to 1.5% for service occupations.

Sales Taxes
Most state revenues are provided by a 6.5% retail sales and use tax, which is levied on most purchases (except groceries and medicines) and some professional services. Municipalities assess local sales taxes that range from 0.5% to 1%, with an additional 0.6% in cities that operate public transportation systems.

Property Taxes
Local governments rely on property taxes as their main revenue source. Regular property tax levies are constitutionally limited to 1% of "true and fair" property value per year. Rapidly increasing real estate prices since the mid-1980s have resulted in frequent property tax increases in the Puget Sound area, alarming homeowners on fixed incomes. Voters may approve additional special one-time property tax levies, above the constitutional limitation, by a 60% vote.

Exemptions & Deferrals Retired Persons age 62 and older with total disposable incomes under $12,000 per year are exempt from regular property tax levies on the first $28,000 valuation or 50% of total valuation of their home, and those with incomes between $12,000 and $24,000 a year are exempt for the first $24,000 valuation or 30 percent (up to $40,000) of the total valuation. Those with incomes under $18,000 a year are also exempt from all special property tax levies. An additional tax relief provision allows retired persons over age 62 with less than $24,000 total income to defer their entire property tax indefinitely, until the tax liability reaches 80% of the equity value of the home; the liability then becomes a lien on the property, payable when it is sold or probated.

Estate/Inheritance Taxes
Washington does not impose a separate estate tax, but only a pick-up tax, which is a portion of the federal estate tax and does not increase the total amount owed. Washington has no state inheritance tax.

Licenses
Driver's License Required within 30 days of establishing residence. Written, vision and driving tests required. Fee: $7 for test, plus $14 for license.

Automobile License Required within 30 days of establishing residence. Registration: $35.85 plus an excise tax of 2.45% of the vehicle's fair market value (the excise tax helps pay for the Washington State Ferry System). Vehicle inspection required, $15.

1888, when the first railroad tunnel through the Cascade Range was completed. With the railroad's arrival, Washington soon became the nation's largest producer of lumber and apples.

The military came to Washington in the 1890s, with the building of the Puget Sound Naval Shipyards at Bremerton, and continued as a major presence through both World Wars. The Hanford Atomic Works in eastern Washington, which produced plutonium for nuclear weapons, employed 45,000 people at the height of the Cold War; widespread public protest forced the last nuclear reactor at Hanford to shut down permanently in 1988.

In recent times, Washington's timber industry boomed to record levels in the 1980s but then crashed as environmentalist opposition brought court rulings that halted clearcutting in the state's remaining stands of ancient forest—an issue that continues to generate heated controversy.

It is increasingly clear, however, that Washington's economic future lies not in timber but in technology. The Everett-based Boeing Corporation is the state's largest employer and, in fact, the United States' largest aerospace firm, largest exporter, and 12th-largest industrial corporation, with annual revenues exceeding $30 billion. Equally impressive is the rise of Microsoft Corporation. Based in the Seattle suburb of Redmond, the world's largest computer software company has grown from three employees in 1975 to 14,500 employees and nearly $4 billion in annual revenues.

Puget Sound

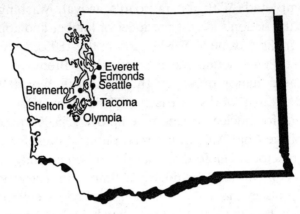

Most of Washington's population lives in a long, narrow corridor, circling Puget Sound. The east-shore communities flank Interstate 5, filling the western one-third of three counties. King County contains Seattle and Bellevue; Pierce County contains Tacoma; and Snohomish County contains northern suburbs including Edmonds, Lynnwood and Everett. All three counties stretch eastward to the crest of the Cascade Range, about 40 miles away. More than half of all three counties is national forest land, containing wilderness areas larger than all of Seattle, its suburbs and satellite cities.

The population has been expanding northward in recent years, drawn by the huge Boeing jetliner plant in Everett. In fact, both Everett and Bellevue, the suburb across Lake Washington from Seattle, rank among the ten fastest-growing cities in the United States, surpassing any city in the traditionally high-growth states of Florida, Texas and California.

In looking at the retirement potential of Puget Sound, we will consider everything from Everett to Tacoma as a single metropolitan area, since it is an unbroken expanse of urban and suburban development.

Seattle/Tacoma

Seattle has fantastic medical facilities, great doctors and places to go year-round. There is always something going on, from sporting events to travelogues and operas.

—Carl Harris

I should begin by noting that people in Tacoma may take offense at the suggestion that their fair city is a Seattle suburb—and rightly so, as it has its own distinct character—still for our purposes most observations about Seattle apply to the adjoining cities as well.

Seattle offers all the advantages of a large city—as well as all the disadvantages. Its setting, between Puget Sound and Lake Washington, with magnificent mountain views in all directions, helps make it one of the more beautiful cities in America. Lofty evergreens shade its parks and suburbs and blend into the surrounding forest. Its location, on the water and sheltered from Pacific storms by the mountains of the Olympic Peninsula, keeps winters mercifully mild and summers pleasantly cool. There is an all-pervasive community spirit such as is found in few other major cities.

Seattle has been a cultural melting pot for a long time. Settled by pioneers from New York and New England in the 1850s, who shared the waterfront with an approximately equal number of Coast Salish Indians, Seattle was transformed in 1897 when it became the departure point for more than 40,000 people who surged north to Alaska during the Klondike gold rush that year. Many returned to Seattle upon discovering that money was easier to come by in Washington's logging camps and ships' docks than in the gold fields of Alaska. Several ethnic groups, from Swedes to Eskimos, became part of Seattle's cultural quilt around that time. Large numbers of Chinese immigrants were among Seattle's early settlers. Throughout the 20th century, other Asian groups—notably Japanese, Filipinos and Vietnamese—have also come to Seattle in significant numbers, adding to the cultural diversity.

Although it is logical to assume that Seattle must have some "bad neighborhoods"—particularly in light of its high crime rate—they tend to be hidden from sight in hard-to-reach corners of the city's sometimes bewildering street system. (Seattle's founding fathers disagreed about whether streets should run due north and south or follow the contour of the shoreline, so they laid out the streets both ways, so many thoroughfares intersect at crazy angles or can't be found at all without a local guide.)

Pretty neighborhoods are hard to miss, though. Among the nicest close to downtown is Queen Anne, where red brick Victorians fill the tops of two high hills overlooking Elliott Bay. Another area close to downtown Seattle that combines urban living with unique character and great views is Alki Beach in West Seattle, where many of the low-rise buildings within a few blocks of the beach contain compact, affordable—though, in many cases, run-down—apartments. On sunny weekends, the long, white beach is full of exuberant activity, and the street that runs alongside it swarms with bicyclists; the rest of the time, locals have the sidewalk cafes and the view of downtown Seattle across the water all to themselves.

Bountiful vegetation transforms even tract-home neighborhoods of recent vintage into exceptionally beautiful places to live. It is practically impossible to keep gardens from growing lushly in Seattle's often misty climate, so yards everywhere are brimming with fir trees, flowering rhododendron bushes and giant ferns as tall as a person. One lovely suburban area is Bellevue, located on the east side of Lake Washington. Bellevue has had an explosive growth rate, and subdivision developers continue to hack new cul-de-sacs and mini-mall sites out of the dense tangle of forest that marks the edge of town.

By the way, people who can arrange their lives to avoid rush-hour driving enjoy a special advantage in Bellevue. Since there are only two bridges across Lake Washington, the flow of traffic going to Seattle in the morning and returning to Bellevue in the late afternoon is often so clogged that motorists feel as if they were waiting for a ferry instead of a bridge. This is perhaps the most extreme manifestation of the traffic problems that constitute a main drawback of living in Seattle. Morning and afternoon rush hours can be absolutely paralyzing, because virtually all traffic from one part of the metropolis to another is channeled via a single freeway, Interstate 5. Even expatriates from Los Angeles have been known to complain about Seattle traffic.

To the south, past the municipality of Federal Way and Sea-Tac International Airport, lies Tacoma, the second-largest city on Puget Sound. Seattle residents often speak of Tacoma with disdain. Much of the region's heavy industry is centered in Tacoma, including huge lumber and paper pulp mills that emanate odors many people find offensive. Despite some attractive turn-of-the-century architecture, Tacoma's downtown area has grown dilapidated, as retailers have abandoned it in favor of several large shopping malls on the city's outskirts.

But Tacoma's bad reputation over the years has translated into the lowest rents and home prices in the greater Seattle area, and this in turn has fostered the emergence of a growing and vibrant artists' community as well as some beautiful historic preservation projects. Tacoma also boasts some of the prettiest parks around, including Point Defiance Park and Dash Point State Park, both high headlands overlooking the misty islands of the South Sound. With Mount Rainier practically in its backyard, Tacoma is hard to beat when it comes to scenery.

If we had to pick a single favorite place to live in the Seattle area, it would be Edmonds. Located between Seattle and Everett, Edmonds' low-rise downtown area is right on the water, with a beach and ferry terminal at the end of the main shopping street. Edmonds, like many outlying waterfront towns, was once an unsightly conglomeration of dingy, rundown lumber and paper pulp mills. But an ambitious renovation project has transformed the Edmonds waterfront with a thousand-slip marina and a broad promenade along the edge of an underwater park used for recreational scuba diving. Edmonds neighborhoods such as Firdale Village, Westgate and Five Corners are among the prettiest in the greater Seattle area.

Recreation and Culture   Seattle has the widest array of cultural activities in Washington, and people everywhere in the Puget Sound area head for Seattle when they want to go to an art museum, opera or hockey game. Seattle Center provides the venue for performances by the Seattle Repertory Theater, Seattle Opera, Intiman Theatre, Pacific Northwest Ballet and Seattle Symphony Orchestra. The University of Washington hosts a full schedule of performances, films and lectures of all kinds. Seattle's thriving little-theater scene centers around Pioneer Square.

The city also has an abundance of museums. The Seattle Art Museum contains thousands of works of fine art and folk art from many parts of the world, including one of the finest collections anywhere of Northwest Coast Indian artifacts. In Volunteer Park, the building that until recently housed the art museum now houses the museum's extensive Asian art collection. Asian culture is also the focus of the Wing Luke Museum in the International District. Many art galleries, including several that specialize in contemporary American Indian art, are located in the Pioneer Square area.

Nine public colleges in the greater Seattle area offer an almost unlimited selection of adult education courses during the fall, winter and spring. The largest program, at Bellevue Community College, offers more than 300 such courses, in fields of study ranging from computers to mystery novels, and has an adult enrollment of more than 2,000. All community colleges in Washington have reduced fees for senior citizens. Seattle University offers Elderhostel courses of study, including cultural topics on Canada, Japan and Russia.

More than two dozen Seattle-area golf courses are open to the general public. The most popular and affordable are three courses operated by the Seattle Department of Parks and Recreation: Jackson Park Municipal Golf Course (27 holes, par 72/36) in the northeast part of the city, Jefferson Park Municipal Golf Course (18 holes, par 70) in the south, and West Seattle Municipal Golf Course (18 holes, par 72) near Alki Beach. These courses are so popular that it is all but impossible to get a tee time on weekends—even rainy weekends, as Seattle-area golf enthusiasts quickly learn to be oblivious to wet weather. Bellevue and Lynnwood (near Edmonds) also have municipal courses, as does Tacoma. There are more public and private golf courses in Tacoma than anywhere else in the Seattle metropolitan area, though some are on military reservations and are restricted to active and retired military personnel. Among the Seattle-area courses rated as the best by local golfers are the North Shore Golf Course, on the north edge of Tacoma near Sea-Tac airport, and Harbour Pointe Golf Club in Mukilteo, north of Edmonds. In 1991, *Golf Digest* rated Harbor Pointe as the best public golf course in the United States.

Seattle has more boat owners than any other U.S. city, naturally enough when you consider that there is as much water as land within the city limits. The channels that meander between islands in Puget Sound invite boaters to unlimited exploration of secluded coves and beaches, many of them unreachable by road. Seattle's used-boat market is as active as used-car markets in most cities. If you don't own a boat, there are a number of rental places offering everything from sea kayaks to houseboats.

Chinook, coho and pink salmon have traditionally been the favorite catch in the waters around Seattle. In the last few years, salmon runs have declined drastically, however. Fishermen blame the seals that inhabit the harbors and canal locks in the area; environmentalists blame commercial fishermen. In any case, more anglers are settling for some of the 200 other fish species that inhabit Elliott Bay, such as halibut, cod and rockfish. Lake Washington offers good fishing for a wide range of freshwater species such as cutthroat and rainbow trout, kokanee, catfish and largemouth and smallmouth bass.

There are great hiking trails of every length and difficulty both within Seattle and in the large municipal woodland parks on its outskirts. The Washington Park Arboretum is a good starting point for walks along the shoreline of Lake Washington. Discovery Park and Dash Point State Park offer spectacular views from bluffs high above the water. On the forested slopes just east of Seattle, there are many miles of trails in what locals have dubbed the "Issaquah Alps"—Tiger Mountain State Forest, Squaw Mountain State Park and Cougar Mountain County Park.

As for spectator sports, Seattle is the only Northwestern city that fields major league teams in football (Seattle Seahawks), baseball (Seattle Mariners) and basketball (Seattle SuperSonics). University of Washington Huskies games are a must for area college football fans. The Seattle Thunderbirds hockey team draws large crowds to the new Key Arena in Seattle Center. The city also hosts national championship events in tennis, cycling, canoeing and kayaking, swimming and gymnastics.

Housing and Other Costs The breadth and diversity of the Seattle area's residential market defies attempts to quantify it. "Average" home prices vary greatly between Seattle neighborhoods, as well as between Seattle and its suburban municipalities. As a gross generalization, housing prices in the Seattle area are somewhat higher than in comparable-sized Midwestern cities and about the same as in most other West Coast urban areas. Overall, home prices are higher than in any other part of Washington except the San Juan Islands.

Near the end of the 1980s, residential property values doubled in just two years. At the time, locals blamed skyrocketing prices on an influx of newcomers from California, though population growth during the same period suggests that it was a simple matter of demand exceeding supply. As new housing construction has caught up with the demand, the volatility of the housing market has stabilized—for the moment, anyway.

Residential real estate prices tend to be lower for older homes closer to the city center. Be warned, though, that older homes need much more in the way of repairs and maintenance in Seattle's damp, drippy climate. Housing—whether you rent or own—is still a bargain in Tacoma, where real estate prices run about 30 percent lower than in Seattle. Houses cost more in Bellevue than they would in most other parts of the Seattle area, including the city itself. Edmonds home prices are lower than Bellevue and about the same as Seattle, with much higher prices for waterfront homes in the north part of town. Condominiums are plentiful in the northern suburbs of Edmonds and Lynnwood, and they come in all price ranges from about $75,000 to $500,000. Apartment rentals are hard to come by in Edmonds but are abundant and reasonably priced in neighboring Lynnwood.

The Seattle area also has 33 independent living communities that provide apartments along with central dining, housekeeping, transportation, social and recreational activities, financial counseling and nursing care. These full-service retirement communities account for about half the nursing home facilities in the state. Monthly fees typically range from $1,000 to $2,000 a month.

Medical Care   Seattle has more and larger hospital facilities, as well as more medical specialists, than any other community in the Northwest. Residents of most Washington communities covered in this chapter come to Seattle for major medical procedures. The total number of hospital beds in the greater Seattle area is 7,400—far more than in all other parts of the state combined. Seattle and Bellevue average one hospital bed per 263 residents, while Tacoma has one bed per 509 residents, and the Snohomish County suburbs of Edmonds, Lynnwood and Everett have one bed per 530 residents.

The largest among Seattle's 25 hospitals are the University of Washington Medical Center and Harborview Medical Center. In Tacoma, the largest of eight hospitals is Tacoma General Hospital. Among Snohomish County's five hospitals, the largest are General Hospital Medical Center in Everett and Stevens Memorial Hospital in Edmonds.

Crime and Safety   The Seattle area has the seventh-highest crime rate in the country. By far the least safe place to live in Washington, Seattle's overall crime rate of approximately 10,800 incidents annually per 100,000 population is slightly higher than that of New York City. Unlike many cities, Seattle's poorest neighborhoods are well hidden from view; yet judging from headlines in the daily newspapers, predatory criminals thrive in their invisibility.

The city's long, thin layout has a big effect on crime patterns. Crimes of violence, localized in downtown Seattle and Tacoma (armed robbery) and the University District (sexual assault), are rare in suburban areas. Home burglaries and car thefts, however, are far more common in northern suburbs such as Lynnwood, Marysville and Everett than in the city center. One recent law enforcement study correlates the incidence of property crimes to the proximity of Interstate 5; the closer people live to the freeway, the more vulnerable they are to burglary and theft.

When Grandkids Visit The top spot in the city for sightseeing with children is Seattle Center, the complex of museums and other attractions that surrounds the Space Needle on the former World's Fair (1962) grounds north of downtown. The family fun to be found there includes the Children's Theatre, the Fun Forest amusement park, the Seattle Children's Museum, the Pacific Science Center and the Center House with its array of nearly 20 international fast-food restaurants under one big roof. Elsewhere, the Washington Park Zoo and the Seattle Aquarium are among the best in the nation. Seattle's biggest kid-pleasers, though, are three unique rides: the elevator to the top of the Space Needle, the monorail that runs between the Seattle Center and downtown, and a round-trip cruise across Puget Sound on the Bremerton ferry, which departs from the Seattle waterfront.

Tacoma, like Seattle, has an award-winning zoo. Located at Point Defiance Park, the zoo incorporates an excellent aquarium where residents include sharks and beluga whales. Also in the park is a full-scale replica of Fort Nisqually, one of the first settlements in Washington.

Mount Rainier National Park, less than an hour's drive from Tacoma, makes a spectacular playground for all ages. On the way is perhaps the best family attraction in the state, Northwest Trek. Owned and operated by the City of Tacoma, this 635-acre wildlife park provides a chance to view bison, moose, mountain goats and many other native animals of the Northwest in their natural habitat from the safety of enclosed tram cars.

Important Addresses and Connections

Chamber of Commerce: Central Seattle: 2108 E. Madison, Seattle, WA 98112; King County Visitors Bureau: 666 Stewart, Seattle, WA 98101; Tacoma: PO Box 1933, Tacoma, WA 98690.

Senior Services: Council on Aging, 223 N. Yakima, Tacoma, WA 98403.

Newspapers: *Seattle Post-Intelligencer,* 101 Elliott Ave. W., Seattle, WA 98119; *Seattle Times,* Fairview Ave. N. at John St., Seattle, WA 98111; *Tacoma News Tribune,* P.O. Box 11000, Tacoma, WA 98411.

Airport: Sea-Tac International Airport, located in-between Seattle and Tacoma, is the largest airport in the Northwest.

Bus/Train: Greyhound buses provide intercity service. Independent bus lines such as Green Tortoise also run up and down the coast. Amtrak's provides service not only south and east, to the rest of the U.S., but it also recently opened a spur north to connect with Canadian passenger trains in Vancouver.

SEATTLE	Jan.	Apr.	July	Oct.	Rain	Snow
Daily Highs	46	59	75	60	34	3
Daily Lows	36	44	56	48	in.	in.

Olympia

We have lots of retirees in Olympia. It's an especially good place for retired military because it's convenient to commissaries and base hospitals.
                                                                    —Lynn Heinold

Olympia, the capital of Washington, is the kind of dignified, clean, not-too-big city that every state capital should be. So many people here work for the government that the city's shops, sidewalks and parks are almost deserted during regular business hours. Rush hours and weekends, it's best to stay home.

The Olympia area is home to about 22,000 senior citizens. Since 1980, the over-65 population has grown by 53 percent— almost double the area's overall population growth rate. Retired military personnel who discovered the area while stationed at nearby Fort Lewis or McChord Air Force Base account for a sizeable segment of Olympia's active senior community. As the center of state government, Olympia serves as a proving ground for social programs, including several new intergenerational programs designed to bring together elders and young people. The Grandfolks Brigade places seniors from area retirement communities as mentors in elementary schools, while the Synergy Intergenerational Arts Program fosters creative collaborations between older adults and schoolchildren. One experimental program brings local third-grade students into STARS (Services To At-Risk Seniors) adult day care centers as companions to residents who are living with Alzheimer's disease, Parkinson's disease and frailty due to advanced age.

Among the first settlements in the state, Olympia got its start in 1846. The town plat was modeled after the New England towns that founding pioneer families had come from, with a town square, tree-lined streets and—even though Washington was not yet an official territory, much less a state—a hilltop site set aside for a future capitol building. This, along with its location at the southernmost tip of Puget Sound and the fact that it had the only newspaper in the region, made Olympia the natural choice for capital of the newly formed Washington Territory in 1853. It was the largest city in Washington through much of the 19th century, but its economic prospects faded when the first mainline railroads bypassed Olympia in favor of Seattle. But for the business of government, Olympia would have become a quaintly historic, little would-be seaport like Port Townsend or Bellingham. Throughout most of the 20th century, life in Olympia was calm and uneventful.

Times change, though. Recent population growth in Washington has meant a rapidly expanding state government— and a job boom in Olympia. From 1980 to 1995, the population of Thurston County grew 29 percent. Olympia has remained a small, comfortable city of 35,000, but it has become the commercial center for the neighboring towns of Tumwater and Lacey, which have grown to become contiguous suburbs of the capital. More than half of the area's 170,000 residents live in outlying rural areas, where llama ranches and fields of organic vegetables exist alongside more traditional small farms.

Temperatures are generally mild, though Olympia gets considerably more rain and fog than Seattle and other Puget Sound communities farther to the north. It usually doesn't rain very hard, but it rains often, with an average of 230 cloudy days a year, with more than a trace of rain on 147 of those days and fog on 75 of them. Other factors to keep in mind are that retirees in Olympia and surrounding areas express concern about the rapidly increasing property taxes and the need for a senior center.

Recreation and Culture Hikers and birders can get close to nature in Nisqually National Wildlife Refuge, about five miles east of town. Denizens of the refuge include deer, coyotes, eagles, herons, and many varieties of ducks. Another good hiking and wildlife viewing area is Tolmie State Park, an expanse of rolling uplands surrounding a saltwater lagoon and sandspit. Golfers play at Indian Summer Golf Course (18 holes, par 72) and Capitol City Golf Club (18 holes, par 72). The Black River is a favorite canoeing spot.

Olympia has an active and fast-growing arts community, with two resident dance companies, a symphony orchestra, a chorale ensemble, several ethnic and folk music groups, and six resident theater companies. The Washington Shakespeare Festival is held each August in Olympia. Adult education courses are offered through South Puget Sound Community College.

Housing and Other Costs The average price of a three-bedroom home in the Olympia area is $130,330—lower than in Seattle but higher than Tacoma. There are only a limited number of condos, typically priced around $115,000. Rentals are actually higher than in the Seattle area, with apartments starting at $500 or more and house rentals ranging from $750 to $1,100 a month. Other cost-of-living factors are the same as in Seattle.

Medical Care St. Peter Hospital in Olympia has 314 beds and 450 physicians and performs all major procedures except heart transplants. The hospital's NursePlus service offers free medical advice by phone. Capital Medical Center operates a smaller, 110-bed hospital facility.

Crime and Safety The per capita crime rate in Thurston County during the 1990s has been exactly the same as for Washington state as a whole. The number of crime incidents has been rising 2 percent a year, slightly less than the population growth rate. Violence against senior citizens is rare, and the South Sound area is not plagued by big-city crime problems.

When Grandkids Visit You might first try a visit to Mount Rainier, an easy drive from Olympia. After that, a couple of less-known spots that are sure to spark youngsters' enthusiasm are Wolf Haven, a sanctuary near neighboring Tenino that cares for more than 30 wolves and offers guided tours and summer night "howl-ins," and Mima Mounds Natural Area, where hiking trails wind among strange, evenly spaced miniature hills about seven feet high.

Important Addresses and Connections

Chamber of Commerce: P.O. Box 1427, Olympia, WA 98501.
Senior Center: Olympia Center, 222 N. Columbia, Olympia, WA 98501.

Newspaper: *The Daily Olympian*, P.O. Box 407, Olympia, WA 98507.

Airport: Capital Aeroporter runs frequent shuttle buses to Sea-Tac International Airport, about one hour away.

Bus/Train: Greyhound buses stop in Olympia on their Interstate 5 route. Amtrak's Coast Starlight also serves Olympia.

OLYMPIA	Jan.	Apr.	July	Oct.	Rain	Snow
Daily Highs	43	59	78	61	51	3
Daily Lows	30	36	49	41	in.	in.

Shelton

Maybe it's a coincidence, but Mason County has 44,000 residents and also 44,000 acres of commercial Christmas trees.

—Charles Webb

Shelton, a town of 7,600 people, is the county seat and only incorporated town in rural Mason County. Economically, Shelton is a bedroom community of Olympia, 18 miles away via the county's only stretch of four-lane highway; the area that includes both Shelton and Olympia is known as the South Sound. As a place to stay home and enjoy the quiet, peaceful little Shelton and Mason County have a character that is completely different from the Olympia area.

Set along the bank of Oakland Bay, a saltwater inlet scarcely wider than a river, Shelton's town center has dozens of historic buildings dating back to the era between World War One and the Great Depression. Shelton got its start as a logging camp in the 1850s and officially became a town in 1884. Then, as now, it provided shopping, banking, schooling and other services for many smaller logging camps, farms and fishing villages scattered throughout the area. Even today, two-thirds of Mason County residents live in rural areas away from Shelton. Among the country dwellers are two Indian tribes, the Skokomish and Squaxin Island people, who live on separate reservations within a few miles of Shelton.

From metropolitan Seattle, it's a longer trip to Shelton than to anyplace else on Puget Sound; getting to or from downtown Seattle takes at least two hours. The distance, too far to commute on a daily basis, has insulated Shelton and Mason County from the rampant development that has transformed so much of the Puget Sound area in the past decade.

For several years now, Shelton and Mason County have made a real effort to attract senior citizens to the area by providing many services and activities. Supplementing the full schedule of activities at Shelton's Senior Citizen Activity Center, the North Mason Senior Citizens' Association holds daytime dances and card games twice a week, and the Area Agency on Aging sponsors such service programs as a senior nutrition program, a foster grandparent program, a seniors' information clearinghouse and volunteer chore services. Private enterprises offer senior ride, errand, cleaning and daily phone monitoring services.

Outside of Shelton, Mason County offers a variety of country environments. Narrow channels and inlets, as well as the Great Bend area of the mile-wide Hood Canal, make for some 300 miles of scenic shoreline, much of it uninhabited. Inland, small farms and wetland meadows nestle in a vast expanse of privately owned second- or third-growth Douglas-fir forest. The fir-covered hills are dotted with rural homes and vacation cabins, blending into the wild Wonder Mountain and Mount Skokomish Wilderness Areas. In the northwest corner of the county is a little-known, roadless corner of Olympic National Park. A trailhead from Lake Cushman, a half-hour drive north of Shelton, provides access to an extensive network of hiking trails in this remote sector of the park.

Recreation and Culture There are five championship golf courses in Mason County, and every local golf enthusiast has a story about trying to play through a deer or elk herd on the fairway. Favorite courses include the Lake Limerick (9 holes, par 37), Shelton Bayshore (9 holes, par 36), Oakridge (18 holes, par 70), and Alderbrook (18 holes, par 72) courses.

Mason County boasts more lakes than any other area in Washington. The largest, Lake Cushman in Olympic National Forest, is a popular boating spot. Smaller lakes such as Nahwatzel Lake and Lake Limerick are stocked with rainbow trout and cutthroat. There is good fishing in the Hood Canal for king, chub and silver salmon and, in the winter, steelheads. The canal is also the place to harvest clams, oysters and crabs. Hood Canal shrimp, famous throughout western Washington, reach 6 inches in length.

The farm fields and wetlands of Mason County have an astonishing abundance of bird life. Local people can tell birdwatchers the best places to observe bald eagles and ospreys.

Local theater groups present amateur stage plays in Shelton several times a year. Otherwise, most live performance events are held in connection with community celebrations such as the late spring Forest Festival, the midsummer Mason County Fair, and the Oysterfest in October.

Housing and Other Costs   Housing is a bargain in the Shelton area, with two- to three-bedroom home prices averaging in the low $80,000s. Similar homes rent for $450 and up, while apartment rents in Shelton start at $375. There are no condominium complexes in Shelton or anywhere in Mason County. Other cost-of-living expenses run lower here than in Seattle or most other areas of western Washington.

Medical Care   Mason General Hospital in Shelton has 68 beds. For non-emergency surgery and inpatient care, many Mason County residents opt for the larger hospital in nearby Olympia or one of the many facilities in the Seattle area.

Crime and Safety   Several people in Shelton, including a deputy sheriff, acted surprised when we asked about safety issues and assured us that there is no crime in Mason County. FBI statistics tell us that this belief is slightly over-optimistic, but only slightly. Shelton and rural Mason County enjoy one of the lowest crime rates in the state.

When Grandkids Visit   The major sightseeing attraction in town—Christmastown Village, a year-round Christmas theme display built by the chamber of commerce—can be fun for smaller youngsters, but it's good for a brief visit at best. Fortunately, within a half-hour drive of town, Potlatch, Twanoh, Belfair and Lake Cushman State Parks invite exploration of a variety of coastal and forest environments. Along the way, you'll see some of the tree farms that make Shelton one of America's largest producers of Christmas trees. Each fall, more than 3 million are cut and shipped to cities throughout the United States.

Important Addresses and Connections

Chamber of Commerce: P.O. Box 666, Shelton, WA 98584.
Senior Center: Senior Citizens Activities Center, 826 Railroad St., Shelton, WA 98584.
Weekly Newspaper: *The Journal,* 227 W. Cota St., Shelton, WA 98584.
Airport: Shelton has a small general aviation airport but no commercial service. Shuttles from Olympia carry air passengers to Sea-Tac.

Bus/Train: Intercity buses carry passengers between Shelton and Olympia, where you can catch a Greyhound bus or Amtrak train.

SHELTON	Jan.	Apr.	July	Oct.	Rain	Snow
Daily Highs	45	61	78	62	64	4
Daily Lows	32	38	51	42	in.	in.

Bremerton/Kitsap Peninsula

The evenness of the climate is superb in Gig Harbor. There are no extreme temperatures, and there's lots to do. —Ken Kirk

Directly across Puget Sound from Seattle lies Bremerton, the site of the Puget Sound Naval Shipyards, the largest military base in western Washington. The city of 40,000, predominantly military personnel and their dependents, lacks the Northwestern charm that attracts retirees to the Puget Sound region. However, within a few minutes' drive of the dock in Bremerton where ferries arrive from Seattle, custom-built homes and vacation cabins lie hidden along unpaved country lanes that wind through the forests of the Kitsap Peninsula.

In fact, nowhere else in the region will you find so many secluded woodland homes and homesites so close to a major urban area. A high percentage of retirees on the Kitsap Peninsula say they first discovered the area while in the Navy. Other homes on the peninsula are built as weekend getaways by Seattle residents who plan to retire there on a full-time or part-time basis. It is a marvelously scenic 50-minute ferry ride from Bremerton to downtown Seattle, not bad when you consider that it takes just as long to get downtown from many Seattle suburbs such as Edmonds, Lynnwood or Bellevue.

Geographically, the Kitsap Peninsula is a sprawling, irregularly shaped land mass roughly 28 miles wide and 60 miles long. It would be the largest island in Puget Sound but for the fact that it is connected to the Olympic Peninsula by a neck of land less than a mile wide near the village of Belfair.

Development on the Kitsap Peninsula is governed by the most tightly controlled growth restrictions in Washington. Small-scale timbering and real estate seem to go hand-in-hand here. Unlike most private lumbering areas on the Olympic Peninsula, where timbering is done in vast clearcuts that are replanted with

Douglas-fir seedlings, it is common practice on the Kitsap Peninsula to clearcut small plots of land and them sell them as cabin sites. Thickets of alder trees grow back on unbuilt portions of the land within a few years and are gradually taken over by larger evergreen trees over a span of about two decades. This approach protects not only the area's deep-forest feel but also its abundant wildlife. Bainbridge Island, linked to the peninsula by a highway bridge and to Seattle by a ferry route, is one of Seattle's most exclusive suburban neighborhoods, with gracious homes secluded on large estates hidden from casual view by stands of evergreens. The 48-square-mile island is home to 17,500 people, of whom nearly half commute to Seattle on a daily basis. Another island connected to the peninsula, Vashon Island, has a part bucolic, part artsy population of 10,000 and is linked by ferry to Tacoma.

The most intriguing communities on the peninsula are those farthest from the ferries that carry commuters to the urban side of the sound. Poulsbo, a waterfront community 16 miles north of Bremerton, got its start in the 1880s as a fishing village of Norwegian immigrants. The Scandinavian heritage lives on along the town's main street, now filled with art and craft galleries, antique shops and waterfront cafes, as well as in annual events ranging from the Viking Fest in May and the Midsommarfest in August to a traditional lutefisk dinner in October and a Christmastime Yule Fest. Hartstene Island, connected by bridge to the southeastern corner of the Kitsap Peninsula, has forests, beaches, and meandering roads that provide access to hundreds of residences concealed deep in second-growth forest.

One increasingly popular area for retirees to settle is Gig Harbor, a picture-perfect little boat haven near the southernmost tip of the Kitsap Peninsula. With its superb view of Mount Rainier across the water, Gig Harbor has as scenic a setting as you could want. Though linked by a long suspension bridge to Tacoma, just 15 minutes away, this small town is nevertheless a world unto itself, where more residents own boats than cars.

Recreation and Culture

The Kitsap Peninsula is golf country. Bremerton has one public golf course, the Rolling Hills Golf Club (18 holes, par 68), as well as an exclusive country club and a practice course. Other public golf courses are located in the towns of Union, Gorst, and Port Ludlow. The top golf spot on the peninsula, however, is Port Orchard, a small town south of Bremerton. There you'll find public golf links at the Cloverdale Valley Country Club (18 holes, par 69), Horseshoe Lake Golf Course (18 holes, par 71), McCormick Woods Golf Course (18 holes, par 72), and Village Green Golf Course (18 holes, par 58).

Here as elsewhere around Puget Sound, boating is one of the most popular recreational activities. There are public marinas at Bremerton, Bainbridge Island, Port Orchard, Silverdale and Poulsbo. Motorized boat rentals are hard to find, but outdoor sports outfitters in all of these communities rent sea kayaks.

There are beaches, picnic areas and short hiking trails at 24 state and local waterfront parks around the peninsula. Inland, hiking is limited because all forested areas are privately owned. Instead, bicycling is a favorite way to experience the relatively flat terrain and quiet, winding roads of the peninsula. Bike rentals are plentiful, and on sunny weekends bicycles often outnumber cars on back roads.

When it comes to culture, the Kitsap Peninsula is overshadowed by Seattle's wealth of visual and performing arts. However, Bremerton has four fine art galleries, a community theater group and a dance company. Smaller communities on the peninsula have sizeable artist populations and a scattering of small galleries and studios open to the public. Olympia College in Bremerton offers about 30 adult education courses; interestingly, about 80 percent of the continuing education staff are Navy personnel.

Housing and Other Costs Housing costs on the Kitsap Peninsula are not much different than in outlying neighborhoods of Seattle. In Bremerton, the average cost of a two- or three-bedroom house is around $135,000. In the surrounding countryside, homes come in all price ranges, from around $65,000 to $500,000 or more. Condominiums, which are increasingly common in the area, sell for anywhere from $40,000 to $150,000. Both houses and condos run higher in smaller communities away from Bremerton. In Gig Harbor, for example, two- to three-bedroom homes average about $167,000, and condominiums about $120,000.

Rents for both houses and apartments start at around $450 in Bremerton. Rental apartments can also be found in Poulsbo and Gig Harbor, where rents start at $650 a month for units away from the water, $900 with harbor views, and $1,000 for waterfront locations. In general, low-end rentals cost more in Bremerton than in mainland Seattle due to the large military presence. The good news is that there are plenty of rental units available in Bremerton, though they are hard to find elsewhere on the peninsula.

Cleared home sites in forest areas of the Kitsap Peninsula typically cost about $10,000 for a 2.5-acre lot (the minimum lot size allowable under the county's growth management restrictions). In other respects, the cost of living is slightly lower in Bremerton than in Seattle, though in surrounding rural areas the cost of propane or electric heat can push living expenses skyward in the winter.

Medical Care The only civilian hospital on the Kitsap Peninsula is Harrison Memorial Hospital, a 297-bed facility in Bremerton. The hospital provides ambulance and paramedic service to all parts of the peninsula. There are medical clinics in Port Orchard, Poulsbo, Winslow, and Gig Harbor.

Crime and Safety Crime on the Kitsap Peninsula seems to be a bigger problem in the areas that are most easily accessible from Seattle. The rate of both personal and property crime in Bremerton, while lower than in the Seattle area as a whole, is as high as in many Seattle suburbs. Farther from the city, however, in places like Poulsbo, Hartstene Island and Gig Harbor, violent crime hardly ever happens, and property crime is limited to occasional burglaries or the vandalization of empty vacation homes.

When Grandkids Visit The main sightseeing attraction at the Puget Sound Naval Ship Yard in Bremerton is the USS Missouri, the battleship on whose deck the peace treaty ending World War II was signed. Public tours are offered. Another historic ship that is open to the public is the USS Turner Joy, a 1960s-vintage destroyer involved in the Gulf of Tonkin incident that touched off the escalation of the Vietnam War. The huge gray steel warships are sure to impress visitors of all ages. Nearby, the Bremerton Naval Museum contains model ships and other exhibits tracing U.S. Navy history from wooden sailing ships to nuclear submarines.

Important Addresses and Connections

Chamber of Commerce: P.O. Box 229, Bremerton, WA 98310.
Senior Center: Bremerton Parks and Recreation, 13th and Nipsic, Bremerton, WA 98310.
Newspaper: *Bremerton Sun*, P.O. Box 259, Bremerton, WA 98310.

Airport: Residents take the ferry to Seattle, then drive or take a Metro Transit bus or Airport Express shuttle to Sea-Tac Airport.

Bus/Train: There is no bus or train service to Bremerton, but the ferry to Seattle disembarks within walking distance of the downtown Greyhound and Amtrak stations.

BREMERTON	Jan.	Apr.	July	Oct.	Rain	Snow
Daily Highs	44	59	76	61	49	4
Daily Lows	33	41	53	45	in.	in.

Olympic Peninsula

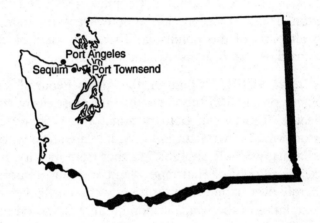

Half of Washington's west coast, maybe about a tenth of the state's total area, is actually a peninsula—the Olympic Peninsula. Here towns are small, somewhat isolated and generally located within shouting distance of the water—either the Strait of Juan de Fuca on the north or the Pacific Ocean to the west.

The main attraction of this area is Olympic National Park, one of the most popular national parks in the United States. The dramatically jagged, snow-capped mountains of the park's wilderness interior are accessible only by hikes of several days' duration but can be seen in all their glory from Hurricane Ridge, a windblown, mile-high ridgeline in the park just a short drive south of the largest town on the peninsula, Port Angeles.

Those of us who love the outdoors, but suffer from circulatory or respiratory problems that keep us out of high altitudes, find the Olympic Mountains, with maximum elevations under 8,000 feet, much more hospitable than the Cascade Range, where massive mountains like Mount Rainier stand nearly twice as high. Most trails through the park follow river valleys, staying at low altitudes and avoiding steep climbs. For gentler walking, there are a number of beautiful nature trails in the eastern part of the park, including deep, glacier-gouged Lake Crescent, pretty Marymere Falls, and several trails through the lush forest surrounding Sol Duc Hot Springs.

Unlike the northern coast, facing the Strait of Juan de Fuca, the western or Pacific coast of the Olympic Peninsula has little to offer in the way of places to live. Aside from the rather dreary lumber town of Forks, and several small towns on the Makah, Quileute and Quinault Indian Reservations, the western part of the peninsula is completely uninhabited. All of the coastline except for the Indian reservations is set aside as part of the national park, three national wildlife refuges, and a major archaeological site at Ozette.

Besides the broad, storm-scoured beaches, studded with shipwrecks and giant driftwood trees, the west side of the national park includes the spectacular Hoh Rain Forest, the largest temperate rain forest in North America. With 145 inches of annual rainfall, the moss-clad trees grow up to 300 feet high and more than 20 feet in diameter. Ground and trees alike are carpeted with thick layers of moss, giant ferns, blackberry bushes, licorice plants, and hundreds of varieties of flowers. Rainfall in a number of Olympic Peninsula towns, such as Port Angeles and Sequim, is surprisingly low, because most precipitation falls here, in the rain forest on the ocean side of the mountains, before reaching the north shore of the peninsula.

Port Townsend

This was the first year we stayed in town all winter. I almost gave up on ever seeing the sun again. Next winter, we're going to sail south to Baja with the whales. But we'll be back. Look around—this has got to be the most beautiful place on earth!
—Pamela Parker

Port Townsend, with its carefully preserved Victorian architecture and magnificent vistas of sea and glacier-clad peaks, may well be Washington's prettiest town. Located on the northwest-ernmost tip of the Olympic Peninsula at the mouth of Puget

Sound, Port Townsend is just remote enough from the Seattle metropolitan area to be beyond easy commuting distance. It is home to many artists, crafters and bed-and-breakfast innkeepers, who depend on the brisk but very seasonal tourist trade. In the off season, the town slows down so much that many locals migrate south to sunnier, livelier climes until spring.

The entire town of Port Townsend is a National Historic Landmark. As the original shipping port on Puget Sound, it prospered from the 1860s to the 1890s. Bigger and busier than the little timber town of Seattle, it emerged as the state's second-largest "city," after Olympia, with a population nearly equal to its 7,000 present-day inhabitants.

Then, as now, Port Townsend was a split-level town. A neighborhood of stately Victorian homes and churches surrounds the ornate courthouse, overlooking the water from atop limestone cliffs as much as a hundred feet high. At the foot of the cliffs, red brick buildings preserve the memory of bygone days when Port Townsend was reputed to be the roughest seaport on the West Coast. Then the commercial district around the docks was filled with saloons and bordellos; today they have been replaced by restaurants and art galleries.

The oceangoing ships of former times are gone. Some of the old docks have decayed away to leave only stubs of pilings standing in rows far out into the water, ideal perches for seagulls and pelicans. At the center of the old waterfront is the modern Washington State Ferries dock. There is no direct service from Port Townsend to Seattle; car ferries run frequently to Whidbey Island, where an 18-mile drive takes motorists to another ferry that carries them to the mainland at Mukilteo, an Everett suburb about an hour by interstate north of Seattle. In other words, a trip to the city can take all day. In the summer, a private ferry company offers daily passenger service to the San Juan Islands from the same docks.

Recreation and Culture There are two public golf courses in town, the Chevy Chase (9 holes, par 34) and the Spring Valley (9 holes, par 35) courses. Beachcombing on 10 miles of sandy public beach and clamming and birdwatching at Fort Worden State Park are other favorite outdoor activities. Port Townsend is a boating haven, with no less than seven marinas in the immediate area, and the town has a major reputation for boatbuilding— both wooden sailing vessels and state-of-the-art motor yachts.

Sea kayaks, motorized fishing boats and sailboats are available for rent.

On the cultural front, Port Townsend has one little theater group—the Key City Players at the Water Street Theatre—and several small art galleries. Otherwise, performing and visual arts are showcased in a packed schedule of more than 40 community events annually, including several major blues, jazz and chamber music festivals.

Housing and Other Costs

Housing costs in Port Townsend are similar to those in most other communities on the Olympic Peninsula. Unrestored Victorian-era homes start around $85,000; those that have been restored sell for nearly twice as much. While there are relatively few new homes in Port Townsend, there are plenty of luxury condominiums, typically with views of both the water and the mountains, priced between $250,000 and $350,000—much higher than single-family houses. Houses rent from $500 a month, while apartments range from $300 to $600 a month, but rentals are not always easy to find.

Other living expenses in the Port Townsend area are the same as in other towns on the peninsula, except that utilities are significantly more expensive within the Port Townsend city limits. The municipal government continues to raise utility rates as part of a policy designed to retard growth.

Medical Care

Jefferson General Hospital in Port Townsend is a small facility with 42 beds. Most residents go to Seattle for non-emergency procedures and for visits to specialists.

Crime and Safety

Official FBI crime statistics are unavailable for Port Townsend. Local residents assert that this is because there is no crime here.

When Grandkids Visit

Fort Worden State Park, just north of town, is the site of the Port Townsend Marine Science Center, where young visitors can handle starfish and other tidepool creatures in four touch tanks. The park, which was part of an extensive coastal defense system from 1890 through World War II, also offers a look at the area's military history, including a lighthouse, artillery museum and balloon hangar as well as restored Victorian-style officers' residences. More military exhibits are in the Jefferson County Historical Museum, housed in Port Townsend's original city hall.

Important Addresses and Connections

Chamber of Commerce: 2437 Sims Way, Port Townsend, WA 98368.

Senior Center: None locally; closest is 31 miles away in Sequim.

Newspaper: *The Leader*, 226 Adams St., Port Townsend, WA 98368.

Airport: Air travelers must ferry to the mainland and drive to Sea-Tac International Airport, a trip of at least two-and-a-half hours, or take a commuter flight to Sea-Tac from Fairchild International Airport in Port Angeles, 48 miles away.

Bus/Train: There is no bus or train service from Port Angeles. Passengers must ferry to the mainland, where they can catch a Greyhound bus or Amtrak train in either Edmonds or Seattle.

PORT TOWNSEND	Jan.	Apr.	July	Oct.	Rain	Snow
Daily Highs	44	59	76	61	49	4
Daily Lows	33	41	53	45	in.	in.

Sequim

Sequim is an absolutely good community to retire in, but if you're coming from a warmer climate, rent for a while before buying a home here. Even though Sequim has the best weather in western Washington, many newcomers find it chilly.

—Barb Butcher

Sequim (pronounced "Skwim") has a reputation as Washington's top retirement haven. Hundreds of older newcomers move to Sequim each season, contributing to phenomenal growth: the area population has risen from 4,000 residents a decade ago to 25,000 today. Less than 15 percent of the populace lives in Sequim's small town center; the rest live in suburban and semi-rural areas of the surrounding Dungeness Valley. Approximately half of area residents are over age 62.

The main factor accounting for Sequim's rise to retirement mecca status is the weather, which has earned the area its nickname, the Banana Belt. More than any other western Washington community, Sequim is protected from foul weather by the rain shadow of Mount Olympus, the massive peak thirty miles to the southwest. The town receives approximately the same annual rainfall as Los Angeles, and the sun shines 306 days a year. Average annual rainfall increases one inch per mile going west from Sequim, and almost as much going east.

Although Sequim lacks the architectural charm of other nearby towns, notably Port Townsend, the downtown area has a growing number of antique shops, as well as galleries that show the work of artists who make their homes in the area.

The town is set about two miles from the water's edge on a flat, green prairie that juts out into the Strait of Juan de Fuca. From the land's tip extends Dungeness Spit, the longest natural sand spit in the nation, home to seals, shorebirds and the oldest lighthouse in Washington. The tidal flats west of town, from Dungeness Spit to the entrance to Sequim Bay, rank among the Pacific Northwest's best clamming and crabbing areas. Seafood gourmands prize the local Dungeness crabs, and it takes only one giant geoduck (pronounced "gooey-duck") clam to make a meal. To the south of Sequim, unpaved logging roads lead into the Douglas-fir woodlands of Olympic National Forest, where mountain ridges rise toward the jagged peaks of Olympic National Park. There are also privately owned dig-'em-yourself oyster beds along Sequim Bay.

The sunshine factor makes Sequim a great place for gardening. Flowers, vegetables and fruits thrive and sometimes reach prodigious size. Several raspberry and strawberry farms in the area let you pick your own baskets of berries in season for a small charge. Area growers sell their produce at the Sequim Farmer's Market every Saturday during the summer months.

This part of the coast was home to the S'Kallam, a Coast Salish Indian tribe, for centuries before the first Europeans homesteaded the area in 1854. Their descendants, the Jamestown S'Kallam people, have continued to live on the shores of Sequim Bay but only won official federal recognition of their tribal status in 1981. Five miles east of Sequim, the Indians operate a tribal center, art gallery and buffet seafood restaurant in the same complex with the large Seven Cedars Casino, which draws gamblers all the way from Seattle.

Recreation and Culture Sequim has two 18-hole golf courses—the public Dungeness Golf Course (18 holes, par 72) and the private SunLand Golf & Country Club (18 holes, par 72).

Fishing is fine in the Sequim area. Offshore waters offer fishing for salmon, halibut and lingcod. The Dungeness River and numerous freshwater lakes in the area are good spots to fish for rainbow trout, steelhead and bass.

The Dungeness National Wildlife Refuge on Dungeness Spit is a hikers' and birdwatchers' paradise. Visitors may spot a wide variety of species ranging from bald eagles to cormorants.

The cultural focus is on local clubs and associations, which sponsor a full calendar of events such as doll shows, cat shows, horse shows, and bonsai shows. The biggest local celebration of the year is the week-long Irrigation Festival, the longest-established community event in the state, held in early May.

Housing and Other Costs Overall housing prices around Sequim run slightly below the national average. A typical, new, three-bedroom home costs $125,000; the few available condominiums in the area start at $90,000. House rentals are available in the $650 to $700 range. There are no rental apartments.

The overall cost of living in Sequim is about average, partly because food prices run a little high both locally and at larger markets in nearby Port Angeles. Gasoline also runs higher in this and other Olympic Peninsula communities, though this is offset by lower utility charges than in most other parts of the United States, thanks mainly to the year-round mild climate.

Medical Care Sequim has no hospital. The closest one is Olympic Memorial Hospital, 20 minutes away in Port Angeles. However, the high percentage of senior residents in Sequim has prompted the development of health care facilities not found in any other town of the same size in Washington, including a complete cancer chemotherapy and radiation therapy center, a kidney dialysis center, and several well-equipped walk-in medical centers that provide comprehensive health-care services. Sequim has one of the highest per-capita concentrations of physicians in Washington and, along with other nearby communities, boasts the lowest health-care costs in the state.

Crime and Safety As in other communities along the north shore of the Olympic Peninsula, the crime rate in Sequim and the Dungeness Valley is remarkably low. In fact, crimes of violence are almost unknown. Property crimes are on the rise, though, occurring somewhat more frequently than in Port Townsend, Whidbey Island, Anacortes or the San Juan Islands. Sequim's location, along a major highway, may make it more vulnerable to crime, and some locals believe that the proximity of the Indian gambling casino contributes to the increasing number of thefts.

Still, the crime rate is lower than in nine out of ten U.S. towns, making Sequim a very safe and secure place.

When Grandkids Visit The Olympic Game Farm, located five miles from Sequim, is home to exotic animals used in movies, television shows and commercials. On a self-guided driving tour or a walking tour led by a guide, visitors have a chance to see bison, elk, zebras and even a rhinoceros roaming the 90-acre park. Predators such as wolves, grizzly bears and tigers are confined in a habitat complex at the center of the game farm. There are also an aquarium, a petting zoo, and movie sets.

Important Addresses and Connections

Chamber of Commerce: P.O. Box 907, Sequim, WA 98382.

Senior Services: Sequim Senior Citizens Center, 3921 East Hammond Street, Sequim, WA 98383.

Weekly Newspaper: *The Gazette,* P.O. Box 1750, Sequim, WA 98382.

Airport: Sequim has a small general aviation airport. Fairchild Airport in nearby Port Angeles has daily air shuttle service to Sea-Tac.

Bus: Port Angeles-Seattle Bus Lines picks up passengers in Sequim twice daily and provides shuttle service to Sea-Tac. Clallam County Transit carries passengers from Sequim to Port Angeles and Port Townsend; seniors age 65 and up ride free.

SEQUIM	Jan.	Apr.	July	Oct.	Rain	Snow
Daily Highs	47	56	71	58	16	-
Daily Lows	33	39	51	38	in.	-

Port Angeles

Even though it has a lot of gray weather, Port Angeles is the most beautiful place in the world. It's a wonderful community and a good place to retire.
　　　　　　　　　　　　　　　　　　　　　—Lois Reed

The largest town on the Olympic Peninsula, Port Angeles (pop. 17,500) is the main gateway to Olympic National Park. This fact alone makes it an appealing choice for nature lovers. Besides limitless hiking trails and unparalleled wildlife watching, the park has special programs that provide volunteer opportunities for senior citizens.

Port Angeles itself is a busy town that stretches along the waterfront. Its two parallel main streets, and the downtown area small enough for walking, are complete with turn-of-the-century architecture in need of a fresh coat of paint. A long waterfront park has paved hiking trails and well-groomed woodlands. Growth has been slow and steady, so residential areas contain a mix of older and contemporary homes.

Homesteaders came to the mountain valleys around Port Angeles long before the creation of the national forest and national park, so the fringe areas around the park are a patchwork quilt of federal and private land. You'll find houses of every description, from rustic log cabins to contemporary custom-built homes, many of them secluded miles in on unpaved forest roads. The area's rural residents actually outnumber the population of Port Angeles itself.

Recreation and Culture
Hiking enthusiasts will find hundreds of miles of trails of every length and difficulty in Olympic National Park. The park is also one of the best places in Washington for wildlife viewing. The Port Angeles area is also a great place for saltwater and freshwater fishing, with four public boat launches inside the city limits. Favorite catches are blackmouth salmon and halibut. Clams, crabs and shrimp are also abundant in offshore waters. Anglers cast in dozens of nearby rivers and lakes for steelhead, cutthroat and rainbow trout. Fishing charters and river float trips are available in season. Golfers head over to the Peninsula Golf Course (18 holes, par 72) when they want to play a few rounds.

The Port Angeles Fine Arts Center holds exhibitions by major regional and national artists. There is not much in the way of performing arts, though. Peninsula College in Port Angeles offers twenty to thirty adult education courses each quarter, ranging from arts and crafts to international politics and including a number of classes designed especially for seniors, who make up about one-fourth of the school's non-degree students. Additional classes are offered through the Port Angeles Senior Center.

Housing and Other Costs
Port Angeles residential real estate prices are similar to those in Sequim and lower than in the Seattle metropolitan area. The average price of a two- or three-bedroom home is about $122,000. The few condominiums in the area, most of them clustered around the Peninsula Golf Club, start at $140,000. Rentals are significantly more affordable than in the Seattle area. Houses rent for $600 to $700, less in nearby

rural areas. Apartments, which can be found in Port Angeles more easily than in other Olympic Peninsula towns, rent for $350 to $400. Lower-than-average housing and heating costs are balanced out by higher-than-average costs for food and gasoline.

Medical Care Olympia Memorial Hospital in Port Angeles, with 126 beds, is the largest hospital facility on the Olympic Peninsula.

Crime and Safety Though less safe than the island communities presented in the following sections of this chapter, Port Angeles has a far lower incidence of crime than the Seattle area. Robberies and assaults are very rare, and residential burglaries and car thefts are also uncommon. By far the most common problem, accounting for about three-fourths of all crimes reported to the Port Angeles police, is theft of personal property from tourist vehicles parked at trailheads. Such thefts happen, on the average, about ten times a day!

When Grandkids Visit On sunny days, nothing can compete with an outing to Hurricane Ridge or any of several other car-accessible areas of Olympic National Park, where even the liveliest of youngsters will find boundless room to run off excess energy. When the weather is uncooperative, you can settle for a visit to Port Angeles' Fiero Marine Laboratory, which has a touch tank containing native tidepool creatures, or the Clallam County Museum, where exhibits include Indian artifacts found in the area as well as a re-creation of an old-time general store. To share a once-in-a-lifetime experience in Northwest Coast Indian heritage, head west to the village of Neah Bay on the Makah Indian Reservation, where the Makah Museum and Cultural Center displays a wonderful exhibit from the nearby archaeological site at Ozette, a pre-Columbian Indian village that was buried by a mudslide hundreds of years ago, sealing and preserving thousands of wooden artifacts that otherwise would have decayed away in the damp climate long ago.

Important Addresses and Connections

Chamber of Commerce: 121 E. Railroad Ave., Port Angeles, WA 98362.
Senior Services: Port Angeles Senior Services and Community Center, 328 E. 7th St., Port Angeles, WA 98362.
Newspaper: *The Daily News,* P.O. Box 1330, Port Angeles, WA 98362.
Airport: Horizon Air operates daily commuter service from Fairchild International Airport in Port Angeles to Sea-Tac.

Bus: Port Angeles-Seattle Bus Lines takes Seattle-bound passengers in Port Angeles and to the Seattle Greyhound station.

PORT ANGELES	Jan.	Apr.	July	Oct.	Rain	Snow
Daily Highs	44	54	67	57	49	-
Daily Lows	36	40	51	44	in.	-

The Strait of Juan de Fuca

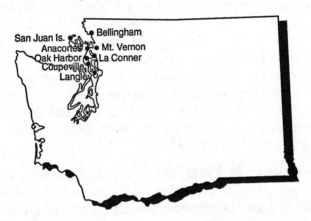

The area where the Strait of Juan de Fuca meets Puget Sound is the place a growing number of people call home. There are a number of communities on relatively developed Whidbey Island in the south, at the mouth of Puget Sound, which are almost suburbs of Seattle. A short drive by bridge to the north from Whidbey, and you find Fidalgo Island, pressed up against mainland Skagit Valley and its towns of La Conner and Mt. Vernon. Another short hop to the northwest, by ferry this time, and you arrive at the lovely San Juan Islands, cradled between the Washington port town of Bellingham and the British Columbia city of Victoria, on nearby Vancouver Island. Even the mainland towns here are inextricably tied to the strait and its islands, and each site is uniquely attractive for those who've always dreamed of spicing up their retirement years with a taste of island life.

Whidbey Island

Oak Harbor is a Navy town, which is good for retired Navy personnel. The quality of life is as good here as any place I know.
—Cheryal Hartling

Whidbey Island was known as a retirement area long before the first senior citizen thought of moving to Sequim. Langley, a residential community on the southwest shore of the island, is nicknamed "Port of the Sea Captains," because it has been a favorite retirement spot for mariners for more than a century.

Measuring 55 miles from north to south, Whidbey Island is the longest island in the United States—a distinction it gained in 1985 when the U.S. Supreme Court ruled that Long Island, New York, was actually a peninsula. It has the advantage of being accessible by highway bridge—but only from the north. Frequent ferries carry vehicles and passengers from terminals on the island to both Mukilteo, north of Seattle, and Port Townsend on the Olympic Peninsula.

Whidbey Island is predominantly rural in character, with three towns and a scattering of tiny villages along the protected coast that faces the mainland across Skagit Bay and the Saratoga Passage. The biggest town on the island is Oak Harbor, with a population of 15,000, including many personnel from nearby Whidbey Naval Air Station. However, the county seat of Island County (Whidbey Island, that is), is little Coupeville, an old-fashioned, Victorian-era port town of 1,300. For the most part, Whidbey Island residents live on small dairy and truck produce farms nestled in the fir trees that line a seemingly endless labyrinth of nameless little paved roads.

Whidbey Island is the place to go if the ultimate in peace and quiet is your goal. Any kind of excitement is highly unlikely here; in fact, retirees we've talked to in such laid-back places as Sequim, Port Townsend and Anacortes dismiss the prospect of life on Whidbey Island as "too boring." Boredom gives way to congestion on sunny weekends and during the summer months, when day-trippers from the Seattle area arrive as fast as the ferries can carry them and clog the island's only highway with bumper-to-bumper traffic bound for Deception Pass State Park and other popular recreation areas.

Recreation and Culture Water sports reign supreme on Whidbey Island, including fishing, sea kayaking, clamming and whale-watching. Ten of the island's thirty, mostly small, state, county and city parks afford boating and fishing access. Oak Harbor has a 420-slip marina, and Coupeville and Langley have public boat launch ramps. All three towns also have bicycle rentals, and the island's long, level back roads are ideal for bike touring, especially on weekdays when traffic is light. There are woodland and coastal hiking trails at Rhododendron State Park, Deception Pass State Park, Fort Casey State Park, Fort Eby State Park and South Whidbey State Park. The shorelines, sloughs and lakes of Whidbey Island are among the most popular birdwatching areas around Puget Sound, home to bald eagles, herons, snow geese and tundra swans among many other species.

The local golf courses are both private: the Whidbey Island Golf and Country Club (18 holes, par 72) in Oak Harbor and the Useless Bay Golf and Country Club (18 holes, par 72) in Langley.

The Coupeville Arts Center offers a wide range of adult arts classes, from nature photography to dollmaking and Navajo weaving.

Housing and Other Costs Island real estate sells at a premium, and Whidbey Island is no exception. Residence prices average $135,000—slightly higher than for comparable homes on the mainland. This is true not only of charming little farms and picturesque waterfront homes, of which there are many, but also of typical suburban-style custom homes. On the positive side, real estate here is much more affordable than in the San Juan Islands to the north. Whidbey Island homes also appear to possess good investment potential because of the high growth rate in the mainland city of Everett, just a 20-minute ferry ride away.

Rentals are common in and around Oak Harbor because of nearby Whidbey Island Naval Air Station, but rents are relatively high—$750 to $1,200 for a house, $550 to $750 for an apartment. Other living expenses, especially food and gasoline, are also significantly higher than on the mainland.

Medical Care Whidbey General Hospital, the island's 51-bed facility, has a staff of 44 physicians and a 24-hour emergency room. The hospital is not located in Oak Harbor, the largest town, but in the more centrally situated village of Coupeville, which can be reached quickly by ambulances from the several local fire stations around the island.

Crime and Safety Whidbey Island's crime rate falls in the lowest five percent of all communities in the United States. Like other islands nearby, such as Fidalgo Island (Anacortes) and the San Juans, it is virtually off-limits to professional criminals because of the obvious problems involved in making a quick getaway via the Washington State Ferries.

When Grandkids Visit Of interest to some youngsters are the historical parks and museums clustered around Coupeville, one of the oldest towns in Washington. The ways of life of Indians, sea captains and early-day homesteaders are recorded at the Island County Historical Museum on the town's waterfront. A walking tour of the town takes you past 45 historic buildings, including two of the first blockhouses built by early settlers to defend against possible attacks by hostile Coast Salish tribesmen. Coupeville forms the center of 17,000-acre Ebey's Landing National Historical Reserve, which also includes Fort Ebey and Fort Casey State Parks—military fortifications from both World Wars—as well as the picturesque Admiralty Head Lighthouse.

Other children may find more fun on the mainland at Forest Park, not far from the dock for the Mukilteo ferry, which links Whidbey Island with Everett. Fun in the park includes a swimming pool, playground facilities, and a petting zoo. Everett is also the site of the largest building in the world, the Boeing Aircraft Assembly Plant. Eleven stories tall and covering an area of 62 acres, the plant can house 16 jetliners at a time. Public tours are offered daily.

Important Addresses and Connections

Chamber of Commerce: P.O. Box 152, Coupeville, WA 98239.

Senior Centers: Oak Harbor Senior Center, 2327 20th NW, Oak Harbor, WA 98277; South Whidbey Senior Center, 2845 East Highway 525, Langley, WA 98260.

Senior Services: Senior Services of Island County, 2845 East Highway 525, Langley, WA 98260.

Weekly Newspaper: *Whidbey News Times*, 3098 W, Oak Harbor, WA 98278.

Airport: Oak Harbor Airport has daily commuter flights on Harbor Airlines to Sea-Tac International Airport and the San Juan Islands.

Bus: Island Transit buses serve all communities on the island and take passengers to both the Clinton—Mukilteo and Keystone—and Port Townsend ferry docks.

WHIDBEY IS.	Jan.	Apr.	July	Oct.	Rain	Snow
Daily Highs	43	57	71	58	18	2
Daily Lows	33	40	51	43	in.	in.

Anacortes

This is a good retirement area with many city activities for older people. Health care is excellent, and the tax rate is moderate.
—Kelly Larkin

A pleasant coastal town of about 12,500 people, Anacortes shares Fidalgo Island with several wooded county and state parks, large tracts of community forest lands, and the Swinomish Indian Reservation. Fidalgo is only technically an island, linked to Whidbey Island and the mainland by bridges over channels that are no wider than moderate-sized rivers. Across the island from the bridges, the town of Anacortes faces a seascape shaped by the misty silhouettes of Guemes, Cypress and Orcas Islands.

Historically, Anacortes was among several 19th-century settlements that aspired to become the major port city on Puget Sound, but which slipped into oblivion when the railroad bypassed them. The Spanish-sounding name is actually an alteration of "Anna Curtis," the wife of an early real-estate developer who named the settlement's first post office after her. The name was later Hispanicized to fit in with the many other Spanish names in the area, such as San Juan and Lopez Islands and the Strait of Juan de Fuca. (De Fuca, the navigator who claimed the area for Spain centuries earlier, was actually a Greek; when he got a job sailing for the king of Spain, he, like the town of Anacortes, changed his name.)

Today, Anacortes's main claim to fame is the ferry to the San Juan Islands, one of the most popular travel experiences in Washington. On weekends and every day in summer, thousands of visitors drive through Anacortes on their way to the ferry dock about three miles out of town. The only ferry that continues past the San Juans to Vancouver Island, British Columbia, leaves first thing in the morning, and motorists must get in line early to beat the crowd. As a result, many people spend the night before their San Juan Islands trip in Anacortes, creating an economy that thrives on lodging and restaurant business, along with a scattering of antique dealers, gift shops and art galleries.

Still, relatively few travelers take time to explore the town beyond Commercial Avenue, the long, straight, perpetually busy motel strip. Those who do discover a 13-block historic district full of turn-of-the-century homes and storefronts that would fit right into a New England fishing village. The Anacortes Murals, a series of nearly 60 life-size, cutout paintings based on antique photos depicting Anacortes at the dawn of the 20th century, decorate the historic district and beyond. The artist, lifelong Anacortes resident Bill Mitchell, plans to create a total of 100 murals.

Anacortes has been attracting retired people in increasing numbers recently because it offers much of the charm of San Juan Islands life without the disadvantages of high prices and crowded ferries. The city sponsors an extraordinary number of activities for senior citizens year-round.

Recreation and Culture Fidalgo Island is an outstanding place for fishermen, with public access to no less than seven freshwater lakes. Choices range from Lake Erie, where you'll find boat ramps and developed recreation and resort facilities, to Pass Lake, restricted to flyfishing from nonmotorized boats, and Whistle Lake, located deep in the Anacortes Community Forest and accessible only by hiking trail. The catch in the various lakes includes largemouth bass and cutthroat, brown and rainbow trout. The salt water offshore is known for good salmon fishing, with a year-round season in most areas. Crabbing for Dungeness and red rock crabs is a popular local pastime.

Anacortes is also a major recreational boating center and a good base for exploring the nearly 400 islands in the San Juans that can't be reached by ferry. Five municipal and private marinas on the island offer fuel, supplies, moorage, repairs and maintenance. If you don't own a boat, you'll find an abundance of rentals and charters ranging all the way from sea kayaks to 120-foot yachts. Your golfing needs can be fulfilled at the Similk Beach Golf Course (18 holes, par 72).

The cultural scene is pretty much limited to stage performances by the Anacortes Community Theatre. During the summer months, a full calendar of festivals and special events enlivens the town, beginning with the Waterfront Festival in May and climaxing with the Anacortes Arts & Crafts Festival in August, which brings more than 50,000 visitors to town. Other annual events include a Roaring Twenties-style ice cream social, the Fidalgo Island Quilt Show, and Shipwreck Day, a community-wide garage sale.

Winter in Anacortes is utterly uneventful. About the only off-season excitement on the island is to be found at the Swinomish Casino on the Indian reservation.

Housing and Other Costs   Housing costs in Anacortes used to be lower than on Whidbey Island, but they have been rising quickly in the past few years; they are still much less than for comparable homes in the San Juan Islands. An average home in Anacortes sells for $150,000 away from the water or $350,000 on the waterfront. Prices are about the same for condominiums as for houses, and there are many for sale, both with and without views of the water.

Apartment rentals start around $600, and houses around $700 away from the water. The overall cost of living in Anacortes is comparable to Whidbey Island and higher than the mainland Skagit Valley towns.

Medical Care   Island Hospital, a 43-bed facility, is the principal provider of emergency and inpatient medical services for Anacortes and all of the San Juan Islands. The hospital has a helicopter landing pad and acute care, intensive care and cardiac care units. Larger hospitals are nearby in Mount Vernon and Sedro Woolley. Anacortes also has more than 50 physicians in private practice. The Anacortes Convalescent Center offers Medicare-certified physical therapy and full-time nursing care, including specialized Alzheimers care.

Crime and Safety   Anacortes enjoys the distinction of having the twelfth-lowest crime rate in the entire United States.

When Grandkids Visit   A ferry cruise to the San Juan Islands is obligatory whenever you find yourself hosting grandchildren—or any other out-of-town visitors. Yet sometimes the waiting line for the ferries can be hopeless, and thankfully several places around Anacortes present fun alternatives on weekends. You can drive to the top of Mount Erie, the highest mountain on Fidalgo Island (1,270 feet above sea level), where on a clear day you can see the San Juan Islands, as well as the Olympic Peninsula and the Cascades from Mount Baker to Mount Rainier. Or tour the W.T. Preston, a sternwheeler "snag boat" that was used in the 1870s to break up log jams on Puget Sound and, miraculously, is still afloat more than a century later. On summer weekends, the Anacortes Railway—a miniature steam train built by a local man—carries passengers on a loop from the restored Burlington Northern Railroad Depot.

Important Addresses and Connections

Chamber of Commerce: 1319 Commercial Ave., Anacortes, WA 98221.

Senior Center: Anacortes Senior Center, 1701 22nd St., Anacortes, WA 98221.

Weekly Newspaper: *The American,* 901 6th St., Anacortes, WA 98221.

Airport: There is a general aviation airport in Anacortes; shuttle service is available to Sea-Tac International Airport, two hours away.

Bus: Grayline Bus provides early-morning service between Anacortes and Seattle. For interstate travelers, Greyhound buses stop in Burlington, 20 minutes away.

ANACORTES	Jan.	Apr.	July	Oct.	Rain	Snow
Daily Highs	46	58	73	60	25	1
Daily Lows	33	42	52	43	in.	in.

San Juan Islands

There are lots of retirees on Lopez Island—upscale retirees, that is. Housing is very expensive, but recreational activities don't cost anything.
                                                            —Gary Berg

As their idyllic reputation has spread, retirees have been drifting to the San Juan Islands in ever-increasing numbers, searching for the islands of their own dreams. What you're likely to find today in the San Juans is a setting and way of life every bit as pretty as you imagined—and a palpable threat of overdevelopment fueled by high demand and skyrocketing real estate prices. In the 1970s, about 2,500 people lived on the islands. Today, the year-round population exceeds 10,000, of which about half are retired. (The rest, presumably, are reclusive artists and the independently wealthy; one of the key factors in the San Juan Islands economy is that there are almost no jobs.) This rapid development is taxing the islands' natural resources—especially fresh water, which is already in critically short supply.

Most newcomers to the islands in recent years have been retirees; it's hard to make a living in the San Juans and impractical to commute to the mainland on a daily basis. Aside from the people who run the burgeoning number of bed-and-breakfast inns and restaurants on Orcas, San Juan and Lopez Islands, the few other locals who are gainfully employed are artists, crafters, writers and computer commuters.

The San Juan Islands, fragments of a partly submerged archipelago in the Strait of Juan de Fuca at the mouth of Puget Sound, rank high among the Northwest's scenic wonders. The islands, with their tall evergreen forests, rocky shorelines and a myriad of small coves and harbors, are separated from one another by channels no more than a mile or two wide. There are officially 428 islands in the San Juans at high tide, and 743 at low tide. Ten are state parks and wildlife reserves that provide habitat for bald eagles, river otters and deer. Sixty are inhabited by humans. Of these, only four—Lopez Island, Shaw Island, Orcas Island and San Juan Island—have regular ferry service.

To sightseers, the ferry trip to and through the San Juans is a marvel; to residents bound for the the mainland, long waits in line can be a real nuisance on weekends and all summer. Three-hour waits in line each way are standard, and five-hour waits are not uncommon. During the peak tourist season, sixteen ferries run daily, each carrying up to 175 cars and 2,000 passengers. The influx of tourists can amount to more than three times the resident population of all the islands.

San Juan Island, the largest of the islands, is relatively flat, and its interior is filled with small farms, many of which have been converted into bed-and-breakfast inns. The island has a somewhat obscure historical significance as the site of the "Pig War," a standoff between U.S. and British soldiers in the mid-19th century over who had jurisdiction to arrest a local farmer for shooting his neighbor's trespassing pig. The real issue, of course, was whether the San Juans belonged to the United States or Canada, and the confrontation lasted for 12 years during which the island was occupied by 2,500 soldiers. The "war" is commemorated by San Juan Island National Historical Park, which preserves the American and English army camps on opposite sides of the island. Friday Harbor, the touristy waterfront village where the ferry lands, is the largest town in the San Juans.

In sharp contrast, Orcas Island is mountainous, and the western half of the island is taken up by Moran State Park, Washington's largest. At the center of the park, the 2,160-foot summit of Mount Constitution, the highest point in the San Juans, affords a spectacular view of hundreds of islands. The horse-shoe-shaped island has two major towns—Orcas, where the ferry lands, and Eastsound, where most local businesses are located.

Farmland surrounds Eastsound, while rustic cabins and vacation homes occupy the west side of the island.

Lopez Island was entirely residential until a few years ago. Today, due to the huge increase in tourism, there is a handful of stores and services near the ferry dock, but otherwise the island is peaceful enough to suggest what living must once have been like on Orcas and San Juan. As for Shaw Island, the only commercial enterprise is the Little Portion Store near the ferry landing. It is run by Franciscan nuns, who also help tie up the arriving ferries.

Besides the four large islands served by the ferry, eleven others have tracts of residential property. For supplies and transportation to the mainland, most residents of these islands go back and forth to Friday Harbor by boat. Several of the islands also have landing strips for small aircraft. Between 40 and 50 other islands are privately owned and contain a single home or estate. (A small, forested island suitable for building a house lists for around $2 million.)

Recreation and Culture   Except when it's raining, the islands are better suited for bicycling than driving a car. In fact, the majority of local residents do rely on bikes most of the time. Rental bikes are available in Friday Harbor, Orcas and Lopez.

Moran State Park on Orcas Island has 26 miles of hiking trails past secluded woodland lakes and waterfalls. San Juan Island is the place to rent a sea kayak, with or without a guide. The ultimate experience is a close encounter with a pod of orca whales, which inhabit the waters offshore in large numbers. (Although orcas are also known as "killer whales," there is no record of any human whalewatcher ever having been injured by one.)

You can golf in Friday Harbor, on San Juan Island, at the San Juan Golf and Country Club (9 holes, par 36). In the town of Eastsound, on Orcas Island, give the Orcas Island Golf Course (9 holes, par 36) a try.

Cultural events in the islands are haphazard. Orcas Center in Eastsound presents visiting lecturers and local music, dance and theater productions. The San Juan Community Theatre hosts productions by various local groups including the Straights of Juan de Fuca and the Friday Harbor Middle School Drama Group. The Mount Vernon-based Skagit Community College operates a small branch in Friday Harbor on San Juan Island, offering various adult education courses geared toward retirees.

Housing and Other Costs Real estate prices are much higher than almost any other place in Washington, but for some the quality lifestyle here makes it worthwhile. Realtors in the islands categorize property as "inland no-view," "view," and "waterfront." Inland no-view homes average $175,000 on all three islands. View property for all three islands (meaning that it has a sea view; lakes don't count) averages around $250,000, with some homes (on Orcas Island) running as high as $800,000. On Orcas Island, whose horseshoe shape makes for more water frontage than the other major islands, homes start at $200,000 on the bluffs and $300,000 on the beach. On San Juan Island, waterfront homes cost $325,000 and up, and on Lopez Island, $265,000 and up.

Rentals houses and apartments are almost nonexistent in the San Juans. There are a few apartments and an occasional live-aboard boat for rent in Friday Harbor, but virtually none on Orcas and Lopez Islands.

Other cost-of-living factors in the San Juan Islands, including food and utilities, are no higher than on the mainland. The sizes of the main islands mean that most residents enjoy minimal automobile expenses, though it gets quite expensive to take your car on the ferry regularly. Many island residents, in fact, leave their cars in Anacortes and either rely on bicycles or keep an older second car at home. Walk-on passengers pay a lot less and never have to wait.

Medical Care Many newcomers first realize the full meaning of living on an island when they need to go to the emergency room. There is no hospital or 24-hour medical clinic in the San Juan Islands. Only San Juan Island itself has a resident doctor on call 24 hours. Individuals in need of emergency hospital treatment are rushed by helicopter to Island Hospital in Anacortes, Whidbey General Hospital in Coupeville or St. Joseph Hospital in Bellingham. Some island residents subscribe to Medflight, a non-profit helicopter ambulance service that offers emergency transportation as needed for a reasonable annual membership fee.

Routine medical treatment is available at medical centers on San Juan, Orcas and Lopez Islands. Full-time nursing care and physical therapy are available at the Islands Convalescent Center in Friday Harbor.

Crime and Safety Crimes against local residents—and all types of violent crime—are almost unknown in the San Juan Islands. The overall crime rate is below the rate of 90 percent of U.S. cities and towns.

Crime would be even lower if not for the victimization of tourists in Moran State Park and other island parks. More than 2,000 car break-ins are reported yearly, mostly by hikers who return to find their gloveboxes ransacked and their luggage looted. This type of crime has become epidemic in many western Washington forests and parks, and the San Juan Islands are no exception. (Locals say nomadic felons move from campground to campground perpetrating these break-ins, though there doesn't seem to be overwhelming evidence to support the theory.)

Security is a problem on some of the more remote islands, where vacation homes and other part-time residences are particularly vulnerable to vandals and burglars with boats. Solitude makes such places hard to protect with burglar alarms. Owners often employ a housesitter or caretaker during prolonged absences—a practice that lets some island residents live in dream houses during the off-season.

When Grandkids Visit The most captivating experiences for youngsters are to be found on San Juan Island, where the Whale Museum in Friday Harbor contains limitless information about whales, dolphins and orcas, including complete gray whale and orca skeletons as well as photographs, paintings and videos. For a real-life look at orcas, dolphins, seals and eagles, book a naturalist-guided excursion, usually available from May through October. Lime Kiln State Park is also a good spot for orca-watching through binoculars.

Important Addresses and Connections

Chambers of Commerce: P.O. Box 252, Eastsound, Orcas Island, WA 98245; P.O. Box 98, Friday Harbor, San Juan Island, WA 98250; P.O. Box 102, Lopez Island, WA 98261.

Senior Services: Orcas Island Senior Services, P.O. Box 18, Eastsound, Orcas Island, WA 98245; San Juan Senior Services, P.O. Box 951, Friday Harbor, San Juan Island, WA 98250; Lopez Senior Services, P.O. Box 154, Lopez Island, WA 98261.

Newspaper: *The Journal,* 580 Guard St., Friday Harbor, WA 98250.

Airport: Friday Harbor Municipal Airport provides commuter service. Several independent companies operate seaplanes between San Juan, Orcas and Lopez islands and Seattle.

Bus: The nearest bus service is in Anacortes.

SAN JUAN IS.	Jan.	Apr.	July	Oct.	Rain	Snow
Daily Highs	44	57	70	58	29	1
Daily Lows	34	40	49	44	in.	in.

La Conner/Mount Vernon

La Conner has a great deal to offer in terms of variety, services and hospitality, but its greatest asset is its people.

—Dan O'Donnell

Mention the Skagit Valley (pronounced to rhyme with "gadget"), and most people in Washington think of one thing: tulips. The valley's farms produce over 40 million tulip, daffodil and iris bulbs a year—more than any other place in the world, including the Netherlands. In April, hundreds of thousands of motorists descend on the valley to see miles and miles of carefully cultivated flowers burst into bloom, a spectacle that rivals New England's autumn leaves. Besides flowers, major products are peas, strawberries, dairy products, and riding horses. Organic farms thrive in the area, and pesticide use is discouraged.

The Skagit River flows 78 miles from the heart of North Cascades National Park, skirting the south face of Mount Baker and spilling into Skagit Bay, which separates Whidbey Island from the mainland.

The key towns in the valley, each quite different from the others, are La Conner, a historic port town with a population of just 720; Mount Vernon, the county seat, with a rapidly growing population that stands at 21,000 as of 1996; and Sedro-Woolley, a logging town and the headquarters for North Cascades National Park and Mount Baker-Snoqualmie National Forest, with a population of 7,000.

The number of retirees living in the Skagit Valley has been increasing gradually since the 1970s, when senior citizens represented 13 percent of the valley's population; by 1990, they accounted for 28 percent.

La Conner is one of the Puget Sound area's quaint little Victorian port towns. It dates back to 1869 and had its heyday in

1884, when the population was about five times what it is today. The town languished on the brink of oblivion through most of the 20th century before ambitious historic preservation efforts in the 1980s transformed it into the artists' colony and tourist destination that it is today. Although La Conner itself is tiny, it serves as the commercial center for Shelter Bay, a large, upscale private residential community inhabited mainly by retirees. Rounding out the greater La Conner area's unusual cultural mix are the residents of the adjacent Swinomish Indian Reservation, descendants of eleven tribes that originally inhabited the Skagit Valley.

Located about ten miles inland, Mount Vernon sprawls westward from the riverbank on which it was founded in 1877. The town itself is a no-nonsense agricultural center. Interstate 5 runs through it and carries a steady stream of produce from the Skagit Valley to Seattle and points beyond. Mount Vernon has a charming downtown historic district sure to make you feel as if you'd stepped into a Norman Rockwell painting, as well as a number of city parks with rose gardens and scenic overlooks. The advantage of living in Mount Vernon is its central location for recreation. The North Cascades Scenic Highway, Ross Lake Recreation Area, the San Juan Islands and the Olympic Peninsula, not to mention the Seattle area and the Canadian border, can all be reached with less than an hour's driving.

Just nine miles upriver, Sedro-Woolley has a character very different from either La Conner or Mount Vernon. Logging has traditionally been the main industry in this town at the foot of Mount Baker. The timber industry has been on the decline here for several years, due to changes in environmental policy and dwindling numbers of the large trees for which the local lumber mills were designed. While several small manufacturers continue to make wood products such as furniture and toys, there can be little doubt that the economic future of Sedro-Woolley depends on tourism. It has emerged as the preferred home base for visitors to North Cascades National Park, Ross Lake National Recreation Area, and Mount Baker-Snoqualmie National Forest.

Recreation and Culture   Public golf courses include the 27-hole Avalon Golf Course in Burlington (par 72/36), a modern development between Mount Vernon and Sedro-Woolley, as well as three nine-hole golf courses in the valley. Several types of salmon can be caught in the Skagit River, along with sturgeon and steelhead. Birdwatchers are drawn to the 1,500-acre Bald

Eagle Natural Area, as well as the Skagit Wildlife Area on the river's roadless delta.

Skagit Valley College in Mount Vernon offers about 50 adult education courses each year, as well as Elderhostel programs. About 45 percent of the nearly 1,000 people who enroll in adult classes each year are retired. Nearby La Conner is home to the Valley Museum of Northwestern Art.

Housing and Other Costs Property values throughout the Skagit Valley are lower than on Whidbey and Fidalgo Islands, though prices have been rising rapidly in La Conner. The average home sells for $130,000, with some houses priced under $100,000 and condominiums starting at $80,000. Rentals can be found in Mount Vernon and Sedro-Woolley at rates that start around $500 a month for apartments and $550 a month for houses; rentals are rare in La Conner. Utilities and property taxes are lower than in the Seattle metro area, and groceries—priced about the same as in Seattle—can be supplemented with bargain-priced fresh local produce in season.

Medical Care There are two hospitals in the Skagit Valley. Skagit Valley Hospital and Health Center in Mount Vernon is the larger one, with 137 beds. It offers full diagnosis and treatment facilities including a cardiovascular lab, CT scans, MRI, radiology and nuclear medicine. The hospital's community outreach programs include Golden Care, an information and assistance program designed for Medicare-eligible adults. Under the same management as Skagit Valley Hospital, United General Hospital in Sedro-Woolley has 97 beds. The Skagit County Health Department's Senior Screening Clinic provides referrals, medical histories, physical exams and lab work for seniors over age 60.

Crime and Safety The crime rate in Mount Vernon is below the overall average for Washington state. In Sedro-Woolley it is lower yet, and in La Conner it is much lower.

When Grandkids Visit The Skagit County Historical Museum in La Conner has pioneer and farm relics from the valley's early days located in recreations of a general store and a farmhouse. In Sedro-Woolley, the Lake Whatcom Railway carries passengers on a 90-minute trip through the valley during the summer months and offers special low fares for children.

Important Addresses and Connections

Chambers of Commerce: P.O. Box 644, La Conner, WA 98257; P.O. Box 1007, Mt. Vernon, WA 98273.

Senior Services: Skagit County Senior Citizens Services, 315 S. Third St., Mt. Vernon, WA 98273; Mt. Vernon Senior Center, 1401 Cleveland St., Mt. Vernon, WA 98273.

Newspaper: *Skagit Valley Herald,* PO Box 578, Mount Vernon, WA 98273.

Airport: The nearest passenger service is at Bellingham International Airport, 25 miles to the north, where commuter planes fly to Sea-Tac as well as to British Columbia. The alternative is to take an Airporter Shuttle bus from Mount Vernon to Sea-Tac, a 67-mile trip.

Bus: Greyhound buses serve Mount Vernon on the Interstate 5 run. The new Amtrak spur connecting the Coast Starlight in Seattle with Canadian passenger trains in Vancouver, B.C., stops for passengers at a station between Mount Vernon and Burlington.

MOUNT VERNON	Jan.	Apr.	July	Oct.	Rain	Snow
Daily Highs	46	58	75	60	32	3
Daily Lows	33	39	49	42	in.	in.

Bellingham

No one has ever come to Bellingham who didn't find it a wonderful place to live.

           —Anna Roedel

If any area of the northwestern Washington coast can claim to be "undiscovered," it is Whatcom County, which stretches along the Canadian border from the Straits of Georgia shoreline to the crest of the North Cascades.

The population center of Whatcom County is Bellingham, a city of 68,000 people located 18 miles south of the Canadian border. The setting, on a series of hills along Bellingham Bay, is as spectacular as the most romantic of Pacific Northwest daydreams. Many neighborhoods and parks have beautiful views of the San Juan Islands across the water to the west, and just a few miles to the east rises 10,775-foot Mount Baker in all its glacier-clad majesty. Although Bellingham is situated just off Interstate 5, a mere 90-minute drive north of Seattle, its historic charm has never been overwhelmed by the growth boom that has transformed other cities to the south.

In the 1880s, Bellingham was a busy port town. The deep bay was ideal for shipping, but like Port Townsend and other Victorian-era port towns along the Washington coast, when Bellingham lost its bid for transcontinental railroad service it fell into a long economic slumber. Three other nearby towns—Fairhaven, Whatcom and Sehome—consolidated with Bellingham in 1903 under a single municipal government. Today, the centers of all four towns have been declared National Historic Districts, along with Bellingham's old waterfront port and a Victorian mansion district. The tallest structure in the old-fashioned downtown shopping district is the clock tower of the stately, red-brick Whatcom Museum of History and Art. Many 1880s and '90s storefronts have been restored and converted to art galleries, antique shops and restaurants.

Over the years, Bellingham has developed an intriguing cultural mix. Through much of the 20th century, the town's economy depended mainly on Canadians from Victoria and Vancouver, B.C., who came south to buy U.S.-made goods duty-free. Though the North American Free Trade Agreement is gradually eliminating import tariffs between Canada and the United States, you still see about as many British Columbia license plates as Washington ones in shopping mall parking lots. As the site of Western Washington University, Bellingham has a college student population of nearly 11,000. It is also one of the favorite communities in Washington among aging hippies and enlightenment seekers. Smaller neighboring villages retain distinctive Dutch and Scottish influences from early settlement days. In addition, about 5,000 Lummi and Nooksack Indians make their homes on two nearby reservations.

Senior residents find that it's hard to get bored in Bellingham. The exceptionally active senior center offers more than 60 classes, health programs and social events each week. Additional activities are offered by AARP and the Older Women's League (OWLS). Whatcom County Senior Services sponsors low-cost boat, train and bus trips to destinations throughout Washington, Oregon and even Alaska. Independent living apartments including dinner, transportation and social activities are available at the Willows Retirement Community near St. Joseph's Hospital.

With the opening of Fairhaven Station, a new transportation complex, in 1995, Bellingham now offers a full range of transportation options from one central terminal. Besides Greyhound and Whatcom County Transit buses and Amtrak passenger trains, the terminal also serves three separate ferry lines, offering daily departures to Friday Harbor on San Juan Island and Victoria on Vancouver Island, B.C., as well as three-day ferry trips up the Inside Passage to Alaska.

Recreation and Culture

Bellingham and surrounding Whatcom County have the highest concentration of public and private golf courses in the state—17 in all. In addition to saltwater fishing for chinook and coho salmon in and around Bellingham Bay, there is good freshwater fishing for cutthroat and rainbow trout, kokanee salmon and largemouth and small-mouth bass in Lake Whatcom, Samish Lake and several smaller lakes on the outskirts of Bellingham as well as in the Nooksack River. Hiking opportunities are boundless, from easy walking trails in several of Bellingham's 18 forested state and local parks to challenging wilderness routes in nearby Mount Baker-Snoqualmie National Forest.

On the outskirts of Bellingham are two Indian-run gambling establishments, the Lummi Casino and the Nooksack River Casino. The latter has the highest bet limits north of Nevada and an all-you-can-eat buffet.

Live stage plays are presented throughout the year by the Bellingham Theater Guild. Western Washington University's Performing Arts Department also presents theatrical and dance performances.

Housing and Other Costs

All types of housing are available in and around Bellingham. Real estate prices are very close to the national average. Three-bedroom home prices range from $120,000 to $300,000, with condominiums starting around $80,000. Rental rates for apartments average about $675 a month, and for houses about $750 a month. Five-acre home sites in rural areas outside the city sell for about $40,000. The overall cost of living in Bellingham is virtually the same as in the Seattle area.

Medical Care

St. Joseph's Hospital has two separate facilities in Bellingham, with a total of 253 beds. The city has more than 160 general practitioners and specialists in private practice.

Crime and Safety

Bellingham's crime rate, though higher than in some of the island and Olympic Peninsula communities covered in this chapter, is much lower than in urban areas such as Seattle, Tacoma and Everett. The highest crime categories are assault, sexual assault and petty theft, most commonly directed against university students. Crimes against older victims are rare.

When Grandkids Visit The Children's Museum Northwest has hands-on exhibits that focus on career choices, including an elaborate medical center display. Many children are also fascinated by the Maritime Heritage Center, an open-air museum and fish hatchery where an interpretive trail shows how salmon are incubated and released into the ocean each spring. There is a large aquarium tank on the promenade at Squalicum Harbor, one of the largest marinas in the Northwest.

Important Addresses and Connections

Chamber of Commerce: 904 Potter St. #D, Bellingham, WA 98225.

Senior Center: Bellingham Senior Activity Center, 315 Helleck, Bellingham, WA 98225.

Newspaper: *Bellingham Herald,* PO Box 1277, Bellingham, WA 98227.

Airport: From Bellingham International Airport, several commuter airlines provide shuttle service to Sea-Tac International Airport as well as to Victoria and Vancouver, British Columbia.

Bus/Train: Greyhound stops in Bellingham. Amtrak started rail service to and from Bellingham in 1995, with connections to ViaRail and British Columbia Rail routes in Vancouver, B.C.

BELLINGHAM	Jan.	Apr.	July	Oct.	Rain	Snow
Daily Highs	43	57	73	59	35	9
Daily Lows	31	40	53	42	in.	in.

Pacific Coast

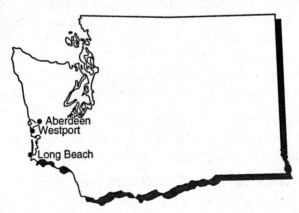

As mentioned before, the northern Pacific coast of Washington (the west coast of the Olympic Peninsula) does not have much to offer in the way of full-time living for retirees. Happily, this is not the case with the central and southern regions of Washington's Pacific coast. There are small to mid-size towns here that deliver good value for your money spent. Here, in addition to the attractions of a beach-oriented lifestyle, you'll find pleasant communities that care about their senior population and provide the support and services to prove it.

Aberdeen/Westport

If this is your first trip to the Washington coast, you'll love it here in Ocean Shores and Westport. Ours is a truly unique area.
—Michael Gaines

Aberdeen, the largest town on Grays Harbor (on Washington's central coast) started on the road to becoming a retirement mecca as retirees came to take advantage of a downturn in the economy in the 1990-91 recession. Seniors have contributed to the comeback of a nice area. Today, Aberdeen and surrounding towns are home to a large number of retirees, many of them originally drawn by low housing costs. While the economy of Aberdeen and the Grays Harbor area has rebounded and is now busy and strong, real estate prices remain among the lowest in Washington.

Traditionally, Grays Harbor depended on fishing and lumber for its prosperity. Both occupations paid well, and the area flourished. Then an invasion of foreign boats with 30-mile-long drag nets came and began cleaning out the fish. At the same time, Aberdeen became the largest timber shipping port in the United States as Japanese factory ships loaded up the area's raw logs, processing them with low-paid Filipino workers and selling finished lumber products back to U.S. consumers—bypassing local lumber mills and factories. Aberdeen's economy sputtered to a standstill. Fishing boats stayed in port, and businesses closed down, causing stores to shut down and homes to stand vacant. Five years later, the port has been dredged to make it competitive as a shipping center for exporting to the Pacific Rim.

Aberdeen has great senior services, equal to the best we've seen. The surprising thing about these community services, not just in Aberdeen, is that so few retirees take full advantage of them. We asked the center's director what she considered to be her biggest problem. "Getting the news out that we exist! Folks just have no idea of what we offer. Many of our services are free, some have a nominal cost, others have a sliding fee, according to the ability to pay. Some items are limited to lower-income folks, but most are available to all. Yet we can't seem to spread the news!" Available services range from free health care to legal services and Alzheimers support groups.

A possible disadvantage for some is an exceptionally high rainfall—almost 70 inches a year, but almost all falls during the winter. One enthusiastic Aberdeen booster said, "I have to admit, I get pretty tired of that steady drizzle all winter. May is also sometimes drizzly, but the gorgeous flowers are fabulous. Even the most tumbled-down house looks great with a flowering bush in the yard!"

More retirees settle in Aberdeen than in the smalller communities around Grays Harbor such as Grayland, Westport and Ocean Shores—damp, scenic little towns where tending cranberry bogs is the main activity. The explanation is probably that these distant shores are too far from anyplace that can properly be called a town, and that winter weather can be soggy at best and sometimes violent along the unprotected Pacific coast. Still, for people who long for isolation and sea views, these communities on the ocean side of Grays Harbor are worth investigating.

Recreation and Culture   Grays Harbor College in Aberdeen offers 75 to 100 adult education courses per quarter. Though many of the classes are remedial or vocational courses to help those displaced by the decline of the timber industry, 15 to 20 classes each quarter are specifically for senior citizens.

Housing and Other Costs   Part of Aberdeen's recovery has to do with retirees moving in to take advantage of the great real estate bargains. As people left the area during its economic decline, houses went on the market, but few buyers were interested. A few years ago, perfectly liveable homes were being offered for as little as $15,000. The economy has bounced back with a downsized labor force, so home buyers still have a tremendous edge. The average price for a two- or three-bedroom home in Aberdeen is $72,000. In Westport, Grayland and Ocean Shores, the average home price is $97,000. Rural building sites are few because most area land is owned by timber companies.

For some reason, there are hardly any apartments in the area. Rents for houses in Aberdeen start at $300 and average around $500. Rentals are considerably higher in Westport, Grayland and Ocean Shores, where small houses and duplexes start around $400 a month and larger homes are in the $700- to $800-a-month range. According to one Aberdeen realtor, the cost of living here is noticeably lower than in other west Washington communities.

Medical Care Grays Harbor Hospital has two locations in Aberdeen with a total of 259 beds. It reportedly can be difficult to find a physician still accepting new patients, however there are some in nearby Hoaquiam.

Crime and Safety The crime rate in Aberdeen is about the same as the statewide average, which is a little high for a community this size. Official explanations vary: law enforcement officers blame economic displacement and a high incidence of alcoholism, while some local politicians scapegoat "teenage gangs."

When Grandkids Visit Grays Harbor Historical Seaport has a replica of the wooden sailing ship Captain Robert Gray used to explore the Washington coast at the end of the 18th century, along with exhibits on shipbuilding. The Aberdeen Museum of History has a collection of photos and memorabilia that includes an exhibit of old-time firefighting equipment.

Important Addresses and Connections

Chamber of Commerce: P.O. Box 306, Westport, WA 98595.
Senior Services: Aberdeen Senior Center, PO Box 1827, Aberdeen, WA 98520; In Grayland-Westport, none; only Seaside Seniors and AARP.
Newspaper: *The Daily World,* P.O. Box 269, Aberdeen, WA 98520.
Airport: There is no commercial air passenger service from Aberdeen. Air travelers must drive to Sea-Tac, 98 miles away.
Bus: There's an excellent local bus system (25 cents fare), and the Grays Harbor Transit Authority operates buses between Aberdeen and Olympia approximately every two hours for just $1. Travelers can transfer to a Greyhound bus or an Amtrak train in Olympia.

ABERDEEN/WEST.	Jan.	Apr.	July	Oct.	Rain	Snow
Daily Highs	45	58	70	62	85	-
Daily Lows	34	40	50	50	in.	-

Long Beach

*We really appreciate having the beach all to ourselves in the
spring and fall. Of course, in the winter we go to Bucerias in
Mexico, where you can swim in the ocean, which you can't do
here.*
　　　　　　　　　　　　　　　　　　　　—Shelley Waller

The world's longest beach extends the full length of this slen-
der, 26-mile-long peninsula on the southern Washington coast.
Just over two miles wide, the peninsula slopes up to an elevation
of 30 feet at its central ridgeline, where there are pine trees and
long, narrow freshwater lakes, With a population of 1,300, the
municipality of Long Beach is the largest town on the peninsula.
Smaller villages include Ilwaco (pop. 840), Seaview (pop. 200)
and Oysterville (pop. 200).

Retirees account for most year-round residents of the Long
Beach Peninsula; the area's only industries are growing cranber-
ries in the bogs along Willapa Bay and cultivating oysters in the
bay itself.

Long Beach attracts boisterous, predominantly young crowds
during the summer months, when there is a full calendar of community events such as the Ocean Park Garlic Festival, the Ilwaco
Oyster Festival, and Long Beach's rodeo, international kite festival and Sand-Sations sand sculpture contest.

After Labor Day, though, locals have the peninsula all to
themselves. Despite a climate much grayer and damper than that
found farther north around Puget Sound, Long Beach in the off
season has an austere kind of beauty that invites you to stroll the
boardwalk, dig for razor clams, comb the beach for treasures,
watch for the migrating whales that often skim close to the shore
or just daydream to the ocean's hypnotic rhythms.

Life on the Long Beach Peninsula is not for everybody, which
is why so few people live here. But if your dreams involve seclu-
sion at land's end in a small, friendly, affordable seaside community where nothing much happens for months on end, Long
Beach could be your kind of place.

Recreation and Culture　　There are two nine-hole golf
courses, one near each end of the peninsula—the Heritage Golf
Course (par 34) north of Ocean Park and the Peninsula Golf
Course (par 33) in Long Beach. Both are open to the public.

The tip of the peninsula, as well as the islands in the bay that separates it from the mainland, is a national wildlife refuge, home to deer, elk and many bird species. The refuge provides opportunities for hiking, kayaking and birdwatching. There are a number of easy hiking trails at Fort Canby State Park at the base of the peninsula.

Long Beach residents tend to be passionate about fishing. Sport fishermen take to the open sea hoping to catch a sturgeon; mature fish reach eight to twelve feet in length and may weigh upwards of 100 pounds. A simpler pastime is digging for razor clams along the beach. Fishermen often combine clamming with surf fishing, since clam necks are the best bait for catching "pogeys," or surf perch.

Housing and Other Costs The Long Beach Peninsula has a variety of housing options. There are a fair number of custom homes of recent vintage on the market at prices averaging around $120,000. Homes are not built right on the ocean, since winter storms can be fierce, but most are within sight (or at least earshot) of the water. By local ordinance, all new construction and remodeling of houses on the shoreline must be submitted to a design review committee for approval. Condominiums come in all price ranges, from $45,000 units that are basically designed as weekend beach cabanas to $250,000 luxury units. Rentals are available, though not numerous; rates range between $400 and $500 a month for both houses and apartments.

Heating costs are high in the winter because all homes on the peninsula use propane tanks. Otherwise, the cost of living on the Long Beach Peninsula is comparable to Vancouver and other southwestern Washington communities.

Medical Care The peninsula's only hospital is the small Ocean Beach Hospital in Ilwaco, with a total of 25 beds. Seven doctors reside on the peninsula, and several out-of-town specialists come to Long Beach a few days a month. For non-emergency procedures, residents go to Astoria, Oregon, 15 miles away.

Crime and Safety In 1994, Long Beach residents were shocked by a murder on a remote part of the peninsula. True, both victim and perpetrator were from out of town, but it gave cause for alarm because it was the first murder in Long Beach history—and practically the only crime of any kind. Since then, some residents have even started locking their doors.

When Grandkids Visit Long Beach is the home of the annual week-long Washington State International Kite Festival, held in late August. If your youngsters come at a different time of year, take them to the Long Beach World Kite Museum, featuring a collection of more than 200 Japanese kites as well as other kites from around the world and videos of Chinese and Japanese kite festivals.

Important Addresses and Connections

Chamber of Commerce: P.O. Box 310, Long Beach, WA 98631.
Senior Center: Under construction.
Weekly Newspaper: *Chinook Observer,* Long Beach, WA 98631.
Airport: There is no commercial air passenger service to the Long Beach Peninsula. The closest airport, 15 miles away in Astoria, Oregon, has several commuter flights a day to Portland International Airport.
Bus: Pacific Transit operates buses from Long Beach south to Astoria, connecting with independent bus lines that run to Portland. Pacific Transit buses also go up the coast to Westport to connect with Grays Harbor Transit Authority buses to Aberdeen and Olympia.

LONG BEACH	Jan.	Apr.	July	Oct.	Rain	Snow
Daily Highs	45	62	75	63	62	-
Daily Lows	34	41	53	53	in.	-

Columbia River Valleys

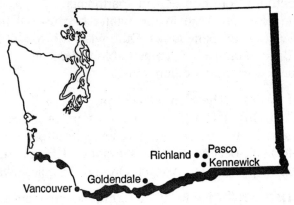

Delimiting most of the Washington-Oregon border, the Columbia River makes its way grandly to the sea through a series of scenic east-west valleys. The Washington cities and towns that border the Columbia all have the river's beauty and recreational opportunities in common, but from that starting point, the retiree is faced with a variety of choices in community size, weather, and attractions.

Heading upriver from urban Vancouver (Washington, not British Columbia!), which faces Portland, Oregon, across the water, as you proceed up the Washington side of the Columbia you find delightful little towns strung along a winding, scenic road. Such towns as Camas, Washougal and Skamania are close enough to the city for convenience, but not so close as to feel overwhelmed by it. The river's bank rises from the waterline, with streets forming tiers which provide scenic views for the towns' homes. There's an exceptionally peaceful air about this stretch of river, a combination of woods, meadows and steep hills that invites retirement.

Continuing upriver from Vancouver you pass the Cascade Range and enter eastern Washington. This is where you begin to notice a change in environment—the rainfall is less in this region, the summers warmer, the winters dryer. Here you'll find towns nestled in the foothills next to the river, more affordable than those to the west, yet still with plenty of outdoor recreation—from fishing to skiing—to keep residents busy year-round.

Vancouver

Vancouver is a good retirement community... Many residents leave for the winter, but they always come back.
—Riley Montgomery

Although in the state of Washington, Vancouver (pop. 55,000) is essentially a "bedroom community" of Portland, just across the Columbia River. Yet the city stands alone in several respects. For one thing, its commercial centers are self-sufficient, and residents don't think in terms of "downtown" being in Portland; Vancouver has one of its own, thank you. Residential neighborhoods here tend to have larger lots and smaller home prices than on the other side of the river. The most significant difference, though, is in taxes. As mentioned earlier in this chapter, the state of Washington doesn't collect state income taxes, and provides substantial property tax relief to low-income senior citizens. Vancouver residents manage to minimize Washington's hefty sales tax by simply crossing the bridge to make their major purchases in Oregon, which has no sales tax at all. Though the practice undoubtedly dismays Vancouver merchants, few other places present such opportunities to dodge taxes legally.

Recreation and Culture The city's Parks and Recreation Department operates one of the most extensive programs of activities for seniors that we've seen anywhere, including a wide assortment of adult education classes, a free monthly newspaper, health, legal and insurance benefit consultations, clubs, free massages, dances and special events. There are even seniors-only classes in tap dancing. The department's Luepke Center also produces a weekly television program called "Elder Court," on which senior volunteers debate hot issues facing older adults today. In 1996, the center initiated a Senior Trade Fair designed to introduce senior citizens to the full range of services and organizations available in the community.

The Forever Young Hiking Club organizes hikes to scenic spots in the area almost every weekend. Additionally, golfers can stretch their legs at two area courses: Bowyer's Golf Course (9 holes, par 27) and Pine Crest Golf Course (9 holes, par 27).

Clark College offers more than 40 classes, including seminars and field trips, focusing on mature learning. Enrollment in these courses is limited to persons age 55 and over, and about 1,100 seniors sign up for them each quarter.

Housing and Other Costs Real estate prices are roughly the same as in the Puget Sound area. The average selling price for a two- to three-bedroom home is $130,000. Condominiums are available in all price ranges, from about $45,000 for an 800-square-foot unit to $350,000 for a luxury condo overlooking the river. House rentals start at $750 a month, and apartment rents start at $600. Other cost-of-living factors are about average for western Washington.

Medical Care Vancouver has two hospitals, both under the same management: St. Joseph Community Hospital and Vancouver Memorial Hospital. Residents also take advantage of the full range of health care facilities and services available across the river in Portland, Oregon.

Crime and Safety As part of the Portland metropolitan area, Vancouverites face the personal security worries inherent in living in any big city. The Columbia River and its bridges seem to present a partial barrier against crime, however, as statistical rates for both personal and property crimes run about 15 percent lower in Vancouver than in Portland.

When Grandkids Visit Fort Vancouver National Historic Site, a reconstruction of the first fur trading post in the Pacific Northwest established by the Hudson's Bay Company in 1824, gives visitors a look at the area's frontier heritage. Volunteers in period costume demonstrate pioneer skills from cooking to blacksmithing. Also at the historic site, an archaeological dig has unearthed portions of the original fort.

Important Addresses and Connections

Chamber of Commerce: 404 E. 15th St. #11, Vancouver, WA 98663.

Senior Center: Leupke Center, 1009 East McLoughlin Blvd., Vancouver, WA 98668.

Newspaper: *Vancouver Columbian,* P.O. Box 180, Vancouver, WA 98668; *Senior Messenger,* P.O. Box 1995, Vancouver, WA 98668.

Airport: Portland International Airport, located on the south bank of the Columbia, is actually closer to Vancouver than to Portland.

Bus/Train: Daily bus service is provided by RAZ Bus Lines, an Oregon-based Greyhound affiliate. Vancouver is on more Amtrak routes than any other city in the West.

VANCOUVER	Jan.	Apr.	July	Oct.	Rain	Snow
Daily Highs	44	63	80	64	39	8
Daily Lows	33	42	55	46	in.	in.

Goldendale

Goldendale has four seasons and a large retired population, but not many vacant homes.
    —Bob Johnson

In the late 1980s, the town of Goldendale became one of the first Washington towns to launch a campaign to draw retirees into their midst. Goldendale's economy had been on the decline for several years. Replacing regular industry with retirees, the nonpolluting industry, seemed to be a solution.

With the population dwindling, the civic leaders placed classified ads in major California newspapers, urging retirees to resettle there. The ads boasted of Goldendale's low taxes and utility costs, and good recreation and health facilities. The result, a slow, steady migration of senior citizens into Goldendale, has proven the campaign a success.

The only problem is, in a town this size, it doesn't take many newcomers to create a housing shortage. Since 1990, about 325 people have moved into town—a nearly 10 percent growth rate—but new housing construction has been minimal. Population statistics give some sense of how isolated Goldendale is: with a population of 3,700, it is the largest town in 2,000-square-mile Klickitat County.

Be aware that this area is out of the Pacific Coast's "green belt" of forest and heavy rainfall. Goldendale participates in typical eastern Washington weather patterns, with half to a third as much rainfall as along the coast. Also, it's somewhat isolated and lacks public transportation.

Recreation and Culture   Fishing is good in the Klickitat, Deschutes and Columbia rivers for salmon, steelhead, trout, walleye, bass and sturgeon. Rockhounds search the lava cliffs near town for agates and petrified wood. In the spring, a favorite pastime in the area is hunting for morel and chanterelle mushrooms. Golfers meet at the Goldendale Golf Course (9 holes, par 36).

The premier museum in the area is the Maryhill Museum, an elegant three-story mansion built by roadbuilder Sam Hill as a residence for him and his wife Mary. It was converted to a museum without ever having been lived in, when Mary refused to take up residence so far from civilization. The museum contains a spectacular and unusual series of collections, including Rodin sculptures, stone heads carved by pre-Columbian Indians, antique camera equipment, dozens of unique chess sets and the Romanian royal furniture. Goldendale's excellent public library, established in 1912, is one of the few original Carnegie Libraries still in existence.

Housing and Other Costs   Recent home listings in Goldendale have ranged from $80,000 to $100,000, but houses come on the market infrequently. There are no condominiums in the area. Houses occasionally come up for rent at $400 to $650 a month, and the few apartments in town rent for $400 to $450. The biggest bargain in Goldendale real estate today is acreage for building sites, which starts around $500 an acre; construction materials cost more because of the expense of transporting them to this remote area, but labor costs are lower. Housing aside, the overall cost of living is about the same as in the Tri-Cities area and less than in western Washington communities.

Medical Care   The Klickitat Valley Hospital has a total of 31 beds. For major non-emergency procedures, residents go to Portland, 120 miles away.

Crime and Safety   The FBI's crime statistics do not mention Goldendale. When we inquired locally, a sheriff's deputy responded, "Crime? You must be thinkin' of some other place."

When Grandkids Visit   One of Goldendale's proudest assets is a truly spectacular night sky, free from pollution or city lights. Goldendale Observatory, set on the summit of an extinct volcano on the outskirts of town, has one of the largest reflecting telescopes open to public use anywhere in the world. Tours are offered in the afternoon, and evening programs give visitors of all ages the chance to see planets, stars and occasionally comets for themselves.

Important Addresses and Connections

Chamber of Commerce: P.O. Box 524, Goldendale, WA 98620.

Senior Services: Klickitat County Adult Services, 228 West Main St., Room 110, Goldendale, WA 98620; Senior Center, 115 East Main St., Goldendale, WA 98620.

Weekly Newspaper: *Goldendale Sentinel,* 117 West Main Street, Goldendale, WA 98620.

Airport: The nearest airport with passenger service is Portland International Airport, 120 miles away.

Bus: Amtrak stops for pre-ticketed passengers in Wishram, a tiny river-bank hamlet ten miles south of Goldendale. The closest place to catch a Greyhound bus is The Dalles, Oregon, 30 miles away.

GOLDENDALE	Jan.	Apr.	July	Oct.	Rain	Snow
Daily Highs	37	62	84	63	16	7
Daily Lows	22	34	50	36	in.	in.

Tri-Cities

Our community offers a spectrum of cultural, sports and intellectual activities sure to make your stay enjoyable, whether it be for a day or a lifetime!

—Jim Hansen, Mayor, City of Richland

Situated on the banks of the Columbia River in eastern Washington, the cities of Richland, Pasco and Kennewick have grown into a single metropolitan area commonly referred to as the Tri-Cities. Like other eastern Washington towns, the Tri-Cities with their brown, desertlike setting may appear less than charming on first impression. The area's subtle attractions reveal themselves slowly over the seasons: 300 sunny days a year, little rain or snowfall, low humidity, and the constant, calming presence of North America's second-largest river.

The Tri-Cities are situated where the Snake and Yakima Rivers flow into the Columbia. The rivers separate the three cities—Pasco on the north bank of the Columbia, Richland south of the Columbia but north of the Yakima, and Kennewick on the south banks of both rivers. Though city boosters make much of the historical fact that Lewis and Clark camped at a site near present-day Pasco in 1805, the three towns were mere farming hamlets with a few hundred residents until 1943, when the federal government began construction on the nation's first nuclear reactor at the Hanford Site, 25 miles north of Richland in the middle of a vast, vacant expanse of desert land. The population boom was sudden and spectacular. Richland grew from 300 people to 15,000 in a single year, and the other two towns were not far behind.

By the height of the Cold War in the mid-1960s, the Tri-Cities had more Ph.D.'s per capita than any other city in the world, and it had long since surpassed Seattle as the community with the highest per-capita income in Washington state. The Department of Energy employed 45,000 people at the Hanford Site, operating nine nuclear reactors that produced huge amounts of weapons-grade plutonium. Workers poured into the Tri-Cities area, drawn by some of the highest wage rates in the United States. But by the early 1980s, the dark side of the nuclear age cast a shadow over the Tri-Cities.

The level of radioactive material production at Hanford was staggering: the nine reactors produced an average of 75,000 pounds of plutonium per day! In earlier years, not much attention was paid to the problems surrounding the disposal of nuclear waste. The stuff was simply placed in 100-gallon steel drums and buried in the desert. Later the drums began to leak and, in at least one case, catch fire. When it was discovered that radioactivity in the Columbia River had reached the highest levels of any river on earth, state politicians pressured the Department of Energy to shut the Hanford Site down. Many thousands of people were thrown out of work and forced to leave the Tri-Cities, and in many cases they were unable to sell their homes at any price.

Today, massive cleanup efforts at the Hanford Site have brought a new influx of residents to the Tri-Cities. In fact, the cleanup employs more people than the construction and operation of the nuclear facilities ever did. Most neighborhoods are new here, a consequence of fast growth during the past two decades, and an overall prosperity is evident.

The Tri-Cities are also a major agricultural center. Besides producing wheat, the irrigated desert land is great for grape-growing, and the Tri-Cities have many highly regarded wineries. Although Pasco may not live up to the damp, green expectations most folks have of Washington, there are certain advantages to living in the eastern part of the state. Besides being a place that actively seeks retirees, the Pasco-Kennewick-Richland area offers great real estate prices and an interesting climate. Even in the coldest part of winter, when the temperature drops to 20 degrees in the morning, you could be fishing for salmon or sturgeon that same afternoon on the Columbia River bank in your shirt sleeves. Like rain, snowfall here is slight. Sunshine is plentiful, and being outdoors is a pleasure year-round. A low-humidity summer rounds out the weather picture. Still, despite assurances from the Department of Energy, few people believe that the environment around the Tri-Cities today is 100-percent safe; one's personal attitude toward radioactivity must be the determining factor in deciding whether the area is a viable retirement possibility!

Recreation and Culture The Tri-Cities boast eight public and private golf courses, including Canyon Lakes Golf Course (18 holes, par 72) in Kennewick, the Sham Na Pum Golf Course (18 holes, par 70) in Richland, and the Pasco Municipal Golf Course (18 holes, par 72). The Columbia River invites boating, fishing and birdwatching. Jet-skis, paddleboats, sailboats, hovercrafts, party barges and houseboats can be rented. Spectator sports include the Tri-City Chinook minor-league basketball team, the Tri-City Americans hockey team, and spring and fall quarter horse racing at the Sundowns racetrack.

Performing arts groups in the area include the Richland Players and Ye Merrie Greenwood Players theater companies, the

Mid-Columbia Regional Ballet, the Mid-Columbia Symphony, the Richland Light Opera, and the Camerata Musica chamber music ensemble.

If you seek mental stimulation, the Columbia Basin College in Pasco has a large continuing education program that serves over two thousand adult enrollees, including two to three hundred seniors, per quarter. The college has 17 instructors specifically to teach classes designed for seniors. Tuition is subsidized for students over age 60, who pay only $13.50 per class, instead of the usual course fees of more than $100. The college also offers an inexpensive "Gold Card" for seniors, entitling them to audit any classes they wish and attend concerts, plays, and other school activities for free.

Housing and Other Costs Although the Tri-Cities became known in the late 1980s as having the lowest cost of living in the United States, today they are somewhat more expensive than other small cities in the region with slower growth rates, such as Pendleton, Oregon, and Walla Walla and Spokane, Washington. An average two-bedroom home sells for $85,000, and a three-bedroom for $115,00 to $120,000.

During the area's atomic heyday, the Tri-Cities had the highest per-capita income and education level in Washington, and as a result the area has more than its share of large, upmarket suburban houses, a fair number of them for lease. Rents for both apartments and small houses start at $500, while custom homes rent for as much as $1,500.

Medical Care Our Lady of Lourdes Hospital in Pasco, Kadlec Hospital in Richland and Kennewick General Hospital have a combined total of 349 beds and offer a full range of services including cancer treatment facilities rated among the best in the state. Prospective Tri-Cities residents should be aware that serious health problems including cancer occur among long-time residents at such high rates that they are the basis for many lawsuits now pending against the Department of Energy.

Crime and Safety Crime rates, which are almost exactly the same as the overall rates for Washington state, appear to be going down. The crime rate is slightly higher in Pasco and slightly lower in Kennewick.

When Grandkids Visit The biggest kid-pleaser in the Tri-Cities is Oasis Waterworks, a huge playground with eleven water slides, a rolling river ride and a hot tub that will seat 100, as well as baseball batting cages, volleyball courts, a basketball court, concession stands and a vast video arcade.

Important Addresses and Connections

Chamber of Commerce: P.O. Box 2241, Tri-Cities, WA 99302.

Senior Centers: Kennewick Senior Citizen Center, 500 South Auburn, Kennewick, WA 99336; Pasco Senior Center, 1315 North 7, Pasco, WA 99301; Richland Senior Center, 506 Newton Street, Richland, WA 99352.

Newspaper: *Tri-City Herald,* P.O. Box 2608, Tri-Cities, WA 99302.

Airport: Tri-Cities Airport, on the northern outskirts of Pasco, has daily commuter flights to Seattle, Spokane and Portland.

Bus/Train: Greyhound buses stop in Pasco en route between Spokane and Portland. Amtrak's Empire Builder also stops in Pasco on its way between the same two cities.

TRI-CITIES	Jan.	Apr.	July	Oct.	Rain	Snow
Daily Highs	36	69	90	65	16	6
Daily Lows	22	38	56	38	in.	in.

The Eastern Cascades

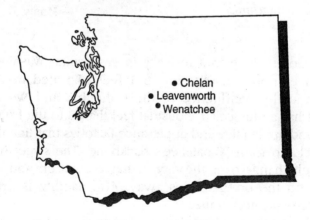

One-hundred-twenty miles due east of Seattle, on the other side of the Cascade Mountains, lies the heart of Washington's fruit orchard country. Like everyplace east of the Cascades, this part of central Washington is too far from the sea (and civilization) to attract large numbers of retirees. Whereas tens of thousands of retirees move to the Puget Sound area annually, older newcomers to "apple country" number a few dozen a year. The majority of senior citizens in the area have spent much of their lives here.

Yet the area has a particular kind of charm that's easy to fall in love with. The orchards that line the two-lane highways produce more apples than any other agricultural area in North America. In the spring, the spectacle of fruit trees bursting into flower is breathtaking. At harvest time, roadside produce stands and u-pick-em orchards invite you to enjoy the pick of the fruit crop. The fruit orchards fill valleys sheltered by mountain slopes clad in ponderosa pine. In addition to the orchards and forests, there are lakes amid these foothills, where residents (and plenty of visitors) fish, swim and boat in the summer. In the winter, the few feet of snowfall hereabouts makes for good skiing, but the winter weather is mostly dry and hardly unbearable.

Wenatchee / Leavenworth

Leavenworth, Cashmere and Wenatchee are gathering speed as retirement spots. Some retirees don't like the snow, but many love to cross-country and downhill ski. Those that live here tend not to be snowbirds.
                                                            —Monty Turner

The closest thing to a real city in east-central Washington is Wenatchee (pop. 22,000, elev. 651 feet). Located in the dry foothills at the confluence of the Columbia and Wenatchee Rivers, it has a blue-collar industrial feel thanks to the fruit warehouses and apple juice and applesauce factories that line the railroad tracks to form Wenatchee's backbone. The sweet scent of apple pulp hangs over the city in harvest season and can be smelled on the breeze miles away. Affordability is probably Wenatchee's greatest virtue.

Up the Wenatchee River lie a pair of smaller towns, each with its own unique character. Cashmere (pop. 2,500; elev. 795 feet), five miles west of Wenatchee, has been refurbished in cheerful Victorian and Early American style. Its only major industry is a factory that makes Turkish-style fruit-flavored candies called Aplets and Cotlets. Ten miles farther upriver, Leavenworth (pop.

2,000, elev. 1,164 feet) is a self-styled Bavarian village surrounded by dramatic mountain peaks.

Both Cashmere and Leavenworth were originally inhabited by loggers and railroad workers. The railroad was rerouted in the 1920s, however, and the lumber mills soon shut down. The Aplets candy factory, which opened in Cashmere in 1920, created enough employment to keep the town alive, but Leavenworth dwindled to a near ghost town before 1972, when a local women's club started Project LIFE (Leavenworth Improvement For Everyone), a task force designed to refurbish Leavenworth's image in a way that would attract enough tourism to boost the town's sagging economy.

The Leavenworth townsfolk voted on a whole range of gimmicks, and the winner—despite the fact that the community's German heritage was vague and tenuous—was "Bavarian Village." So they opened beer gardens, schnitzel restaurants and curio shops that sold Hummel figurines. They transformed the traditional apple harvest festival into an Oktoberfest complete with oom-pah bands and slap dancers. They slapped an Alpine ski-lodge facade on the local supermarket and opened a score of European-style bed-and-breakfast inns.

The odd thing is that Leavenworth's born-again Bavarianism actually works. The old mountain town's transformation into one of the most popular spots for weekend getaways from the greater Seattle area has endured for more than a generation now, and locals seem to find it perfectly natural to dress for work in dirndl skirts and lederhosen.

More recently, Cashmere has made an attempt to emulate Leavenworth's success by refurbishing its main street in turn-of-the-century style so picture-perfect that it feels like a giant Norman Rockwell painting. Both Leavenworth and Cashmere are remarkably friendly little towns. Locals seem eager to welcome newcomers of all ages who want to play a role in their Disneylandish communities. True, the winters are cold and snow-packed, but for some retirees, these towns are ideal places to leave urban America behind and adopt an alternative way of life.

Recreation and Culture People come to the Leavenworth area from all parts of the state for hiking and bicycling, especially along Icicle Creek and its tributaries in the mountains east of town. Many of these trails are also groomed for cross-country skiing in the winter. A major forest fire in 1994 forced the forest service to close some major hiking trails indefinitely to prevent erosion, so trails that remain open in the Icicle Creek area see heavy use.

Wenatchee has the municipal Three Lakes Golf Course (18 holes, par 69), as well as two private courses in East Wenatchee. In Leavenworth, there's the public Leavenworth Golf Club (18 holes, par 71).

In the Wenatchee area, the Columbia River gives anglers a chance at all species of fish that reside in area rivers and streams flowing into the Columbia, including cutthroat, steelhead, coho, chinook, sockeye, largemouth and smallmouth bass, and catfish. Wenatchee Lake, in the national forest northwest of Leavenworth, offers good fishing for rainbow trout and kokanee salmon.

Practically the only cultural events in the area are community festivals. Leavenworth has lots of them, beginning with the annual Mai Fest and continuing with the International Folk Dance Festival, the International Accordian Celebration, Oktoberfest and a lavish Christmas lighting ceremony. Wenatchee's big annual celebration, the Apple Blossom Festival, attracts hordes of sightseers from the Seattle area in early May.

There are educational opportunities here—Wenatchee Valley College offers more than 100 adult education courses, including special state-subsidized "Senior College" classes for those age 55 and up. The favorite courses among retirees here are the computer classes. Finally, the Wenatchee senior center also offers a full schedule of fitness and health classes.

Housing and Other Costs
Compared to western Washington, Wenatchee is a quite affordable place to live. There are plenty of nothing-special tract homes for sale in the $80,000 range, and beautifully restored Victorians sell for $110,000 to $160,000. Two- and three-bedroom houses rent in the $800-a-month range, and apartment rents average $600 a month. In the countryside, family farms with fruit orchards can be bought for around $500,000.

Housing prices are higher in Leavenworth and Cashmere, where home prices start around $120,000 and range as high as $800,000. Most retirees in these towns live in condominiums, which are plentiful and average around $125,000. Rental houses and apartments are scarce in both communities.

Cost-of-living factors other than housing are roughly the same in Wenatchee as in the Seattle area. Expect high winter heating bills in Leavenworth, where propane and electricity are costly ways to keep frigid mountain temperatures at bay.

Medical Care In Wenatchee, the 48-bed Central Washington Hospital serves a large rural area. About 100 physicians practice in the Wenatchee area; 40 percent of them are surgical specialists. Supplementing the hospital in Wenatchee, Leavenworth's Cascade Medical Center has 33 beds for inpatient care, though surgical facilities are limited.

Crime and Safety Violent crimes are uncommon in Wenatchee and virtually nonexistent in Cashmere and Leavenworth. Burglary and theft, however, have reportedly reached epidemic levels in Wenatchee and begun to spill over into the surrounding countryside. Part-year residents who migrate south for the winter are well-advised to leave their homes in the care of a housesitter or watchman.

When Grandkids Visit A working electric train modeled after the Great Northern Railway, some of the oldest Indian artifacts found in North America and an old-fashioned apple-packing factory are among the exhibits at the North Central Washington Museum in Wenatchee. Better may be a free tour of the Aplets factory in Cashmere, where they make ten tons of candy per day.

Important Addresses and Connections

Chambers of Commerce: P.O. Box 7195, East Wenatchee, WA 98801; P.O. Box 327, Leavenworth, WA 98826; P.O. Box 834, Cashmere, WA 98815.

Senior Centers: Wenatchee Valley Senior Center, 1312 Maple St., Wenatchee, WA 98801; Cashmere Senior Center, 120 Cottage Ave., Cashmere, WA 98815.

Newspapers: *Wenatchee Daily World,* P.O. Box 1511, Wenatchee, WA 98801; *Leavenworth Echo,* 215 14th St., Leavenworth, WA 98826.

Airport: Local Pangborn Memorial Airport has commuter flights.

Bus/Train: Greyhound buses stop in Wenatchee. Amtrak's Empire Builder offers daily service from Wenatchee to Seattle, and points east. There is also a free, frequent Link shuttle bus to and from Wenatchee.

LEAVENWORTH	Jan.	Apr.	July	Oct.	Rain	Snow
Daily Highs	32	63	84	61	9	36
Daily Lows	19	38	56	37	in.	in.

Chelan

Sure, it's crowded with tourists in the summertime. Why would you want to live in a place people don't want to visit?
—Elaine Reed

The deepest body of water in Washington is not Puget Sound but Lake Chelan, 1,500 feet deep, 55 miles long, and only two miles across at its widest point. The town of Chelan (pop. 2,800) is located among the arid foothills at the lake's southern end. It is a mecca for boating enthusiasts, who can cruise the long waterway into the mountains that enclose the northern half of the lake with sheer granite cliffs where mountain goats roam. At the upper end of the lake, the tiny village of Stehekin serves as a wilderness gateway for North Cascades National Park.

Chelan is a madhouse of activity during the summer months, when boaters flock over the mountains from the Seattle area and tourists come from all over to ride the Lady of the Lake passenger ferries, which cruise the length of the lake daily. Bed-and-breakfast inns seem to be the main industry in town, and Chelan's municipal RV park is one of the largest in the state.

One thing Chelan has plenty of is waterfront property. Houses line both shores of the lake for miles, giving the whole community a pleasant resort ambience. Virtually everybody in town owns a boat, and most people park them by the front door and use them instead of cars to go to the supermarket. While a high percentage of the houses are vacation homes owned by Seattlites, an even higher percentage of full-time residents are retired. The reason? There are few jobs in the area at any time of year and virtually none outside of tourist season.

The main drawback to living full-time in Chelan is a lack of cultural depth. Everything is geared toward tourism, and during the two-thirds of the year when there are no tourists in town, there seem to be few activities to occupy active minds. Seattle is 175 miles away, and during the winter one and sometimes both highway routes over the mountains are closed by snow. The nearest city, Wenatchee, has bookstores but little else.

Recreation and Culture Lake Chelan Municipal Golf Course (18 holes, par 72) enjoys a scenic location on a bluff overlooking the lake. Water sports, however, are the main attraction. Activities permitted on Lake Chelan include sailing, canoeing, kayaking, water skiing, jet-skiing and (for those who dare to plunge into shockingly cold water) swimming. Fish in Lake Chelan include smallmouth bass, ling cod, kokanee and chinook salmon and cutthroat, rainbow and lake trout.

Housing and Other Costs
Most houses around Lake Chelan were originally built as vacation homes, and although more people have moved to the area full-time in recent years, few houses are very large. Both two-bedroom houses and two-bedroom condominiums range in price from $125,000 to $150,000. Rental homes are priced for the vacation trade—typically $700 to $1,000 a month. There are virtually no apartments for rent in town. Food and fuel prices run a little higher because of Chelan's remote location.

Medical Care
Lake Chelan Community Hospital has 34 beds. No other hospital in the area is much larger. For major procedures and specialized treatment, residents must go to either Seattle or Spokane, each a four-hour drive away. (Spokane's huge Sacred Heart Medical Center, rated as one of the best hospitals in the United States, is considered by many to be superior even to most facilities in the Seattle area.)

Crime and Safety
The crime rate in Chelan is so low as to be unmeasurable. The biggest problems, according to local officials, are alcohol-related incidents during the summer months.

When Grandkids Visit
The Lady of the Lake ferry cruise is the must-do activity for all Chelan visitors, though it is long enough to bore smaller children to tears. There's nothing boring about Slidewaters Water Park, where kids age 4 and up can play all day and still not want to leave.

Important Addresses and Connections
Chamber of Commerce: P.O. Box 216, Chelan WA 98816.

Senior Centers: Chelan Senior Social Club, 534 Trow, Chelan, WA 98816; Senior Citizens Center, 109 S. Bridge St., Brewster, 98812.

Newspaper: *Lake Chelan Mirror,* 315 Woodin Ave., Chelan, WA 98816.

Airport: Pangborn Memorial Airport, about 50 miles from Chelan in East Wenatchee.

Bus: Link shuttle buses run regularly between Chelan and Wenatchee, and they're free!

CHELAN	Jan.	Apr.	July	Oct.	Rain	Snow
Daily Highs	32	64	87	62	9	14
Daily Lows	19	39	59	38	in.	in.

BRITISH COLUMBIA

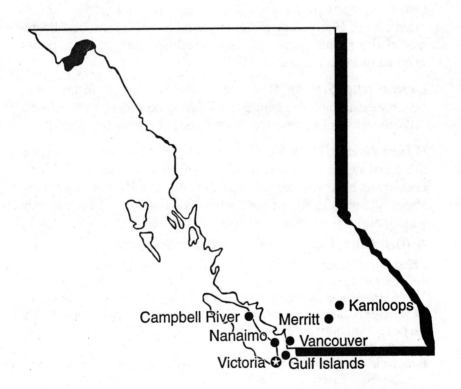

Campbell River ●   ● Merritt   ● Kamloops

Nanaimo ● ● Vancouver

Victoria ✪ ● Gulf Islands

British Columbia, odd as it may seem, is Canada's answer to Florida. Not all of British Columbia, of course; the entire northern half of the province is near-roadless, subarctic, mountain wilderness, and most of the southern half remains a frontier as thinly populated as anyplace in the United States. Although British Columbia is as large as the states of Washington, Oregon and California combined, more than 85 percent of the population lives in the southwest corner—in Vancouver, the largest city, or Victoria, the provincial capital.

Mention the word "retirement" in Canada, and for most folks the first place that comes to mind is Victoria. Situated at the southernmost point of Canada's Pacific coast, it is known far and wide as having the country's most temperate climate. In fact, Victoria's climate is just slightly cooler and damper than that of most towns in the Puget Sound area of Washington. Canadian weather doesn't get any better than this.

For most U.S. citizens, the fabled Victorian climate provides little reason to choose British Columbia, but there are other allures. Canadian cities and towns are cleaner and safer than their U.S. counterparts. During the (all too brief) summer months, the spectacular scenery of the Canadian Rockies and the remote islands and fjords of the northern coast are all the reason needed to become a seasonal resident.

The most common reason we have heard from expatriates for choosing to live in British Columbia is simply, "It's not the United States." For those who share this sort of disenchantment, British Columbia offers a convenient, quietly dignified English-speaking alternative. At first, Canada may seem just like the United States. After living there for a few months, small differences can endear Canada to some newcomers and drive others back across the border where things are more "normal."

Freeway signs are blue instead of green. Official signs are in French as well as English. Measurements are metric. Canadian cigarettes cost more than twice as much as in the United States. Gasoline costs more, too, but since it is priced in Canadian dollars and sold by the liter, you have to be a math whiz to notice the difference. U.S. dollars spend just as readily as Canadian ones in Victoria and Vancouver, but until newcomers switch over to Canadian currency, they must remember to keep Canadian pocket change separate from U.S. currency and convert prices to U.S. dollars (worth about 30 percent more) in their heads.

U.S.-style football attracts little interest in western Canada, although you can watch it on cable television. There is a local professional basketball team—the NBA's brand-new Vancouver Grizzlies. However, the most popular professional sport in British Columbia (and all of Canada, for that matter) is hockey. The Vancouver Canucks (NHL) have many faithful fans hereabouts. Finally, curling, a game that combines elements of shuffleboard, bowling and ice hockey, is enormously popular in this part of the country. Both a spectator sport and a participatory pastime, curling is played by people of all age groups from schoolchildren to senior citizens.

With property laws and political systems that mirror those of Great Britain, Canada is a British commonwealth—an independent nation that nonetheless pledges allegiance to the English monarchy. Unlike Great Britain, however, egalitarian Canada does not otherwise recognize nobility, and neither the national nor the British Columbian parliament has a House of Lords. Despite the trappings of British tradition, Canada's government is a rather small and simple bureaucracy. In British Columbia, which historically has had stronger ties to the British Crown than to eastern Canada, the provincial government is a stronger presence than the national government.

British Columbians have a keen love of nature and support strict environmental protection measures in developed areas of the province. Paradoxically, British Columbia's vigorous economy is fueled mainly by fishing, logging, mining, oil drilling and hydroelectric dams. There has been little of the sort of conflict over environmental policy that has divided the people of Oregon and Washington in recent years. The unimaginable vastness of the British Columbian wilderness, reaching northward to the virtually uninhabited Northwest Territories, nudges even the most outspoken environmental activists toward a "plenty more where that came from" attitude.

A subtle and very real difference between British Columbian and U.S. cities is that the crime rate is much lower. One major reason is gun control: all firearms are licensed, and handguns, as well as assault weapons, are totally banned. Some locals say that Canadian criminals move south of the border where there is more opportunity to practice their trade. Less than two percent of crimes committed in the province involve the use of a weapon. Liquor consumption is higher in Canada than in the United

States, though, and more than 80 percent of all crimes are classified as "alcohol-related."

Only about 3,000 foreign retirees "officially" moved to Canada in 1994 (the actual number being significantly higher), about half of them choosing British Columbia. Present immigration laws mean that for most older non-Canadians, becoming a legal resident of Canada is difficult or even impossible. This does not rule out living here or even owning a home. It simply means that if you choose Canada and do not have a close relative here or a sizeable sum of investment capital, you will fall into a visitor category, requiring you to leave the country at least once every six months. This arrangement is ideal for snowbirds who prefer to enjoy British Columbia's cool, green summers but dodge off to Texas, Mexico or Costa Rica when those long, bleak Canadian winters set in. (Immigration laws are discussed in detail elsewhere in this chapter.)

Most retirees, both U.S. and Canadian, who move to British Columbia choose to live in the greater Victoria area or in the Gulf Islands, which lie off the eastern shore of Vancouver Island, a short distance north of Victoria. The

> **British Columbia**
> 7th province
> August 1, 1871
>
> **Provincial Capital:** Victoria
> **Population (1990):** 3,535,000; rank, 3rd
> **Population Density:** 9.8 per sq. mile; urban, 80.5%, rural: 19.5%.
> **Geography:** 365,947 square miles. Highest elevation: 15,300 feet at Fairweather Mountain; lowest elevation: sea level on Pacific coast.

city of Vancouver, British Columbia's financial, manufacturing and high-tech center, lacks the allure for retirees that Victoria has, but it's worthy of investigation for those who prefer the advantages of a big-city environment. We have encountered retirees in other towns throughout southern British Columbia, but nothing that could be called a senior citizens' community. The occasional retired person from the United States we have found in these towns seemed to be completely unaware of any other U.S. expatriates living anywhere in British Columbia (and often likes it that way).

History

Since prehistoric times, coastal British Columbia has been home to First Americans (the Canadian term for American Indians) of the Kwakiutl, Nootka, Salish, Haida, Bella Coola and Tsimshian tribes. The first European explorers arrived by sailing ship in the late 1700s. Sea captain George Vancouver claimed the remote reaches of the Pacific coast for England, while others claimed it for Spain and Russia. None established a permanent colony until 1843, when the Hudson Bay Company founded Victoria as a fur trading outpost.

The Canadian government declared Vancouver Island a territory in 1849, with Victoria as its capital, but it remained little more than a fort in the wilderness until 1858. Then gold was discovered along the upper Fraser River Valley and in the Cariboo Mountains of eastern British Columbia, and thousands of prospectors made their way up the coast from the gold fields of California to stake their claims. Victoria, the closest port to the gold fields, experienced a population boom.

In 1863, Vancouver Island was merged into the new territory of British Columbia, and Victoria (which had a larger population than all the rest of British Columbia) remained the territorial capital. When British Columbians voted to become a Canadian province in 1871, Victoria was still the only city on Canada's Pacific coast. Sixteen years later, in 1887, Canada's transcontinental railroad reached the west coast, and the municipality of Vancouver sprang up at the railroad's terminus the same year. Within another 14 years, it grew to become British Columbia's largest city.

Through most of the 20th century, British Columbia's economy has been built on exploitation of its vast natural resources, especially logging, large-scale salmon fishing, and mining for precious metals. Irrigation projects started after World War I brought large-scale agriculture to some river valleys in the interior, especially the Okanagan Valley, now western Canada's leading fruit producer. The forest products industry has expanded rapidly since 1950, creating more employment in the interior. Since the 1980s, Vancouver has grown into a technology center with economic links to the Pacific Rim countries of Asia. Wealthy immigrants from Hong Kong have brought an influx of new investment capital, transforming Vancouver into the most prosperous city in Canada.

Moving to Canada

Canadian immigration laws have become less hospitable to senior citizens, mainly out of fear that elderly foreigners might flood in to take advantage of the country's national health care system. Canada has complex, sometimes daunting requirements for establishing permanent residence—the condition precedent to becoming a Canadian citizen. Any person who has lived in Canada as a permanent legal resident for at least three years and speaks fluent English or French can become a Canadian citizen by taking a written test that covers the country's history and form of government. Many would-be Canadians find it difficult or impossible to qualify for permanent resident status, however, and present immigration laws discriminate against older persons.

Fortunately, retirees from the United States find it easy to choose Canada as a retirement haven without going through the process of becoming a permanent resident. Tourists, students, artists and others who are in Canada temporarily, termed "visitors" in the immigration laws, can stay in the country for no more than six months (183 days). Then they must leave the country for at least 72 hours before returning for another visit. Citizens of the United States and 52 other nations do not need a visa to enter Canada, however, so there is no record of exactly when they enter or leave the country.

Snowbirds from the U.S. are free to do the same as large numbers of Canadian retirees do: enjoy British Columbia's nearly perfect summer climate, then fly south to tropical beaches at the first sign of snow, to return six months later with the spring thaw. For summertime residents who plan to head south during the cold months, it may be advantageous not to apply for permanent resident status, since permanent residents who remain outside Canada for longer than 183 days lose their immigration status and must reapply.

Living in Canada part-time under a visitor status presents few practical difficulties. You must maintain an address in the United States for such documents as your car registration and drivers license; a relative's address or a private post office box will do. **There are no restrictions on U.S. citizens renting or buying real estate or opening bank accounts in Canada.**

If you live in Canada for more than 183 days in one year, you must pay Canadian and provincial income taxes on all your income, even if it comes from outside the country. **As a visitor, you are not allowed to hold a job;** to do so, you need a Social Insurance Number (SIN), equivalent to a Social Security Number in the United States; to get one, you must show that you have been granted permanent resident status. You also need an SIN to qualify for subsidized health care. For those who are not covered

BRITISH COLUMBIA TAXES

Income Tax

Canada taxes on residency, and all residents of Canada are required to file a tax return, declaring their worldwide income. If you are present in Canada for a period of 183 days or more, you will be considered a resident and will be taxed. However, foreign tax credit may be claimed to offset any double taxation. In most cases the taxpayers will pay the higher of the two taxes, but not both.

Federal and provincial income taxes are more steeply progressive than in the United States. For those in the highest brackets, the combined Canadian federal and British Columbian provincial tax rates can be as high as 54 percent of total income. Most people, however, pay about 17 percent. In Canada, 75 percent of capital gains is included in normal income for tax purposes.

Sales Taxes

Canada also has both federal and provincial Goods and Services Taxes (called "GST"), totalling about 7 percent, on all purchases. Visitors to Canada can claim rebates of the GST on some items, but only if they have stayed in Canada for less than 30 days.

by government-sponsored health insurance, Canadian medical treatment is much more expensive than in the United States, so many expatriates go to doctors in Bellingham, Washington, or even Seattle.

Moving household goods across the border into Canada can create big problems. Immigration officials are often very suspicious about non-immigrants' motives for visiting Canada, and a truckload of home furnishings is sure to bring an interrogation about whether you're really just a tourist. Though it is perfectly legal for a tourist to move into a house or apartment while visiting Canada, customs agents can require you to post a large bond guaranteeing that you will take your personal property back to the United States with you when you leave. Even Canadian citizens and permanent residents face formidable paperwork when bringing furniture and major appliances across the border. The better plan, even though it may mean parting with old, familiar belongings and even though such items cost much more in Canada than in the United States, is to buy the household goods you need in Canada.

Bringing firearms into Canada or having them in your posses-
sion in Canada can also cause problems. Canadians are required
to obtain licenses for all firearms, hunting rifles included. Visitors
are supposed to declare their guns at the border and get temporary permits, normally with a very short duration. Having an unli-
censed gun, or one for which the temporary permit has expired,
can get you deported back to the United States.

Health problems, especially those resulting in hospitalization,
can also result in trouble for long-term visitors who do not have
health insurance that covers them in Canada. While Canada's
national health system takes care of tourists and citizens alike,
the law provides for deportation of any visitor who develops a
disease or disability that "might become a danger to public
health or cause a burden on health care or social services."

Immigrating to Canada

Canadian immigration law has undergone sweeping changes
in the last decade. When Great Britain signed a treaty in the mid-
1980s, agreeing to give the British Crown Colony of Hong Kong
to the People's Republic of China in 1997, it sent Canada's parliament into a mad scramble toward immigration reform.
Previously, it had been a relatively simple matter for residents to
move between countries that were part of the British
Commonwealth, and the impending return of Hong Kong to
China raised the spectre of a mass migration that would flood
western Canada with refugees. This perceived threat spurred
sweeping changes to immigration laws, putting immigrants from
Commonwealth nations and colonies on a par with everyone
else but encouraging immigration by wealthy investors regardless
of nationality. Cynics call the reform a scheme by Parliament to
transplant investment capital from one of the wealthiest cities on
earth, Hong Kong, to underdeveloped western Canada. If so, it's
working like a charm. During the past decade, Asian immigrants
have brought more than nine billion dollars in new investment
capital to British Columbia.

Canadian immigration statutes recognize various categories of
immigrants who can apply to become permanent residents (previously called "landed immigrants"). Any person who has lived in
Canada for three years as a permanent resident is eligible to
become a Canadian citizen upon passing a test on the country's
history, geography and political system. Some immigrant categories are subject to quota restrictions. For most, the government

does not keep a waiting list; if the quota is filled when you apply, you must reapply next year. The immigration classes are:

Spouses, fiancees and children of Canadian residents,
Parents and grandparents of Canadian residents,
Political refugees,
Investors,
Entrepreneurs,
Self-employed people,
Independent workers,
Workers in designated high-demand occupations.

For most classes except parents, grandparents and certain other immediate family members of Canadian citizens or permanent resident, eligibility to become a permanent resident is determined by a point system. The applicant must get a minimum of 70 out of a possible 97 points, based on these criteria:

Educational level—up to 16 points
Specific vocational preparation—up to 18 points
Occupational demand—up to 10 points
Occupational experience—up to 8 points
Approved job offer—up to 10 points
Age—up to 10 points (but no points if you're over age 44)
Fluency in both English and French—up to 15 points
Personal suitability—up to 10 points

In addition, applicants in certain categories get bonus points:

Assisted relatives of Canadian citizens or permanent residents
    —5 points
Entrepreneurs—45 points
Investors—45 points
Self-employed people—up to 30 points

Non-workers age 45 and older can only score 46 points—far less than the minimum score needed—even if they have a postgraduate degree, speak fluent French and have a brother who is a Canadian citizen. In fact, it is virtually impossible to qualify unless you are (1) a parent or grandparent of a Canadian citizen or permanent resident and therefore exempt from the point system, or (2) as an investor, entrepreneur or self-employed person.

Parents and Grandparents A citizen or permanent resident of Canada can sponsor one or both parents of any age, grandparents over age 60, and grandparents under age 60 who are widowed or unable to work. The parents or grandparents do not have to qualify under the point system.

The sponsor must apply inside Canada, and the parent or grandparent must wait until the application is processed—typically six to nine months—before moving to Canada. The number of people who can move to Canada under this classification are limited by an annual quota. Unlike other immigration categories, however, parents or grandparents who are turned away because of the quota are placed on a waiting list ahead of new applicants for the following year. This system, which started in 1993, has not generated large backlogs yet. Still, in British Columbia, due to the large influx of immigrants from Hong Kong and other Pacific Rim countries, the number of applicants in this category presently exceeds the quota each year, meaning that long waits may not be far away. The number of people applying to enter Canada as parents or grandparents has doubled since the 1980s and now stands at about 90,000 each year.

The sponsor becomes legally responsible for the parents' or grandparents' accommodation, care and maintenance for ten years after they enter Canada. In other words, if a parent or grandparent becomes unable to support himself or herself, the government can compel the sponsor to provide financial support. When applying to bring a parent or grandparent into the country, the sponsor must show sufficient income to provide such support if necessary. The amount of income required depends on how many people will be living in the household upon arrival of the new immigrants and on the size of the community in which the sponsor lives. For example, a husband and wife without children, living in Victoria and wishing to sponsor one parent, must show income of at least $22,965 a year (Canadian; about $16,800 U.S.); a couple with two children, living in Vancouver and wishing to sponsor both parents, would have to show an annual income of $35,703 (about $26,100 U.S.).

Entrepreneurs, Self-employed and Investors Three categories of people enjoy special immigration preferences. All come with minimum investment requirements, and the more money involved, the easier it is to obtain immigration approval. Immigrant entrepreneurs, self-employed people and investors are closely monitored by the government and must continue in business for an extended time period, usually five years, before they can terminate their activities and still remain in Canada.

Canada's immigration laws have traditionally been hospitable to "entrepreneurs"—newcomers with the intent and ability to establish, purchase or invest in a business or commercial venture in Canada that will significantly contribute to the economy and create job opportunities for Canadians. While no dollar amount is fixed by law, in British Columbia the investment required to qualify as an entrepreneur is usually $150,000 (about $109,000 U.S.). Applicants to immigrate as entrepreneurs must submit a detailed business plan, including a description of their business and financial track record, to both the Canadian immigration department and the British Columbia Ministry of Economic Development for approval. They are then granted a "conditional admission" and must establish the business successfully—and employ at least two Canadian citizens or permanent residents—within two years or face deportation.

Another immigration category, "self-employed," is intended mainly to bring artists and professionals to Canada, though the category is also open to retailers and other experienced small business operators. It differs from the entrepreneur category in two important ways: the applicant is not required to create jobs for anyone but himself or herself, and the initial investment required may be lower—typically in the $100,000 (about $73,000 U.S.) range. In addition, the self-employed applicant must prove that he or she has previous experience in the same business activity. The self-employed applicant gets a lower priority under the immigration points system, and the immigration officer has more discretion in evaluating the applicant's chances of success. For these reasons, persons over age 44 face a more difficult time qualifying as self-employed people than as entrepreneurs.

Since 1986, immigration eligibility has been expanded to include a new "investor" category for those who wish to immigrate to Canada, while bringing substantial funds for capital investment, even though they do not intend to actively operate a business. The new policy has attracted billions in new investment funds to Canada over the past decade.

In British Columbia, the vast majority of newcomers entering Canada under the investor category have been wealthy Hong Kong citizens seeking to leave before the island reverted to the control of the People's Republic of China. A trickle of wealthy retirees from the U.S. has also taken advantage of this category.

To qualify for investor status, an individual must have a personal net worth of at least $500,000 (about $375,000 U.S.) acquired by his or her own endeavors (a provision designed to prevent families from giving money to a single family member to "buy" permanent resident status and then sponsor other family members). The applicant must be prepared to invest at least $350,000 ($260,000 U.S.) in a Canadian business, investment syndicate, or government-managed capital venture fund. The investment must be irrevocable for a period of five years. Although investors need not actively participate in operating the business they invest in, they must show that they have managed a business successfully in the past.

British Columbia, which has attracted more investment under this law than any other province in the country, has one of the highest minimum investment requirements. Some other provinces, especially those in midwestern Canada, require smaller dollar amounts, though the $500,000 net-worth requirement applies throughout the country.

The immigration laws are amended frequently, and the trend in recent years has been to increase investment capital requirements while lowering the number of points needed to qualify for permanent resident status. Still, the current influx of wealthy Asians into Vancouver is meeting increased resistance due to a widespread belief that immigrants force consumer prices up. A growing political backlash may bring about a tightening of immigration laws governing self-employed, entrepreneur and investor categories in the future.

Health Considerations The principal reason Canada's parliament has opted to make formal immigration more difficult for retirees in recent years is to prevent an excessive drain on the resources of the national health care system. Authorities have expressed concern that elderly immigrants might flood Canada to take advantage of the fact that the government subsidizes medical and hospital services for citizens and permanent residents.

As a result, all immigration applicants are required to submit to a medical examination by a government physician in Canada. Mandatory tests include a chest x-ray, a blood test, a urinalysis and, in some cases, a stool examination. Immigration applications will be denied not only to persons carrying a disease that poses a danger to public health, such as tuberculosis, smallpox or cholera, but also to persons who suffer from "any disease or disorder or impairment that would cause, or might reasonably be expected to cause, excessive demand on health or social services." On these grounds, Canada has generally denied immigrant status to persons with conditions such as kidney disease and cancers of all types. In one recent instance, a woman who had a history of breast cancer was refused admission even though her U.S. physician had declared her cured. (She later received permission to immigrate, when five years had passed after her mastectomy with no recurrence of the cancer.)

Victoria & Vancouver Island

This is the place for those who love gardening. The British tradition of formal gardens is very strong in Victoria. We have a long, moist growing season, and absolutely anything will grow.
—Mary Beth Guinn

Victoria, British Columbia's capital, basks on the southern tip of Vancouver Island and sparkles in Canada's mildest climate. Averaging 2,183 hours of sunshine a year, it is the sunniest spot in the province and the gentlest in the country in terms of climate, environment, and lifestyle. The city itself is small, with a population of about 110,000, but this figure is somewhat misleading; another 180,000 people reside in the city's rapidly growing independent suburbs. Victoria is in the economic shadow of its larger mainland neighbor, Vancouver, and it has very little industry. The main employer, the provincial government, is expanding—but not nearly enough to account for Victoria's rapid population growth. Much of the growth is due to the continual flow of people from all over Canada who come to Victoria to retire.

Canada's Pacific Naval Fleet was based at Esquimault Harbor, just west of Victoria, until 1905. Many navy men returned to Victoria after leaving military service. The word spread among naval and civilian seamen that this was the place to retire, and this may be the origin of Victoria's modern-day reputation as the Canadian retirement mecca. Although Victoria is smaller than Vancouver, it has the largest and best-equipped hospital facilities in British Columbia. It also has an excellent public transportation system within the city, around the island and across the Strait of

Georgia to the mainland. Perhaps most importantly, it has a big, lively network of clubs and organizations for older residents, making it hard to sink into the kind of loneliness that can be a problem in some larger cities.

Victoria's character and traditions are derived from a unique history. The first settlement in western Canada, Victoria was founded in 1843 as a fur trading post for the Hudson's Bay Company. It quickly became home to one of the world's largest whaling and sealing boat fleets. In the mid-19th century, Victoria held the distinction of being the most remote outpost of civilization in North America. Its unique cultural heritage continues to shape Victoria's character today. Where else would you find a Scottish bagpiper playing by the base of a totem pole in the shadow of the Parliament Building, an ornate stone structure every bit as elegant as the one in London? In recent years, a fast-growing, generally well-educated and prosperous Asian population has brought an additional dimension to Victoria society.

Vancouver Island is the largest island on North America's Pacific coast, 300 miles long (almost as long as the entire Oregon coast) and up to 100 miles across. At that size, you might think that people would lose any sense of being on an island at all, but in fact they are constantly aware of it. One reason is that no road or bridge connects Vancouver Island to the mainland. Ferries link Vancouver Island with the cities of Vancouver, B.C., and Bellingham, the San Juan Islands, Anacortes, Port Angeles and Seattle, Washington, but waiting in line for the ferries can be an all-morning project, and the trip to the mainland is fairly expensive if you bring along your car for the ride.

Metropolitan Victoria occupies only the southernmost tip of Vancouver Island. The island has two dozen other towns, all primarily timber shipping ports and fishing harbors. Several are growing as tourism and recreation centers. Everyone lives near the coast; away from the water, the island's interior is almost completely unoccupied, touched only by occasional logging roads. Most towns are set along the eastern shore, while most of the western shore is uninhabited and much of it is unreachable by road. Most towns on the island, including Nanaimo, Campbell River and Tofino, are linked to Vancouver and the mainland by inexpensive, frequent Island Coach Lines buses which themselves are carried over by ferry.

Nanaimo (pop. 60,000), 75 miles north of Victoria on the east coast, is an appealing small city with one of the best harbors on Vancouver Island. Just 22 miles across the water, it is actually closer to the city of Vancouver by ferry than Victoria is. In many respects, Nanaimo is a smaller version of Victoria, a timber port grown into a cosmopolitan little city with a full range of gourmet and ethnic restaurants, a rapidly developing artists' colony, great shopping and plenty of summer tourism. Recently, growing numbers of retirees have been choosing Nanaimo as a more relaxed alternative to the Victoria metropolitan area.

Tofino (pop. 1,100) and neighboring Ucluelet (pop. 1,500), the only towns on the island's Pacific coast, are reached by a 125-mile highway that crosses the island from the Nanaimo area. The coastal highway that links the two towns is the only part of Pacific Rim National Park that is accessible by road. Too small, too isolated and too dreary during the long off-season, these towns are not likely candidates for retirement living; but natural beauty, great beachcombing and tasteful resort development make these hideaway towns into an extra reason to consider living in the Nanaimo area.

Another 97 miles up the east coast of the island from Nanaimo, Campbell River (pop. 17,000) is most famous as the salmon-fishing capital of the Pacific Northwest. Until recently, this simply meant that the town harbored a sizeable commercial fishing fleet, which today numbers over 200 boats. More and more, it is also evolving into a prosperous resort area where weekenders from Victoria and Vancouver come to charter fishing boats, hire guides and catch salmon on their own. Campbell River is also the gateway to the wild mountains and forests of Strathcona Provincial Park, the largest public park on Vancouver Island and an increasingly popular tourist destination. Campbell River is relatively isolated, however, with no ferry link to the mainland. It is a four- to five-hour drive to Victoria, but at least you can take a bus to get there.

Recreation and Culture Rain or shine, golf is even more popular in British Columbia than in Washington or Oregon. There are presently 230 golf courses in British Columbia, with new ones opening each year. Many are private, open only to members of other golf clubs, but practically every town in the province has at least one public, 18-hole golf course. In Victoria, the new Cordova Bay Golf Course has a beautiful waterfront setting. Other public courses in Victoria include Cedar Hill, Olympic View and Arbutus Ridge. Elsewhere on Victoria Island, there are especially good golf courses in Nanaimo, Parksville, Campbell River and Tofino.

The most popular hiking area on Vancouver Island is Pacific Rim National Park, a stretch of coastline and rain forest that is only accessible on foot. The 47-mile West Coast Trail starts 44 miles from Victoria at the end of the paved coastal highway. The trail runs the length of the park and takes a full week to hike; you can hike the first segment as a day trip. It's so popular during the summer months that a permit is required and reservations are advised. There are many more hiking possibilities in Strathcona Provincial Park, located in the center of the island near Campbell River. The vast, mountainous park encompasses the tallest peak on the island and the highest waterfall in Canada.

Among the many great fishing spots along the east coast of Vancouver Island, Campbell River bills itself as the "Salmon Capital of the World." Fishing guides and rental boats are abundantly available here, and the mouth of the river consistently produces the highest catch rates, per boat, per day in British Columbia.

Victoria has several playhouses, a symphony orchestra and an opera company. In the summer, the city hosts a major jazz festival and the world-renowned, eight-week Victoria International Music Festival. The Royal British Columbia Museum and the Art Gallery of Greater Victoria rank among the finest museums in the Pacific Northwest.

Housing and Other Costs There is a wide range of housing available around rapidly growing Victoria, especially in new custom home developments on the Saanich Peninsula between Victoria and the ferry docks. Home prices average around $160,000 Canadian (approximately $120,000 US) at this writing but are expected to continue rising rapidly. Condominiums are generally luxurious, with prices comparable to individual homes. Apartment rents in the city typically run from $750 to $950 Canadian ($550 to $700 US). Housing prices run about 20 percent lower in Nanaimo and Campbell River.

Medical Care Victoria General Hospital, the main hospital on Vancouver Island, has 700 beds. There are two smaller hospitals, Saanich Peninsula Hospital in the northern suburbs near the ferry docks and the cheerful-sounding Royal Jubilee Hospital in Victoria. There are also fully staffed health clinics, with a limited number of inpatient beds, in Nanaimo and Campbell River. Emergency helicopter service from remote parts of Vancouver Island to Victoria General Hospital is provided by British Columbia Ambulance, which operates throughout the province as a government-regulated monopoly similar to public utilities.

Crime and Safety   Statistically, Victoria is one of the safest cities in the world. Its crime rate is only about half that of Vancouver, which is a very safe city by United States standards. Part of the reason is that the city is on an island. Though it is a large island, it would be a hard place from which to make a get-away. There is only one main highway, and the only way to get to the mainland is by ferry. Then, too, a basic decency seems to characterize the people of Victoria. Even beggars, highly visible on the fringes of the downtown area, typically wear neckties and ask, "Please, sir, spare change?"

When Grandkids Visit   Of the numerous commercial tourist attractions around Vancouver's Inner Harbour, none is as unique as Miniature World in the Empress Hotel. It contains more than 80 amazingly elaborate dioramas ranging from the historical to the whimsical, including two of the world's largest doll houses. Other visitor attractions that will delight children and adults alike are the world-famous Butchart Gardens and, nearby, the new Victoria Butterfly Gardens.

Important Addresses and Connections
Chamber of Commerce: 812 Wharf Street, Victoria, BC V8W 1T3.
Senior Center: Silver Threads Senior Activity Centers, 4 Centennial Square, Victoria, BC V8W 1P7.
Newspaper: *Victoria Times-Colonist,* PO Box 300, Victoria, BC V8T 4M2.
Airport: Victoria International Airport.
Buses/Ferries: There is bus service between Victoria and other Vancouver Island towns, as well as bus service via BC Ferries to Vancouver. BC Ferries runs car ferries between Swartz Bay on the outskirts of Victoria and Tsawwassen, a Vancouver suburb. There are also BC Ferries between Nanaimo and Tsawwassen. Victoria also has ferry service to several Washington destinations.

VICTORIA	Jan.	Apr.	July	Oct.	Rain	Snow
Daily Highs	43	56	68	57	31	-
Daily Lows	36	43	52	46	in.	-

Gulf Islands

The Gulf Islands, which lie along the protected eastern coast of Vancouver Island, are a north-of-the-border continuation of Washington's San Juan Islands. There are more than 200 islands, of which six—North and South Pender Islands, Salt Spring Island, Galiano Island, Mayne Island and Saturna Island—contain sizeable settlements and are connected by ferry to Victoria and Vancouver. Among the remote North Gulf Islands, another half-dozen thinly populated islands are reachable by ten-minute ferry trips from various towns on northern Vancouver Island.

Preserving the natural beauty of the islands is a matter of paramount importance to local residents. All of the Gulf Islands are under the jurisdiction of the Islands Trust, a government agency responsible for land-use planning in the Strait of Georgia and Howe Sound, and are subject to some of the toughest environmental protection regulations in Canada.

Although several Gulf Islands settlements are within less than an hour's trip by ferry to both Victoria and Vancouver, the sailing schedules are so limited—typically two arrivals and departures daily, at different times on different days of the week—that commuting to work in the city is impractical. For this reason, most island residents are retired people, artists and bed-and-breakfast operators.

More than half the residents of the Gulf Islands live on Salt Spring Island (pop. 7,500), the largest island and the nearest to Victoria. The town of Ganges at the center of the island is an artists' colony with several galleries and a summer-long arts and crafts fair. The island, which is about the size of San Juan and Orcas Islands combined, has local shuttle bus service and two boat marinas.

The current favorite retirement spot in the Gulf Islands, North and South Pender Islands (pop. 2,000) are connected by a short bridge. The Penders are rural in character, with family farms along idyllic country lanes. Deer graze by the roadsides. Twenty-one public parks provide access to swimming beaches and secluded coves. Although neither the Penders nor any of the other Gulf Islands have a senior activities center, there is a wide selection of local associations ranging from a Newcomers Club and a Garden Club to a Health Care Society and a Field Naturalists group.

Of the three "Outer Islands," Galiano (pop. 850) and Saturna (pop. 260) blend resort development with the natural landscapes of large public parks; Mayne Island boasts distinctive Victorian architecture dating back to the Cariboo Gold Rush of the mid-1800s, when prospectors and miners gathered here and prepared to cross the Strait of Georgia to the mainland—in rowboats.

Recreation and Culture Ruckle Provincial Park on Salt Spring Island has hiking trails and camping. Salt Spring Island itself has eleven freshwater lakes that are used for swimming, windsurfing, fishing, canoeing, kayaking and sailing.

In the Penders, hikers can climb Mount Norman on the southern island. The island's three private marinas and three public wharfs provide boat moorage, and rental boats are available for salmon and cod fishing.

Galiano Island offers several spectacular hikes, including the spectacular Bodega Ridge and Mount Galiano, from whose summit the Olympic Mountains of Washington are visible to the south. Galiano is also a favorite of birdwatchers, sea kayakers, bicyclists and horseback riders.

Housing and Other Costs Property in the Gulf Islands costs less than you might expect after pricing comparable homes in the San Juan Islands. Prices range from about $155,000 Canadian (less than $120,000 US) in woodland settings away from the water to $200,000 Canadian (about $150,000 US) for seashore or lakefront property. Home rents range from $600 to $1,000 Canadian ($450 to $750 US). The selection is limited to just a handful of properties for sale or rent at any one time.

Homes in the Gulf Islands depend on wood for heat, requiring a substantial investment for those who plan to spend the winter there. The other major item that can push up living expenses is transportation, since most residents do their household shopping on Vancouver Island. For vehicles, the ferries charge more than $15 Canadian each way to Vancouver Island and twice as much to the mainland. Some residents save money by relying on bicycles at home and public buses on the big island.

Medical Care Both Salt Spring Island and the Penders have medical clinics staffed with doctors, dentists, health nurses, physiotherapists and optometrists. Island residents use hospital facilities in Victoria, and British Columbia Ambulance provides emergency helicopter service.

Crime and Safety Tourism officials say that crime is virtually unknown in the Gulf Islands, a fact confirmed by the Ganges Police Department on Salt Spring Island.

Important Addresses and Connections

Chambers of Commerce: Salt Springs Tourist Information Centre, POBox 111, Ganges, BC V0S 1E0; Mayne Island Community Chamber of Commerce, Mayne Island, BC B0N 2J0; Galiano Island Visitor's Association, P.O. Box 773, Galiano Island, BC V0N 1P0.

Weekly Newspaper: *Island Tides,* Box 55, Pender Island, BC V0N 2M0.

Airport: The nearest airport is Victoria International, located about two kilometers from the Gulf Island ferry dock on Vancouver Island.

Ferries: B.C. Ferries operates several different routes among the Gulf Islands between Swartz Bay (Victoria) and Tsawwassen (Vancouver). Schedule times and frequencies vary according to the day of the week, and fares depend on the time of year and whether it is a weekday or weekend.

PENDER ISLAND	Jan.	Apr.	July	Oct.	Rain	Snow
Daily Highs	43	56	68	57	31	-
Daily Lows	36	43	52	46	in.	-

Vancouver

When summer comes, I rent my house in Santa Fe to musicians for the opera. I charge them a lot, you can bet! Then I come up here [to Vancouver] and spend the warm months with my sister.
—Helen Lassiter

The city of Vancouver and its suburbs of Burnaby, New Westminster and Richmond, among others, cover a series of peninsulas formed between Burrard Inlet, the Frazier River Delta, English Bay and False Creek. Sandwiched between the island-studded Strait of Georgia and a backdrop of snow-capped mountains that rise more than 9,000 feet high from the city's edge, Vancouver may have the most beautiful setting of any North American metropolis.

In many ways, Vancouver is a Canadian mirror image of Seattle, a misty maze of waterways and freeways, fantastic greenery and skyscrapers. It is the center of finance, communication and transportation for all of mainland British Columbia. The population, numbering about 475,000 within the city limits of Vancouver itself and another 900,000 in adjoining suburban municipalities, is cosmopolitan, culturally diverse, and predominantly young. Although the city's decentralized layout makes for broad expanses of suburban sprawl, its excellent public transportation system, integrating B.C. Transit buses, a 15-mile-long subway/monorail called the SkyTrain, and the municipal SeaBus ferry that shuttles passengers across Burrard Inlet, makes it all manageable.

Vancouver's main subculture is Chinese Canadian. Long before the latest wave of immigration began, the city already boasted one of the largest Chinese communities in the Western Hemisphere, rivaled only by San Francisco. Chinese residents, most of them descendants of laborers imported in the 19th century to work in mines and build railroads, have historically made up 25 percent of Vancouver's population. A new wave of Chinese immigration began in the mid-1980s, when it was announced that Hong Kong would merge with the People's Republic of China in 1997. With its already large Chinese community and new immigration laws favoring investors, Vancouver became the destination of choice for Hong Kong capitalists eager to take their wealth beyond the reach of communism. The new wave has transformed Vancouver into the most prosperous, fastest-growing city in Canada.

The new immigrants have met with a certain amount of cultural tension. Vancouverites have traditionally held tolerant, if sometimes superior, attitudes toward "foreigners," whether from China or the United States. Some, however, seem to have more trouble with the idea of rich foreigners. Mercedes-driving Hong Kong refugees are blamed for skyrocketing Vancouver real estate prices and a more gradual rise in the overall cost of living. It has become perhaps Vancouver's most volatile political issue. The more positive side of the argument is that investment by Hong Kong immigrants has financed rapid growth in computer and bioengineering industries, thrusting Vancouver into the forefront of the Pacific Rim technology boom.

As big cities go, Vancouver has many charms. Its climate is almost as pleasant (in a gray sort of way) as Victoria or Seattle. The locals are more open and friendly than in U.S. cities. The streets are surprisingly safe, and Vancouver's historic and ethnic districts fascinating to explore. Its verdant city parks are large and numerous. Yet, compared to Victoria, Vancouver seems to lack services and organizations designed especially to meet the needs of senior citizens. The older Vancouverites we've encountered lived in the city before retirement and never left; few people, apparently, move to Vancouver upon retiring from their jobs. Despite its favorable qualities as a city, Vancouver seems to offer little reason for Canadian retirees to choose it over Victoria, or for U.S. retirees to choose it over Seattle.

Recreation and Culture The greater Vancouver area has more than a dozen public golf courses. *Golf Digest* has called the Peace Portal Golf Course, south of the city near the Tsawwassen ferry docks, one of the finest golf courses in North America. Another fine course, Fraserview, has the dubious distinction of being the busiest golf course in Canada.

Vancouver has many outstanding places for walking and jogging, including the scenic seawall along the waterfront in Stanley Park and the breathtaking Capilano Suspension Bridge. Serious hikers will find mountain trails in Garibaldi and Golden Ears Provincial Parks.

All kinds of boats, from fishing skiffs and sea kayaks to bareboat sailing yacht charters, are available for rent in Vancouver. Although there is a lot of ship traffic in English Bay, by heading eastward up either Burard Inlet or the Fraser River, boaters can reach more peaceful spots.

For spectator sports, the Vancouver Canucks give the south-of-the-border NHL teams a run for their money. And the new NBA team in town, the Grizzlies, are guaranteed to draw some exciting competition from the U.S. stars you've grown to love (or hate!).

Vancouver is the cultural center of western Canada. The Vancouver Symphony Orchestra and the CBC Orchestra, along with the Vancouver Opera, Ballet British Columbia and a full complement of chamber music and chorale groups, offer a year-round schedule of classical music events. Vancouver has more than a dozen theaters that present live stage plays. Of the several major museums in the city, the most exceptional is the University of British Columbia Museum of Anthropology, which contains the most extensive collection of Northwest Coast Indian artifacts in the world.

Housing and Other Costs All types of housing, in all price ranges, are available in and around Vancouver, from high-rise condominiums downtown to small farms on the semi-rural eastern outskirts and beautiful mountain homes in the Garibaldi Heights north of the city, not to mention the miles and miles of homogenous suburbia to the north, south and southwest of downtown. Although Vancouver has traditionally enjoyed a reputation as an affordable city, recently real estate prices have been rising even faster than in Seattle, with no sign of slowing down, which might make property here a good investment, if you are interested in such things. Houses here range in price from $80,000 ($59,000 U.S.) to $600,000 ($450,000 U.S.), with an average price of $137,000 ($110,000 U.S.) for a two- or three-bedroom suburban home. Two-bedroom apartments rent for $750 to $1500 ($600 to $1200 U.S.).

Food prices and public utility costs run lower than in Victoria. Factory-made goods are more expensive everywhere in Canada than in the United States.

Medical Care Although Vancouver is the larger city, its hospital facilities are about equal to those in Victoria—and more crowded. St. Paul's Hospital, the city's largest, has 450 beds. Many outpatient services that hospitals provide in the United States are handled instead by large walk-in medical centers in Vancouver, which are much cheaper than inpatient facilities and help balance the fact that patients who are not covered by Canada's national health insurance pay more for medical treatment than in the United States.

Crime and Safety It should come as no surprise that greater Vancouver, like any other metropolis of a million people, has big-city social problems including organized crime and gang activities. What is surprising is that Vancouver's crime rate is only one-third that of Seattle, the nearest U.S. city of comparable equal size. Why this should be true is a mystery, since Vancouver has fewer police officers, a more cumbersome court system, and far fewer people behind bars than its U.S. counterpart. Locals offer the following explanation: "Well, it's not part of the States after all, eh?"

When Grandkids Visit Vancouver's wide range of family recreation possibilities includes the Vancouver Aquarium, which houses beluga whales, orcas and sea otters as well as fish, and

Playland Amusement Park in Exhibition Park. The Vancouver Museum contains art, archaeology, history and natural history exhibits, and the adjoining MacMillan Planetarium has spectacular laser light shows as well as educational presentations. The British Columbia Sports Hall of Fame not only commemorates Canadian athletes with videos and still photographs but also has a "participation gallery" where kids can let loose excess energy by running, climbing, rowing and throwing balls.

Important Addresses and Connections

Chamber of Commerce: 700 W. Pender #1607, Vancouver, BC, V6C 1G8
Newspaper: *Sun-Province*, 2250 Granville St., Vancouver, BC, V6H 3G2.
Airport: Vancouver International Airport, located just south of the city.
Bus/Train: Greyhound Lines runs buses from Vancouver to Victoria, Seattle, and points east in Canada. Quick Shuttle buses go back and forth between Vancouver and Seattle several times a day. VIA Rail, Canada's national train system, has transcontinental trains three days a week. BC Rail originates from a separate station in North Vancouver and goes to towns in the interior of the province. A recently opened Amtrak spur connects Vancouver and Seattle.

VANCOUVER	Jan.	Apr.	July	Oct.	Rain	Snow
Daily Highs	42	55	72	58	35	3
Daily Lows	31	39	52	41	in.	in.

Merritt / Kamloops

I've never seen anything like the night sky here in Kamloops.
—Carol Scott

British Columbia is vast and sparsely populated. Most of it is entirely roadless, and even along the province's four major highways you can drive for a full day without seeing a community large enough to be called a town. Settlements in the northern part of the province are places where one might go to homestead in the wilderness; as retirement destinations, even during the warm months, they are simply too isolated to be worth considering. From Vancouver, the closest place to find good shopping, cultural events, and complete medical facilities, it is a 470-mile drive to Prince George (pop. 70,000), the largest city in the north country, and another 450 miles to Prince Rupert (pop. 17,000), the only place on the northern coast that can be reached by road. RVers who enjoy discovering out-of-the-way places will find boundless possibilities for adventure, but as a place to live, let's face it, most of the British Columbian interior is for those who consider Alaska too crowded. We explored inland British Columbia with an eye toward identifying places that offered comfortable living conditions and were close enough to drive to Vancouver in half a day.

Merritt, a town of 7,000 people at the foot of the Coquihalla Mountains, 130 miles northeast of Vancouver, nestles among the surrounding mountains in one of the most beautiful settings imaginable. Small and secluded enough to share the frontier flavor of British Columbia, Merritt is still close enough to civilization so that the modern amenities of Vancouver are within easy day-trip distance, without crossing any of the mountain passes that isolate so many British Columbian towns during the winter months. The economy centers on cattle ranching and recreation, and the culture is diverse. Besides the cowboys who work on the dozen or so large ranches around the valley, five Indian bands make their homes near Merritt, as does one of North America's largest groups of Sikhs, a religion from India with an international following. The diverse, balanced community includes a substantial number of senior citizens, many of them retirees from Vancouver who make their homes in Merritt on a full- or part-time basis.

Just fifty miles from Merritt on the far side of the Coquihalla Mountains, Kamloops (pop. 67,000) is a different world. Although snow often closes the 4,800-foot pass over the mountains during the cold months, cutting the region off from Vancouver for days at a time, Kamloops is large enough to offer a good selection of shopping and services, minimizing the need to visit the big city.

Originally a supply center during the Cariboo gold rush of the 1860s, Kamloops was established long before Vancouver. Today its economy depends on cattle, lumber and tourism. The city adjoins the Kamloops Indian Reserve, and "First Americans" make up a significant part of the area's population. Despite rapid economic development—the number of businesses in Kamloops grew 22 percent from 1986 to 1994—the area suffers from a surplus of unskilled workers. The 12 percent unemployment rate, much higher than in the Victoria-Vancouver area, means that many Kamloops residents are forced to depend on Canada's welfare system.

The substantial senior citizen community is proudly and provincially Canadian; few people from the United States retire here, though the prevailing view is that they would want to if they knew about this place—a dubious notion considering that temperatures fall below freezing nightly for almost eight months of the year.

Kamloops is situated at the point where the North and South Forks of the Thompson River flow together, dividing the city in thirds. Only two car bridges span the river, so getting from one part of the city to another often involves elaborate navigation. The downtown area, with its scattering of highrises, stands on the river bank, while many residential areas are located on high bluffs commanding spectacular views of the valley and the mountains that flank it on both sides.

As far removed as it is from British Columbia's largest cities, Kamloops is ideally located for exploring the backcountry a little bit at a time. Though Kamloops is in an arid, near-desert area, the surrounding mountains contain a greater concentration of lakes than anyplace else in the province, and the region is famed for fishing. The Shuswap Lake-Salmon Arm area, an hour's drive to the east, is an emerging resort area with great fishing, boating, birdwatching and camping. Two or three more hours on the road bring you to a series of large national parks along the Continental Divide of the Canadian Rockies. Also within one to two hours of Kamloops is the Okanagan Valley, a fruit-growing area along the banks of 50-mile-long Lake Okanagan, where the big draw for visitors is golf: incredibly, the region boasts 40 public and private golf courses.

Recreation and Culture   There are two nine-hole golf courses in the vicinity of Merritt—the Merritt Golf and Country Club and the Nicola Valley Golf Course in nearby Quilchena. The greater Kamloops area has seven golf courses, including those at MacArthur Island Park and Eagle Point. Southeast of Kamloops, the rolling hills of the Okanagan Valley cater to the golf package tour trade with forty privately owned, rather pricey golf courses.

Fishing around Kamloops is legendary. The catch may include prodigiously large rainbow trout and kokanee salmon.

Curling is the favorite spectator sport. (Most area residents also play the game.) Kamloops is the site of the Brier, the

Canadian national curling championship playoffs, which draws hundreds of thousands of people from all over the country in early March.

Kamloops has a sizeable public art gallery where works by local and regional artists are shown, as well as a regional history museum.

Housing and Other Costs Real estate prices in Merritt run significantly lower than in Vancouver. Residential properties range from $70,000 to $250,000 Canadian, averaging about $130,000 Canadian ($95,000 US). There are no condominiums or apartment buildings, and the only rental units available in the area are mobile homes.

In Kamloops, homes range from $100,000 to $175,000 Canadian, averaging around $130,000 (about $100,000 U.S.). Modest condominiums are available starting around $69,000 Canadian (a little over $50,000 US). Apartment rentals are in the $450 to $600 Canadian ($330-$440 US) range. Twenty-acre home lots range from $49,000 to $75,000 Canadian ($36,000-$55,000 US).

Medical Care The only hospital in the Merritt area is Nicola Valley General Hospital, a small 25-bed facility. Merritt residents go to Vancouver for most non-emergency procedures. In Kamloops, the Royal Inland Hospital has 122 beds and serves as the main hospital care facility for a wide area of central British Columbia. Merritt also has a government-sponsored medical and dental clinic, and Kamloops has seven of them.

Crime and Safety The crime rate remains low throughout this part of the province. Despite higher-than-average unemployment and alcoholism rates, Kamloops has averaged less than one murder a year. Locals are aware of the social problems that plague the area but do not consider crime to be one of them.

When Grandkids Visit With lakes, forests and mountains in every direction, there should be no problem finding family fun. For youngsters who believe that fun must involve an admission charge, there's the Kamloops Wildlife Park, one of the finest zoos in British Columbia, with 55 exhibits of native and exotic wildlife, including wolves, bighorn sheep and grizzly bears, in naturalistic habitats.

Important Addresses and Connections

Chamber of Commerce: P.O. Box 1649, Merritt, BC, V0K 2B0; 7 West Victoria Street, Kamloops, BC, V1S 1P1.

Senior Services: Coquihalla House, Merritt, BC, V0K 2B0; all senior services in Kamloops are church-affiliated.

Newspapers: *The Merritt Herald,* P.O. Box 9, Merritt, BC, V0K 2B0; *Kamloops Daily News,* 393 Seymour St., Kamloops, BC, Z2C 6P6.

Airport: Merritt has a small general aviation airport but no commercial passenger service; residents use Vancouver International Airport, three hours' drive away. In Kamloops, Fulton Field has daily commuter flights to Vancouver.

Bus/Train: Greyhound Lines has daily bus service to Merritt and Kamloops. BC Rail has passenger train service to Kamloops.

KAMLOOPS	Jan.	Apr.	July	Oct.	Rain	Snow
Daily Highs	32	59	82	53	9	30
Daily Lows	5	32	50	23	in.	in.

Index to Places

Our books are available in most bookstores. However, if you have difficulty finding them, we will be happy to ship them to you directly. Just send your check or money order.

Retirement

Retiring, Wintering or Investing
CHOOSE COSTA RICA 3RD ED. $13.95 _____

Enjoying the Devaluation Bargains
CHOOSE MEXICO 4TH ED. $11.95 _____

Retirement Discoveries for Every Budget
CHOOSE THE SOUTHWEST $12.95 _____
CHOOSE THE NORTHWEST $12.95 _____

America's Best and Most Affordable Places
WHERE TO RETIRE $14.95 _____

Strategies for Comfortable Retirement
RETIREMENT ON A SHOESTRING $8.95 _____

Travel

An Impromptu Travel Guide
FRANCE WITHOUT RESERVATIONS $12.95 _____

A Traveler's Guide to Living Affordably Abroad
EUROPE THE EUROPEAN WAY $13.95 _____

Hiking Guides for Active Adults
WALKING EASY IN THE AUSTRIAN ALPS $10.95 _____
WALKING EASY IN THE FRENCH ALPS $11.95 _____
WALKING EASY IN THE ITALIAN ALPS $11.95 _____
WALKING EASY IN THE SAN FRANCISCO BAY AREA $11.95 _____
WALKING EASY IN THE SWISS ALPS $10.95 _____

Postage & Handling
First book............................$1.90
Each additional book..........1.00   _____
California residents add 8% sales tax   _____

Total $ _____

For Credit Card ORDERS ONLY - call toll-free 1-800-669-0773
For Information - call 510-530-0299

Please ship to:

Name _____

Address _____

City/State/Zip_____

Our books are shipped bookrate. Please allow 2 - 3 weeks for delivery. If you are not satisfied, the price of the book(s) will be refunded in full. (U. S. funds for all orders, please.)

Mail to: Gateway Books 2023 Clemens Road Oakland CA 94602